The Network of Control _____

Contributions in Legal Studies
Series Editor: *Paul L. Murphy*

Popular Influence upon Public Policy: Petitioning in
Eighteenth-Century Virginia
Raymond C. Bailey

Fathers to Daughters: The Legal Foundations of Female Emancipation
Peggy A. Rabkin

In Honor of Justice Douglas: A Symposium on Individual Freedom and
the Government
Robert H. Keller, Jr., editor

A Constitutional History of Habeas Corpus
William F. Duker

The American Codification Movement: A Study of Antebellum
Legal Reform
Charles M.Cook

Crime and Punishment in Revolutionary Paris
Antoinette Wills

American Legal Culture, 1908-1940
John W. Johnson

Governmental Secrecy and the Founding Fathers: A Study in
Constitutional Controls
Daniel N. Hoffman

Torture and English Law: An Administrative and Legal History from the
Plantagenets to the Stuarts
James Heath

Essays on New York Colonial Legal History
Herbert S. Johnson

The Origins of the American Business Corporation, 1784-1855: Broadening
the Concept of Public Service During Industrialization
Ronald E. Seavoy

Prologue to Nuremberg: The Politics and Diplomacy of Punishing War
Criminals of the First World War
James F. Willis

The Network
of Control

State Supreme Courts and
State Security Statutes, 1920-1970

Carol E. Jenson

Contributions in Legal Studies, Number 22

GREENWOOD PRESS
WESTPORT, CONNECTICUT • LONDON, ENGLAND

Library of Congress Cataloging in Publication Data
Jenson, Carol E.
   The network of control.

   (Contributions in legal studies, ISSN 0147-1074;
no. 22)
   Bibliography: p.
   Includes index.
   1. Internal security—United States—States—Cases.
I. Title. II. Series.
KF4850.Z95J45   342.73'0684   81-6385
ISBN 0-313-22492-7 (lib. bdg.) 347.302684   AACR2

Library of Congress Catalog Card Number: 81-6385
ISBN: 0-313-22492-7
ISSN: 0147-1074

First published in 1982

Greenwood Press
A division of Congressional Information Service, Inc.
88 Post Road West
Westport, Connecticut 06881

Printed in the United States of America

10 9 8 7 6 5 4 3 2 1

To Tom

CONTENTS

TABLES

PREFACE

Anyone who tackles the vast body of materials involved with judicial interpretation of state law—even within one closely defined area—risks confrontation with critics who are quick to point to the enormity of the task as justification for avoiding this area of inquiry altogether. The limited amount of research conducted on the historical effect of Supreme Court decisions upon subsequent state court action is in itself a demonstration of the scholarly community's reluctance to pierce the wall of insulation that has contained the historical study of U.S. Supreme Court decisions almost totally within a federal court context.

Nevertheless, what follows is an attempt to gauge the historical development of a body of state case law that developed in reaction to selected decisions of the U.S. Supreme Court involving state security legislation. In order to limit the study to a workable format, I have defined security legislation as those laws pertaining to sedition, criminal anarchy, and criminal syndicalism or a counterpart that bears another title such as the Georgia Anti-Insurrection Act of 1866. Again, for purposes of pursuing a workable topic, I have limited my study to investigation of state court reaction to ten major U.S. Supreme Court decisions, made between 1920 and 1970, that ruled on state laws fitting the above definition of security statutes. This study focuses on state court reaction; it is not meant to be an exposition of constitutional doctrine except as that doctrine has related to further state developments.

In initiating the work I found that *The States and Subversion*, edited by Walter Gellhorn and published by the Cornell University Press in 1952 during the anti-Communist crusades of the early fifties, provided a valuable starting point. I conducted the major segment of the research in the state supreme court opinions and in some instances in the intermediate state appellate court opinions included in the National Reporter System. I carried out supportive research in state statutes and codes and in law journals and other secondary materials.

Research of this type presents particular problems not unique to state court interpretation, but certainly enhanced when one deals with more than fifty appellate tribunals. First of all, there is no way to discover systematically which state courts ignored the U.S. Supreme Court precedents since there is no way to catalog omissions. However, dissenting opinions and the proclivity of recalcitrant state judges to distinguish U.S. Supreme Court decisions from cases at bar in the state courts served as a built-in protection against state judges' totally divorcing a state case from a U.S. Supreme Court precedent.

A second and most obvious disadvantage in research of this type is the voluminous amount of material to be surveyed. This problem is complicated further by the overlapping nature of much state legislation. For example, what is entitled a sedition statute in one state may be labeled a treason statute—or criminal syndicalism or criminal anarchy statute—in another. Sorting out the laws is made even more difficult by the fact that what I have defined as state security legislation is closely related to other statutes: antipicketing regulations, red flag laws, conspiracy laws, and numerous other attempts to exert state control over individual and group expression. Consequently, it would appear at first glance that limitation of this study to what has been defined as state security legislation would create an arbitrary and artificial division. However, as the research reveals, the courts have tended to weave all of these types of restrictive laws into a network; and the explanation of that network helps to correct any artificial classification undertaken for purposes of facility in research.

Finally, a third complication in research of this type is that although my principal motivation for undertaking this work was related to an intense interest in the history of civil liberties law, the study by its very nature becomes involved with federalism. To avoid these issues of federalism would create a considerable distortion, so I have attempted to deal with federalism as a vital part of the procedural points involved with the civil liberties issues and not as a totally separate development.

Many who read this work will note that it seems to fall within the general category of what has become known among political scientists as impact literature. With the utmost respect to Stephen Wasby and others who have pioneered in impact studies, I point out that my work does not attempt to deal with the effects of Supreme Court opinions along the lines of impact research. My study is historical—not theoretical. It is concerned with the effects of U.S. Supreme Court decisions upon subsequent opinions of state appellate benches. It is essentially a study of the how and the why of state court application of High Court opinions concerning state security statutes. It traces the contribution that these applications made to a series of state networks that for the most part have been more restrictive of political speech than the doctrines handed down by the U.S. Supreme Court.

In completing this manuscript, I wish to recognize what all of those who attempt scholarly research and writing know only too well. No project is completed without help from institutions and from other individuals. In acknowledging that assistance I wish to express my gratitude to the National Endowment for the Humanities (NEH) Fellowship in Residence Program for grant support that financed a leave of absence from my teaching duties so that I might conduct the core research for this project. I also thank the University of Wisconsin System and the University of Wisconsin-La Crosse for indirect financial assistance. I also express my appreciation to the library staffs of the University of California, Santa Barbara; the Santa Barbara County Law Library; the University of California, Los Angeles, Law Library; and the University of Minnesota Law Library for providing assistance and for maintaining the collections essential to my research.

In addition to the institutional support a number of individuals provided considerable assistance in the development of this project. In 1977-1978 during the course of the NEH Fellowship in

Residence Program I participated in a year-long seminar on "The Supreme Court and Constitutional Change" conducted at the University of California, Santa Barbara, under the direction of C. Herman Pritchett. His long and distinguished career studying the workings of the Supreme Court and his warm and encouraging manner provided valuable scholarly inspiration and advice. I am most grateful for his friendship and counsel. I also wish to thank Paul L. Murphy of the University of Minnesota, who for a number of years has challenged and sustained my interests in constitutional scholarship in general and in the First Amendment in particular.

I am also grateful for the time and counsel provided by colleagues in the History Department of the University of Wisconsin-La Crosse. William E. Pemberton and Stanley R. Rolnick contributed valuable assistance in reading and proofreading the manuscript. I also express my appreciation to Janice Larkin, who typed the manuscript amid the usual chaos associated with an academic department office. Her careful eye caught many errors in my less-than-perfect typing and proofreading. I am also indebted to the editors in the Production Department at Greenwood Press who scrutinized the manuscript very carefully for technical problems in writing and documentation.

Finally, I wish to express a very large personal and professional thank you to my husband, Thomas M. Telzrow, who is a fellow historian and student of the law as well as my dearest friend. He is a secure man, unthreatened by a wife's achievements, and he accepts enthusiastically the necessity of the struggle to support the work of women scholars.

La Crosse, Wisconsin
March, 1981

The Network of Control

1. INTRODUCTION: LAYING THE NETWORK

In 1920 in the closing remarks of his dissent in *Gilbert* v. *Minnesota*, Justice Louis D. Brandeis reflected upon a crucial issue of federalism. The point had been raised in a case in which the Supreme Court majority ruled that the free speech protections of the First Amendment did not impose a limitation upon a state's attempt to restrict political speech critical of governmental efforts during World War I. Brandeis's simple admonition, "I cannot believe that the liberty guaranteed by the Fourteenth Amendment includes only liberty to acquire and to enjoy property,"[1] helped to initiate a long and continuing inquiry into the intricacies of the federal system in relation to Bill of Rights considerations.

The *Gilbert* case brought to the Court for the first time the question of whether a state's attempt to restrict political speech, which a state considered seditious, conflicted with the First Amendment in conjunction with that part of the Fourteenth Amendment that reads "nor shall any State deprive any person of life, liberty, or property, without due process of law." During the fifty years following the *Gilbert* ruling the Supreme Court considered the issue of political speech and state law numerous times. Much scholarly attention has been directed at analysis and explanation of these Supreme Court opinions.[2] Thomas Emerson in his distinguished work on First Amendment constitutional doctrine has described in detail *The System of Freedom of Expression*. He has contended that Supreme Court history has demonstrated that the section of the system concerned with political speech developed from dozens of cases that resulted from a network of federal and state laws enacted in an attempt to protect the security of government.[3]

One thread of the network that the Supreme Court considered during the years 1920-1970 involved the free speech difficulties arising from state statutes that fell under the headings of sedition, criminal syndicalism, or criminal anarchy. The interchangeable use of these terms[4] and the often similar structure and wording of these statutes require that the three areas be considered together; they can be incorporated under the term *state security statutes*. During the fifty-year period ten major cases involving these statutes reached the Supreme Court, and the opinions provided direction for state governments and state courts. Cases involving state sedition laws represented each of the wartime eras. The *Gilbert* opinion involved the 1917 Minnesota Sedition Law directed at criticism of the United States or state government. A similar statute passed by Mississippi in 1942 found its way to the Supreme Court in *Taylor* v. *Mississippi* in 1943, as did a Pennsylvania statute considered in *Pennsylvania* v. *Nelson* in 1956.[5] *Gitlow* v. *New York* in 1925 involved the Criminal Anarchy Act of 1902 passed to prevent the violent overthrow of the government. *Whitney* v. *California*, 1927; *Fiske* v. *Kansas*, 1927; *De Jonge* v. *Oregon*, 1937; and *Brandenburg* v. *Ohio*, 1969—each involved those states' criminal syndicalism laws aimed at the activities of the Industrial Workers of the World or other alleged attempts to change the form of government.[6] A Georgia Reconstruction statute known as the Anti-Insurrection Act reached the High Court in 1937 in *Herndon* v. *Lowry*, a case involving a young black Communist party member; and the same New York statute involved in *Gitlow* appeared before the Court again in *Epton* v. *New York* in 1968 in a case that the justices decided not to hear. *Dombrowski* v. *Pfister* in 1965 reflected Louisiana's attempt to use that state's Anti-Subversive Law to curtail civil rights activities.[7]

Since state security laws have been one strand in the web of interpretation involving freedom of speech, this area of doctrine is necessarily woven together with other closely related categories of police-power-based statutes that were designed primarily for the protection of the state and that also contribute considerably to the network of control. Hence, judicial interpretation of statutes concerned with breach of the peace, trespass, parade and rally permits, picketing, door-to-door solicitation, noise and littering, loyalty oaths and affidavits, membership disclosure, censorship, conspiracy, and numerous other areas has been crucial to the development of decisions and policies regarding state security statutes. This broader category of the network of control, which included the core network of state security statutes, created a web that could be tightened in times of fear of social and political change. A study focused on the security statute thread of the broader network must recognize the close and at times inseparable relationship between these categories of statutes.

The fifty-year period under consideration opened with the Red Scare that followed World War I and the Bolshevik Revolution of 1917 and closed with the turmoil associated with black power movements and student anti-Viet Nam protest. State as well as federal authorities often perceived the intense political, social, and economic conflicts of this fifty-year period as serious threats to the security of the state and sometimes to the very existence of government itself. As a result, state legislatures felt increasingly compelled to enact legislation designed to curb the speech and other First Amendment activities of those who advocated social, economic, and political change. As Emerson has so aptly pointed out, much of the state action in the network actually preceded congressional legislation. Between 1917 and 1921, two-thirds of the states enacted security statutes, even though Congress did not pass peacetime sedition legislation until the 1940 Smith Act.[8] All too often a particular law remained on the books long after the immediate conflict had passed, only to be revived, in an application of selective enforcement, as a weapon against the next wave of protest. Since Congress, as well as the state legislatures, enacted statutes in a number of these same areas, questions of federalism naturally arose and often led to procedural difficulties that had to be resolved in the courts. The procedures involved in legal technicalities at times added to the effectiveness of the network's interference with the exercise of free speech as an integral part of political activity.

The first rash of state security statutes, often bearing the sedition title, came during World War I. State and local concerns over the reported presence of alleged German spies, supposedly disloyal ethnic groups, and allegedly unpatriotic reformers brought many legislatures to pass laws resembling the Congressional Espionage Act of 1917 and the Sedition Act of 1918. Thirteen states plus the territories of Alaska and Hawaii passed wartime statutes prohibiting interference with the war effort, particularly the recruitment of troops.[9] The Minnesota Sedition Act, the statute later scrutinized by the U.S. Supreme Court in *Gilbert*, was typical of this state action. This law required punishment for those who advocated "that men should not enlist in the military or naval forces of the United States or the State of Minnesota."[10]

Activities of the Industrial Workers of the World (IWW), a group that conducted a number of strikes and threatened still more during the war and early postwar years, also stirred wartime domestic fears. During the first decade after its formation in 1905, the IWW had fought to establish protection of the freedom of speech that was essential to organizing large numbers of transient and unskilled workers. Fear of what might result from the IWW presence in the harvest fields, mines, and lumber camps prompted many state legislatures to restrict any further Wobbly (IWW) free speech activities.

Between 1917 and 1920, twenty states and two territories passed criminal syndicalism laws aimed at the activities of the organization that attempted to join all workers into one great union in order to wage the class struggle.[11] According to Eldridge Dowell's authoritative study of criminal syndicalism legislation, "Certainly the IWW were the nearest that America has produced to an indigenous syndicalist group."[12] The IWW tactic of direct action was misinterpreted by officials to mean violence, even though the organization officially opposed any type of violence except as a means of self-defense. The views of the press and much of the general public helped to substantiate the attitude of state officials. As a result, state legislatures, beginning in the western states where IWW activity was the greatest, had little difficulty in passing criminal syndicalism statutes.[13] The Idaho statute of 1917 provided the prototype for this type of law and defined criminal syndicalism as "the doctrine which advocates crime, violence, sabotage or other unlawful methods as a means of industrial or political reform," particularly if it is directed at changing the form of government or industrial control.[14]

The wartime sedition laws and the criminal syndicalism statutes both resulted from a fear of radicals that was greatly reinforced by the events of World War I, the Bolshevik Revolution, and the subsequent Red Scare of 1919-1920. A postwar climate that produced A. Mitchell Palmer's raids, attempts at mass deportation of alien IWW members, and military suppression of left-wing labor groups and that demanded a "Return to Normalcy" in the 1920 election brought considerable legislative response from state governments. These new restrictions supplemented earlier legislation that included general sedition laws, criminal anarchy laws, and conspiracy statutes plus other new regulations prohibiting the use of red flags and requiring strict control over teachers and state officials. The passage of restrictive legislation within a large number of states during a few short years added greatly to the web of state regulations that had emerged from the nineteenth century. After 1925 the legislative reaction subsided briefly, only to resume as radical groups attracted followers during the years of the Great Depression. Then, legislatures directed much of the attention of new legislation toward colleges and universities; and by 1936, fourteen states required loyalty oaths of their professors. The tally in 1936 also showed seventeen states with criminal syndicalism laws, ten with criminal anarchy regulations, and twenty-one with sedition statutes.[15]

However, state judicial objections challenged a few of these restrictions. In 1921, state supreme courts in New Mexico and New Jersey struck down security legislation. The New Mexico Supreme Court discarded, on grounds of vagueness, a statute that "prohibits alike the creation of public opinion by argument and persuasion, and the compulsion of action by the people by force of arms, intimidation, sabotage, or other criminal or illegal means."[16] In 1931 in *Stromberg* v. *California*, a case involving an issue closely related to state security statutes, five members of the Hughes Court discarded the California Red Flag Law on similar grounds of vagueness.[17] The *Stromberg* case revealed a number of the additional civil liberties difficulties found in the network of statutes attempting to control political speech. These laws often have contained provisions that civil liberties advocates and some courts have found to be vague and lacking in ascertainable standards of guilt. Defenders of these statutes have applied state police power arguments to counter charges of due process violations. Criticism of these provisions combined with numerous other arguments based upon the First Amendment attempted to challenge further the system of state security legislation. However, the complexity of the network and the case-by-case nature of constitutional legal development determined a piecemeal development for the protection of the numerous facets of free speech.

Events that followed the Crash of 1929 encouraged a more intense continuation of the left-wing criticism of the probusiness governmental attitudes of the twenties. In response, governments sought greater control over those who supported numerous plans, demagogic and otherwise, to right the economic wrongs besieging the country. State legislatures were not alone during the thirties in the attempt to control the allegedly radical critics of the government. Congress also tried to combat the political response to economic distress with security measures and considered seven sedition bills during the first half of the decade.[18] Critics felt the history of state security statutes and their ineffectiveness in coping with genuine violence cast serious doubt on the need for corresponding federal laws and saw both levels of legislation as endangering the political and social benefits of open analysis and discussion. One particularly strong critic stated:

Sedition legislation which tends to become an anti-labor weapon throws the power of government behind that attempt. Such a result, coupled with the constant lack of prosecution for vigilante violence, raise basic problems as to the nature and function of governmental power. Resort to force to induce docile acceptance of an existent order, as opposed to justification of that order by performance, has been common to many periods of history. The similar modern manifestation abroad has been denominated fascism.[19]

During the early forties, four state legislatures, in addition to those counted above, followed the example of Congress, which had added to the security network with the passage of the first peacetime national sedition statute, the Alien Registration Act of 1940, better known as the Smith Act.[20] This legislation passed Congress despite strong opposition from the American Civil Liberties Union, a number of law professors, and labor leaders. However, the Smith Act caught others off guard even though the House of Representatives McCormack-Dickstein Committee and other anticommunist forces had been calling for national sedition legislation since 1935. A noted civil liberties scholar, Zechariah Chafee, observed:

Not until months later did I for one realize that this statute contains the most drastic restrictions on freedom of speech ever enacted in the United States during peace. It is no more limited to the registration of aliens than the Espionage Act of 1917 was limited to spying. . . .Just as the 1917 Act gave us a wartime sedition law, so the 1940 Act gave us a peacetime sedition law—for everybody, especially United States citizens.

Chafee commented in response to the provisions that made it unlawful to interfere with the military, to advise interference, and to advocate or organize groups to overthrow any government in the United States and that made any printed matter described in the statute subject to removal from any premises under a search warrant.[21]

The new legislation at both the state and national levels was designed to control activities that authorities alleged to be possible attempts to overthrow governments. These statutes joined with an additional block of laws regulating public meetings, picketing, and public employment; and together they supplemented the state security networks. However, the events of World War II that made the Soviet Union an American ally forced the Smith Act to become a dead letter until after the end of the war.

During the years following the end of the hostilities the network became even more closely woven as the events of the post-World War II era led to the much-publicized trial and conviction of Alger Hiss, the fall of China to the Communists, the knowledge of the Soviet possession of the atom bomb, and the fighting in Korea. The cold war and the second Red Scare accompanied still another resurgence of security legislation passed at both the state and national levels. Combined with those laws already on the books, new statutes served as the basis for several well-publicized U.S. Supreme Court decisions that reflected the nation's security orientation during the cold war era. *Pennsylvania* v. *Nelson* in 1956 and *Uphaus* v. *Wyman* in 1959 were primary examples of Court interpretation in this area.[22]

The new statutes of the post-World War II period served to expand the national network of control as numerous persons accused of allegedly disloyal acts suffered disgrace and sometimes loss of their jobs—often regardless of whether or not the charges were proved in court. By the end of 1950 over three hundred various types of antisubversive state laws were in existence,[23] and on many occasions authorities aimed the enforcement of these statutes at groups and organizations and their members and created the additional civil liberties difficulties of guilt by association. As Walter Gellhorn observed in his 1952 study entitled *The States and Subversion*:

Traditionally the criminal law has dealt with the malefactor, the one who himself committed an offense. Departing from this tradition is the recent tendency to ascribe criminal potentialities to a body of persons (usually, though not invariably, the Communists) and to lay restraints upon any individual who can be linked with the group. This, of course, greatly widens the concept of subversive activities, because it results, in truth, in forgetting about activities altogether. It substitutes associations as the objects of the law's impact. Any attempt to define subversion as used in modern statutes must therefore refer to the mere possibility of activity as well as to present lawlessness.[24]

A new type of statute aimed at "foreign subversive organizations" and their members supplemented the pre-World War II type of legislation by which two-thirds of the states had outlawed violence or advocacy of change or overthrow of the government. Eleven states passed Communist registration laws, eight states banned the Communist party completely, and even some municipalities enacted antisubversive ordinances. The situation prompted one law journal to observe, "As federal control tightened, the states enacted more comprehensive sedition laws, and by 1954 almost every state in the Union as well as Alaska and Hawaii had subversive control laws. "[25]

Congress also worked to extend the strands of the network. Down through the years congressional investigating committees and legislation had attempted to reinforce state security legislation and vice versa. Congressional activity reached a high point during the early fifties with the investigations of Senator Joseph McCarthy's subcommittee. In addition Congress supplemented the Smith Act of 1940 with the Internal Security Act of 1950, popularly known as the McCarran Act, which acknowledged an alleged worldwide communist conspiracy and required that communist groups register with a newly created Subversive Activities Control Board. Congress, reflecting the intense national fear of international conspiracy, overrode President Truman's veto of the McCarran Act by a large margin. Four years later, in 1954, Congress added the Communist Control Act, this time over the objections of the Eisenhower administration. The 1954 act outlawed the Communist party but stopped short of making membership an actual crime.[26] This body of legislation paralleled the state networks, thereby providing a basis for raising the issue of federal preemption of the security field, an important point in state court application of Supreme Court precedent. In addition to the action of Congress, loyalty screening of federal employees, conducted by both the Truman and Eisenhower administrations, added to the concern over security that affected both state and federal levels of government.[27]

During the last half of the fifties and throughout the decade of the sixties, few states added to the proliferation of security legislation. Officials applied existing statutes in attempts to control the political speech of civil rights workers, black power advocates, and anti-Viet Nam War protestors during this fifteen-year period.

Since state legislatures did not for the most part seek to repeal the security legislation that they wove into the network of control during this fifty-year period,[28] the challenge to the network developed in the courts. Judges faced the task of interpreting individual statutes in relation to the Bill of Rights and a variety of judicial and legislative interpretations of the state's role in protecting political security and civil liberties. Decisions and opinions of the courts, including those of the U.S. Supreme Court, affected the actions of state courts and state legislatures. The piecemeal direction provided by the Supreme Court contained dual lines of precedent that presented opportunities for state courts to avoid application of precedents considered by many of them to be in conflict with and to encroach upon areas of state law and jurisdiction.

NOTES

1. Gilbert v. Minn., 254 U.S. 325, 343 (1920).

2. Political scientists working in the area of what is known as impact studies have dealt with certain aspects of the subject of state reaction to Supreme Court rulings. See Stephen L. Wasby, *The Impact of the United States Supreme Court* (Homewood, Ill.: Dorsey Press, 1970); Stephen L. Wasby, *The Supreme Court in the Federal Judicial System* (New York: Holt, Rinehart and Winston, 1978); and G. Alan Tarr, *Judicial Impact and State Supreme Courts* (Lexington, Mass.: Lexington Books, 1977). The latter volume deals exclusively with the subject of freedom of religion.

3. Thomas Emerson, *The System of Freedom of Expression* (New York: Random House, 1970).

4. For example, Emerson uses the terms *sedition, criminal anarchy,* and *criminal syndicalism* as near equivalents. Harris, *Black Power Advocacy: Criminal Anarchy or Free Speech*, 56 CALIF. L. REV. 702 (1968), uses the terms *criminal syndicalism* and *criminal anarchy* interchangeably. One of the cases under consideration, Herndon v. Lowry, 301 U.S. 242 (1937), involved the Georgia Anti-Insurrection Law, which despite the title was the same type of legislation as the criminal anarchy and sedition statutes. Dombrowski v. Pfister, 380 U.S. 479 (1965), another case involved in this study, dealt with the Louisiana Subversive Activities Control Law and the Communist Propaganda Law, both of which were forms of sedition statutes.

5. 1917 Minn. Sess. Law Serv. (West), chp. 463; 1942 Miss. Laws, chp. 178; and PA. STAT. ANN. tit. 18 § 4207 (Purdon).

6. 1902 N.Y. Laws § 160-166; CAL. GEN. LAWS ANN. act 8428 (Deering); 1920 Kan. Sess. Laws, chp. 37; 1933 Or. Laws, § 14-3110-3112; and OHIO REV. CODE ANN. § 2923.13 (Page).

7. GA. CODE ANN. §§ 26-901—26-904; 1902 N.Y. Laws §§ 160-166; LA. REV. STAT. ANN. §§ 358-388, 390-390.5 (West).

8. Emerson, *The System of Freedom of Expression*, p. 101. In March 1921, Congress repealed the 1918 Sedition Act passed during the height of

the World War I concerns about disloyalty. See 60 CONG. REC. 293, 4207 (1921), and 41 Stat. 1359 (1921).

9. Zechariah Chafee, Jr., *Free Speech in the United States* (Cambridge, Mass.: Harvard University Press, 1967), p. 595. Appendix III provides a listing of "State War and Peace Statutes Affecting Freedom of Speech." Other works that discuss in detail the background of events that produced the climate for security legislation are William Preston, Jr., *Aliens and Dissenters* (Cambridge, Mass.: Harvard University Press, 1963) and Robert K. Murray, *Red Scare* (Minneapolis: University of Minnesota Press, 1955).

10. 1917 Minn. Sess. Law Serv. (West), chp. 463.

11. Eldridge Dowell, *A History of Criminal Syndicalism Legislation in the United States* (New York: Da Capo Press, 1969), p. 21. Dowell's work, originally published by Johns Hopkins University Press in 1939, is a thorough and authoritative volume on the period that ended in the 1930s. Paul F. Brissenden, *The IWW: A Study of American Syndicalism* (New York: Russell and Russell, 1957) and Melvyn Dubofsky, *We Shall Be All* (Chicago: Quadrangle, 1969) are two well-researched works on the history of the IWW. See also *The Founding Convention of the IWW: Proceedings* (New York: Merit Publishers, 1969).

12. Dowell, *A History of Criminal Syndicalism Legislation*, p. 27.

13. Ibid., pp. 30-37.

14. IDAHO CODE ANN. § 17-4401-4404.

15. 84 U. PA. L. REV. 392 (1936). For additional discussion see Cramton, *The Supreme Court and State Power to Deal with Subversion and Loyalty*, 43 MINN. L. REV. 1025 (1959) and 28 IND. L. J. 492 (1953). See also Preston, *Aliens and Dissenters*, and Murray, *Red Scare*, for greater detail on the Red Scare.

16. State v. Diamond, 27 N. M. 477, 479 (1921), 202 P. 988, 989 (1921); and State v. Gabriel, 95 N. J. L. 337 (1921), 112 A. 611 (1921). The quotation is from the former.

17. Stromberg v. Cal., 283 U.S. 359 (1931). Authorities arrested Yetta Stromberg for displaying a red flag at a youth camp run by the Young Communist League, of which she was a member. See Chafee, *Free Speech*, pp. 362-366.

18. 35 COLUM. L. REV. 917 (1935).

19. Ibid., 926.

20. Alien Registration Act of 1940, 81 U.S.C. § 10, 11, 13 (1940) as amended, 1948, 18 U.S.C. § 2385 (1976).

21. The Smith Act is discussed in detail in Chafee, *Free Speech*, pp. 439-493; Chafee is quoted at p. 441. A more complete legislative history

can be found in Michal R. Belknap, *Cold War Political Justice* (Westport, Conn.: Greenwood Press, 1977), pp. 17-27. See also 61 HARV. L. REV. 1215 (1948). Arkansas, Florida, North Carolina, and Washington enacted the new laws.

22. Pa. v. Nelson, 350 U.S. 497 (1956) and Uphaus v. Wyman, 360 U.S. 72 (1959). Both of these cases will be discussed in chapter 3.

23. Walter Gellhorn, ed., *The States and Subversion* (Ithaca, N.Y.: Cornell University Press, 1952), p. 359. A compendium of these statutes is included in Gellhorn's Appendix A, pp. 393-413. A brief discussion of state legislation during this period is included in David Caute, *The Great Fear* (New York: Simon and Schuster, 1978), pp. 71-78. For further discussion of the domestic repercussion of the cold war see Richard M. Freeland, *The Truman Doctrine and the Origins of McCarthyism* (New York: Alfred A. Knopf, 1972); Alan D. Harper, *The Politics of Loyalty* (Westport, Conn.: Greenwood Press, 1969); and Athan Theoharis, *Seeds of Repression* (Chicago: Quadrangle, 1971). See also William Prendergast, "State Legislatures and Communism: The Current Scene," *American Political Science Review*, 49 (September 1950), 556-574.

24. Gellhorn, *The States and Subversion*, p. 360.

25. Emerson, *The System of Freedom of Expression*, p. 152 and 32 N.Y.U. L. REV. 1302 (1957).

26. Internal Security Act of 1950, 50 U.S.C. § 761 et seq. (1976), and Communist Control Act of 1954, 50 U.S.C. § 841 (1976).

27. Alfred H. Kelly and Winfred A. Harbison, *The American Constitution*, 5th ed. (New York: Norton, 1976), pp. 803-851, provides two chapters on the cold war period. The bibliography of the cold war years is far too lengthy to list here, but helpful overviews include Walter Gellhorn, *American Rights: The Constitution in Action* (New York: Macmillan, 1960); Osmond K. Fraenkel, *The Supreme Court and Civil Liberties* (New York: Oceana, 1960); Milton Konvitz, *Fundamental Liberties of a Free People* (Ithaca, N.Y.: Cornell University Press, 1957); and John W. Caughey, "McCarthyism Rampant," in Alan Reitman, ed., *The Pulse of Freedom* (New York: Norton, 1975). Mary S. McAuliffe, "Liberals and the Communist Control Act of 1954," *Journal of American History*, 63 (September 1976), 351-367, discusses the complexities involved with the passage of the law and assesses in particular Hubert Humphrey's role. See also Mary S. McAuliffe, *Crisis on the Left: Cold War Politics and American Liberals* (Amherst: University of Massachusetts Press, 1978) and Belknap, *Cold War Political Justice*.

28. Few states reviewed their security legislation even after 1956 when the U.S. Supreme Court in Pa. v. Nelson raised serious constitu-

tional questions regarding state security statutes. In 1963, under the leadership of Attorney General Walter Mondale, Minnesota revised and updated its statutes in line with federal court decisions. The Minnesota Legislature repealed the Sedition Act of 1917 but retained the state's Criminal Syndicalism Law. Minnesota appears to have been the exception compared with the inaction of other states. The new states of Alaska and Hawaii, which entered the Union in 1959, did not adopt a proliferation of state security statutes. Alaska developed a criminal syndicalism statute, later repealed in 1978; and Hawaii adopted a statutory section on loyalty to the government. See MINN. STAT. ANN. § 613.08 (West); ALASKA STAT. §§ 11.50.010-11.50.030, repealed 1978, effective January 1, 1980; and HAWAII REV. STAT. § 85. See Appendix for information on security statutes repealed since 1970.

2. THE SUPREME COURT AND STATE SECURITY STATUTES, 1920-1940

In the years 1920-1970 the U.S. Supreme Court provided constitutional interpretation that contributed to the maintenance of the security statutes passed by state legislatures. In this analysis two factors in Supreme Court history stand out in particular. One central point stems from the very nature of Supreme Court decisions, which proceed in piecemeal fashion, gradually creating a body of constitutional interpretation on a given subject. In addition, the Court rulings on political speech in cases involving state security legislation developed dual lines of interpretation that offered state appellate courts an opportunity to pick and choose from precedents that upheld the state police power regulation of speech and from those that discarded state security statutes for lack of a test of clear and present danger. The evolution of these Supreme Court contributions to the network can be demonstrated by closer examination of individual rulings.

The first Supreme Court consideration of state security legislation occurred during the decade of the twenties. The Court dealt with each of the three types of state security laws under consideration here: sedition, criminal syndicalism, and criminal anarchy. The 1920 opinion in *Gilbert* v. *Minnesota* resulted from the Nonpartisan League's challenge to the Republican establishment in the state.[1] Occurring as it did in the wake of the well-known *Schenck* and *Abrams* decisions of 1919, *Gilbert*'s place in constitutional history has been overshadowed by interest in the interpretation of the federal espionage and sedition acts. The Minnesota Sedition Law, passed in April 1917, two months before the corresponding congressional statute, made it illegal to print, publish, circulate, or advocate before more than five persons "that men should not enlist in the military or naval forces of the United States or the State of Minnesota."[2] The legislature reinforced the effect of the statute by establishing a functionally independent Commission of Public Safety designed to coordinate wartime programs and to ensure loyalty to the war effort. The author of the Commission legislation regarded it as a preventive measure that would make it possible to stop disloyalty before it erupted; and the state attorney general issued an order stating, "While the courts are ordinarily the law's agent for law enforcement, they are not under the constitution a necessary factor."[3] However, he neglected to elaborate further to explain what he felt was constitutionally necessary.

After the autumn of 1917, the Commission of Public Safety directed a major part of its loyalty campaign at the farmers' reform organization known as the Nonpartisan League. Recently successful in gaining considerable political power in North Dakota, the League's political strategy centered on running a slate of candidates in the primary election of the majority party—which in nearly every section of Minnesota was the Republican party. The League platform aimed chiefly at correcting the economic plight of farmers and called for state-owned terminal elevators, stockyards, and packing houses and for state control of grain inspection and grading, among other economic reforms. Despite the charges of disloyalty repeatedly leveled against it, the League supported the United States' effort in World War I, reserving the right to criticize policies with which they disagreed.[4] Obviously, it did not support the dictum of the superpatriots who stated that all reform activity should cease until the war ended. Members of the Commission of Public Safety often discussed their animosity toward the League, and the possibility of arresting League organizers and members for violation of the state sedition law lurked in the background.

Harsh feelings between the Commission and the League intensified during the spring of 1918 when the reformers selected as their gubernatorial candidate former Congressman Charles A. Lindbergh, Sr., an outspoken opponent of U.S. entry into the war. In the primary Lindbergh unsuccessfully challenged Republican-incumbent J. A. A. Burnquist, a firm supporter of the Commission and the Sedition Law. Violence plagued the campaign; and Lindbergh himself survived shooting incidents, angry mobs, and an arrest for unlawful assembly. The Commission made good its threats, and state authorities eventually arrested a number of League officials and members.[5] The situation prompted John Lord O'Brian, Special Assistant United States Attorney General for Warwork, to comment that the policy of repression in Minnesota "increased discontent" and that "the most serious cases of alleged interference with civil liberty were reported to the Federal Government from that state."[6] Of the eighteen Minnesota Supreme Court cases based on the Sedition Act of 1917, seven involved the Nonpartisan League, and one reached the U.S. Supreme Court for full consideration—*Gilbert* v. *Minnesota*.

Authorities arrested Joseph Gilbert, the League's Organizational Manager, after a March 14, 1918, indictment by the Goodhue County Grand Jury for remarks allegedly made on August 18, 1917:

We are going over to Europe to make the world safe for democracy, but I tell you we had better make America safe for democracy first. You say, what is the matter with our democracy? I tell you what is the matter with it; have you had anything to say as to who should be Governor of this State? Have you had anything to say as to whether we would go into this war? You know you have not. If this is such a great democracy, for Heaven's sake why should we not vote on conscription of men? We were stampeded into this war by newspaper rot to pull England's chestnuts out of the fire for her. I tell you if they conscripted wealth like they have conscripted men, this war would not last over forty-eight hours.[7]

Gilbert denied having made this statement and insisted he had given staunch support to the Wilson administration and had told his audience, "In the words of President Wilson we will carry on this war to make the world safe for democracy."[8]

Gilbert's trial was highly political in nature, a point not discounted by the fact that it took place at the height of the primary campaign and the fact that a previous grand jury, which had met in October 1917 and was fully aware of the August speech, had not indicted Gilbert at that time. The jury convicted Gilbert after six state witnesses repeated verbatim the ten sentences that appeared in the indictment, a feature that prompted one of Gilbert's lawyers to refer in an appeal brief to "the only parrot chorus in the history of jurisprudence."[9] The trial judge relied upon a broad bad-tendency application of the statute when he instructed the jury that it was not necessary to show that the defendant had directly taught that men should not enlist nor aid the war effort. According to his instructions, "the statute would be violated if the natural and reasonable effect of the words spoken is to teach or advocate that citizens should not aid or assist the U.S."[10]

Gilbert's attorneys appealed unsuccessfully to the Minnesota Supreme Court where a December 20, 1918, decision upheld the statute as a police regulation and ruled that a violation of this statute was criminal regardless of intent and regardless of effect.[11] In November 1920 the U.S. Supreme Court heard the case on a writ of error and in December upheld the Minnesota law with Chief Justice Edward White and Justice Louis Brandeis in dissent. In considering the first case since the adoption of the Fourteenth Amendment to test the issue of state sedition legislation, Justice Joseph McKenna saw the Minnesota statute as part of a cooperative venture within the federal system. Despite the arguments of Gilbert's attorneys contending the exclusive and well-guarded powers of Congress in the area of war and foreign affairs,[12] the majority viewed the Minnesota law as a "simple exertion of the police power to preserve the peace of the State." McKenna declared further that free speech was not an absolute, but it was subject to "restriction and limitation" especially during wartime, and he made no attempt to seek a relationship between Gilbert's words and their effect.[13]

Chief Justice White's dissent was very brief, and his reasoning followed the contention of Gilbert's attorneys that the subject matter involved was "within the exclusive legislative power of Congress."[14] By contrast, Justice Brandeis's dissent raised new questions that were to become part of a compelling body of constitutional development in future decades. Brandeis considered the

Minnesota law unconstitutional because it provided no test to determine relationships between thought and action, but even more importantly Brandeis raised the issue of the Fourteenth Amendment's applicability to situations of this type. He saw the Minnesota Sedition Law as an attempt to "prevent not acts but beliefs," and this he felt interfered with the privileges and immunities of a United States citizen. In his dissent Brandeis supported vigorously federal protection of freedom of speech and other Bill of Rights guarantees from state encroachment, a doctrine that came to be known as the nationalization of the Bill of Rights. As Brandeis stated in his conclusion, "I cannot believe that the liberty guaranteed by the Fourteenth Amendment includes only liberty to acquire and to enjoy property."[15]

By dissenting in the *Gilbert* case, Justice Brandeis maintained the line of reasoning that he had established in earlier free speech cases involving federal law and that concerned the arguments of bad tendency versus proximate causation. However, Brandeis's dissent also added to the area of interpretation on the question of federal-state relationships. This was only the second occasion on which any member of the Court had maintained in any opinion that the Fourteenth Amendment protected freedom of speech from encroachment by state action.[16] Although John Marshall's ruling in *Barron* v. *Baltimore* was not mentioned in the majority opinion, it certainly lurked in the background. In at least twenty rulings since the passage of the Fourteenth Amendment in 1868, the High Court had upheld the old 1833 rule that the Bill of Rights did not apply to the states.[17] However, a change of mind was developing. Not only had the *Gilbert* decision revealed Justice Brandeis's new interpretation of the Fourteenth Amendment, but Justice McKenna's majority opinion had assumed for the sake of argument that the Court could review cases involving free speech and state law.

In the light of the Supreme Court's position in the World War I sedition cases involving federal law, the decision upholding the Minnesota law was no surprise. Yet the *Gilbert* case was significant in itself, for it did involve a state sedition law, an issue that had not been treated previously in the High Court. The main point in sustaining the state law was based upon the Court's majority view that the state police power outweighed the protections of the

First Amendment when considered in relation to the consequences of state action, a point the Court would repeat several times before the end of the decade.

Five years after *Gilbert* the Supreme Court, in the better-known *Gitlow* v. *New York* opinion, provided an additional thread for the security statute phase of the network.[18] The New York Criminal Anarchy Act of 1902, passed in the wake of President McKinley's assassination in Buffalo, provided the statutory basis for the arrest of Benjamin Gitlow. The law, which lay dormant from the time of its passage until Gitlow's arrest in 1919, made it a felony to advocate criminal anarchy by either the printed or the spoken word and defined the crime as the "doctrine that organized government should be overthrown by force or violence... or by any unlawful means."[19] Gitlow was a member of the Left Wing faction that broke from the Socialist party in 1919 and published its "Left Wing Manifesto" in the *Revolutionary Age*, a newspaper for which Gitlow served as business manager. The Manifesto discussed current postwar difficulties and revolutionary struggles. Along the lines of typical Marxist analysis the document called for the destruction of the bourgeois state through "mass strikes" and "mass action" that would lead to the leadership of the proletariat. In 1919 the famed New York Joint Legislative Committee Investigating Seditious Activities, better known as the Lusk Committee, insisted that Gitlow and others be prosecuted for publishing the Manifesto. The state indicted all of the members of the managing council of the *Revolutionary Age*, but convicted only Gitlow, Ignaz Mizher, Harry M. Winitzky, and Irish labor leader Jim Larkin.[20]

Despite the presence of Clarence Darrow as defense counsel, the jury convicted Gitlow in January 1920; and the court sentenced him to five to ten years in Sing Sing. Attorneys appealed the conviction, which the Appellate Division and the New York Court of Appeals subsequently upheld. In their 1922 decision the Court of Appeals judges affirmed the constitutionality of the Criminal Anarchy Law but split over the issue of the construction of the statute. The majority reasoned that the Criminal Anarchy Act could be applied to Communists, even though Communists and anarchists were at opposite poles in the political spectrum of the day. These judges felt that communism was not "a condition which could be fairly regarded as an organized government"; therefore its advocacy was an advocacy of overthrow. However, dissenting Judge Cuthbert Pound along with Benjamin Cardozo, rehearsing for his later role in legal realism, objected to this application, for they felt Gitlow's action did not fall within the limits of the statute. As Pound proclaimed, "Although the defendant may be the worst of men; although Left Wing socialism is a menace to organized government; the rights of the best of men are secure only as the rights of the vilest and most abhorrent are protected."[21]

American Civil Liberties Union attorneys Walter Nelles, Albert DeSilver, and Walter Pollak represented Gitlow before the U.S. Supreme Court. Chief Counsel Pollak based much of the argument in his brief on Brandeis's dissent in *Gilbert* and, as Zechariah Chafee has commented, "convinced the Court that 'Liberty' in the Fourteenth Amendment includes liberty of speech and press."[22] The majority reached this conclusion despite a 1922 opinion written by Justice Mahlon Pitney, *Prudential Insurance Co. v. Cheek*, in which he had stated, "the Constitution of the United States imposes upon the States no obligation to confer upon those within their jurisdiction either the right of speech or the right of silence."[23] Pollak's arguments drew support from a strong 1923 opinion written by Justice James McReynolds that had declared unconstitutional a World War I-vintage Nebraska law that forbade teaching school in any language except English. McReynolds insisted that such a statute violated the due process guarantees of the Fourteenth Amendment; and in 1925 in a decision written one week before *Gitlow*, the Court continued to apply this interpretation of liberty in an Oregon case that overturned a law requiring all children to attend public school.[24] Pollak's brief then concluded that such liberty was so inclusive that it would certainly encompass freedom of speech and press.[25]

Supreme Court consideration in the *Gitlow* case was concerned only with the question of the constitutionality of the New York Criminal Anarchy Law. Although all nine members decided that "we may and do assume that freedom of speech and of the press . . . are among the fundamental personal rights and 'liberties' protected . . . from impairment by the States," only the two dissenters, Oliver Wendell Holmes and Brandeis, felt that the clear and present danger test should be applied to determine what type of speech was protected. As a result, the majority upheld the statute and Gitlow's conviction using a bad-tendency reasoning that allowed words to be punished regardless of any actual consequences. According to Justice Edward Sanford's majority opinion:

A single revolutionary spark may kindle a fire that, smoldering for a time, may burst into sweeping and destructive conflagration. It cannot be said that the State is acting arbitrarily... when... it seeks to extinguish the spark without waiting until it has enkindled the flame or blazed into the conflagration.[26]

In contrast, Holmes's dissent, in which Brandeis joined, argued from the standpoint of the clear and present danger test, insisting, "Every idea is an incitement... Eloquence may set fire to reason. But whatever may be thought of the redundant discourse before us [the Manifesto], it had no chance of starting a present conflagration."[27]

Certainly, a great number of constitutional scholars would argue that the opening of the way for application of the Bill of Rights to the states via the Fourteenth Amendment and the majority rejection of the clear and present danger test are the two most well-known points in the *Gitlow* opinion. However, another ruling in the case had considerable impact upon subsequent developments in state courts. In *Gitlow* the Court held to a traditional position that "every presumption is to be indulged in favor of the validity of the statute." As Sanford pointed out, the case was to be considered "in the light of the principle that the State is primarily the judge of regulations required in the interest of public safety and welfare..."[28] The Court's reaffirmation of its *Gilbert* position on the preeminence of the police power over the protection of political speech provided two precedents for future state appellate courts attempting to maintain state authority within the federal system.

With the *Gitlow* opinion the Supreme Court had ruled in regard to a criminal anarchy statute. Two years later, on May 16, 1927, the High Court spoke again on the subject of political speech in two cases involving criminal syndicalism statutes. *Fiske* v. *Kansas*, which the Court had heard on a writ of error on May 3, 1926, was the High Bench's only state criminal syndicalism statute decision involving the Industrial Workers of the World, the group that the laws had been designed to control.[29] Rice County, Kansas, tried and convicted Harold Fiske for violation of a 1920 law that called into question his association with the Agricultural Workers' Industrial Union No. 110, a branch of the IWW. As an IWW organizer, Fiske had circulated books and pamphlets and had spoken of the necessity for a syndicalist type of industrial organization. He had attempted to persuade others to join his group and had distributed membership cards. At Fiske's trial the only state evidence presented was a copy of the preamble to the IWW Constitution, which referred to the objective of changing the form of government. Upon questioning before the trial court, Fiske had stated he believed in neither violence nor sabotage, nor had he advocated either method. The Kansas Supreme Court upheld his conviction, and his lawyers appealed further.[30]

In writing for a unanimous Supreme Court, Justice Sanford considered the only federal question in the case—whether or not the Kansas Criminal Syndicalism Law was in conflict with the due process clause of the Fourteenth Amendment. Sanford and the other members of the Court concluded that the record indicated that in relying solely upon the preamble to the IWW Constitution, the state had applied the Criminal Syndicalism Law without evidence that the IWW advocated crime or violence: "Thus applied the Act is an arbitrary and unreasonable exercise of the police power of the State, unwarrantably infringing the liberty of the defendant in violation of the due process clause of the Fourteenth Amendment."[31] Although the Court did not discard the Kansas Criminal Syndicalism Statute, Sanford's opinion acknowledged the argument that certain IWW activities enjoyed constitutional protection. Fiske's conviction was reversed and the case remanded to the lower court where it died.[32] In overturning Fiske's conviction, the Supreme Court began the process of providing a second set of precedents in the area of political speech. Although the Supreme Court did not discard the Kansas Criminal Syndicalism Law, the holding in *Fiske* failed to support the presumption of the constitutionality of state authority that emanated from *Gilbert* and *Gitlow*. Also, the *Fiske* procedural point relating to evidence proved to be an important consequence of the opinion in subsequent state court application.

Even though the *Fiske* decision involved the same type of state security law as did *Whitney* v. *California*, the application and ruling in the second case were in considerable contrast to the first.[33] In the *Fiske* ruling the Supreme Court discarded the application of the Kansas Criminal Syndicalism Law and allowed certain activities by persons affiliated with the IWW. In *Whitney* the majority of the justices upheld the state's authority to enact criminal syndicalist legislation and to apply it to those affiliated with a group other than the Industrial Workers of the World. California, having experienced considerable IWW activity in the agricultural fields and the lumber camps since the organization's founding in 1905, was one of the first western states to enact a criminal syndicalism statute.[34] The 1919 California version defined the crime as:

any doctrine or precept advocating, teaching or aiding and abetting the commission of crime, sabotage (which word is hereby defined as meaning willful and malicious physical damage or injury to physical property), or unlawful acts of force and violence or unlawful methods of terrorism as a means of accomplishing a change in industrial ownership or control, or effecting any political change.[35]

Many states that passed criminal syndicalism statutes in the aftermath of World War I did not enforce them to any degree, but this was not the policy in California. Between 1919 and 1924 the state arrested 504 persons and tried 264 of them. Thirty-four of these cases went on to appellate courts, and these proceedings served to silence much IWW activity except for legal defense and amnesty campaigns. As a result, between 1924 and 1930 the state prosecuted no one under the statute because IWW activity was at such a low ebb.[36]

Charlotte Anita Whitney was one of those persons arrested during the early months of the California Criminal Syndicalism Act's enforcement.[37] Her case became what most scholars consider to be the most famous criminal syndicalism ruling made by the U.S. Supreme Court. Miss Whitney, a member of the distinguished family that had produced U.S. Supreme Court Justice Stephen Field and his famous brothers David Dudley and Cyrus, had been well known for her social work and philanthropic activities throughout many of her sixty years. As a member of the Socialist party she, like Benjamin Gitlow, had been involved with the 1919 Left Wing secession. As a result she temporarily belonged to the newly formed Communist Labor party and as a delegate attended an October 1919 convention in Oakland that met to organize a California branch. At the open convention the press reported that Miss Whitney had given vigorous support to achieving political power through the use of the ballot. However, her more traditional political views were in the minority; and the convention urged instead the seizure of power by means of industrial unions and strikes, tactics familiar to the rhetoric of the IWW. In so doing, the Communist Labor party created a pretext for arrest of one of its members under the Criminal Syndicalism Law. Because of her disagreement with the majority of the members of the Communist Labor party, Miss Whitney severed her connection with the group within a month after the convention.

As was the circumstance in both the Gilbert and Fiske prosecutions, authorities arrested Miss Whitney some time after her alleged illegal activity took place. Three weeks following the convention, authorities stopped her as she left an Oakland women's club where she had given a speech on the plight of American blacks. In January 1920, during the height of the Red Scare, an Alameda County Superior Court jury convicted her of criminal syndicalism for the teaching and advocating of violence and for the commission of violence. At her trial, which was complicated by the flu epidemic and the death of one of her attorneys and a juror, she served as the major witness for the defense and was pitted against at least twenty prosecution witnesses. Much of the evidence produced by the state consisted of testimony that discussed acts allegedly committed by the IWW, an organization with which she had no connection whatsoever, during a time period prior to the enactment of the California Criminal Syndicalism Law.[38] Miss Whitney admitted that her activities violated the statute, but her attorneys based her defense upon the contention that the statute on its face violated the Fourteenth Amendment and that her action was insufficient to state a public offense.[39] Defense trial strategy did not consider the applicability of the clear and present danger test, and this oversight later prevented even Holmes and Brandeis from dissenting when the case reached the U.S. Supreme Court. The members of the jury, not convinced that Whitney had taught and committed violence, dismissed those counts and convicted her for organizing a group that they believed to be in violation of the statute. The judge sentenced her to fourteen years in San Quentin for doing nothing more than attending the organizational meeting of the Communist Labor party. The outcome raised the question later phrased by attorney Walter Pollak, "Can an act, innocent at the time, constitutionally become a crime by reason of the subsequent action of other persons?"[40]

Whitney appealed her case through two levels of state appellate courts, receiving negative decisions each time. In 1922 the California Supreme Court refused to rule in the case, thereby affirming the judgment of the trial court. Her attorneys, who by that time included Walter Nelles and Pollak, appealed to the U.S. Supreme Court on a writ of error. They contended that the California courts had denied Anita Whitney equal protection of the law and numerous points of procedural due process.[41] They argued her case on October 6, 1925, and because of a technical difficulty involving the issue of the lack of a federal question had to reargue on March 18, 1926. In the May 16, 1927, opinion Justice Sanford wrote for the majority as he had in *Gitlow*; and his reasoning consisted of four essential points. He ruled that her membership in the party and her participation in the convention provided enough information for her to realize that the organization violated California law. He declared that the California Criminal Syndicalism Act was not unconstitutionally vague and that a person of ordinary intelligence might understand it. He announced further that there was no necessity to distinguish between advocacy and accomplishment. Finally, he ruled that the California Criminal Syndicalism Law did not violate the First Amendment as made applicable to the state by the Fourteenth, and he agreed with the *Gitlow* ruling that the determination of the legislature must be given great weight by the Court, thereby reinforcing the line of precedent supporting the state police power.

Justice Brandeis wrote a well-known concurring opinion for himself and Justice Holmes in which he pressed emphatically the point that the First Amendment limited the legislature's authority to restrict free speech:

The legislature must obviously decide... whether a danger exists which calls for a particular protective measure. But where a statute is valid only in case certain conditions exist, the enactment of the statute cannot alone establish the facts which are essential to its validity. Prohibitory legislation has repeatedly been held invalid, because unnecessary, where the denial of liberty involved was that of engaging in a particular business. The power of the courts to strike down an offending law is no less when the interests involved are not property rights, but the fundamental personal rights of free speech and assembly.[42]

Brandeis agreed with the majority that free speech and assembly rights were not absolute, but he also felt that more than mere advocacy was necessary to justify repression. He explained that a "clear and imminent danger" must be present and that the Court should define a standard for determining the degree of the threat to the established order.

Those who won our independence by revolution were not cowards. They did not fear political change. They did not exalt order at the cost of liberty. To courageous, self-reliant men, with confidence in the power of free and fearless reasoning applied through the processes of popular government, no danger flowing from speech can be deemed clear and present, unless the incidence of the evil apprehended is so imminent that it may befall before there is opportunity for full discussion. If there be time to expose through discussion the falsehood and fallacies, to avert the evil by the processes of education, the remedy to be applied is more speech, not enforced silence. Only an emergency can justify repression. Such must be the rule if authority is to be reconciled with freedom.[43]

The contrast between the *Fiske* and *Whitney* opinions is a murky one. In *Fiske* the Court ruled that because of the trial record the Kansas Criminal Syndicalism Law could not be applied in that case and stated that, although the statute was not unconstitutional, the trial court had construed it to apply to speech, which was constitutionally protected. In many ways Miss Whitney's activity was similar to that of Fiske. However, since the Supreme Court could not consider constitutional questions regarding the clear and present danger application (because they had not been raised in the trial record), her conviction could not be overturned. As a result, not even Holmes and Brandeis could find room to dissent and were forced to voice their objections in a concurring opinion that pointed out the conflict between their interpretation of the First and Fourteenth Amendments and the California law. A few months after the Supreme Court decision in *Whitney*, California Governor C. C. Young pardoned Miss Whitney and justified his action on reasoning resembling that of Brandeis.[44]

Both the majority and the concurring opinions in *Whitney* and the single *Fiske* ruling demonstrate the difficulties in criminal syndicalism cases. As the *University of Pennsylvania Law Review* was quick to note:

Practically all of these statutes were passed as emergency measures to alleviate a condition that arose directly after the World War and which today exists to a much lessened extent. They illustrate the operation of two powerful forces: the right of free speech as against the right of property. That neither shall prevail at the expense of the other has resulted in the test laid down in the *Schenck* case. It therefore becomes exceedingly questionable whether a real need for their being on our statute books now exists.[45]

In the two criminal syndicalism opinions the Supreme Court had sustained the Whitney conviction because the defendant admitted her action; the Court had reversed Fiske's conviction because there was no evidence he committed the action that the state had charged. The *Whitney* opinion confirmed the *Gilbert-Gitlow* line of precedents, and both decisions reflected the piecemeal nature of Court interpretation regarding the First Amendment and political speech.

Like social and economic critics during the twenties, those who exercised political speech and advocated social change during the years of the Great Depression also faced an onslaught of state attempts to quiet discussion of what many authorities considered to be radical programs. States revived the enforcement of criminal syndicalism laws to arrest many who supported left-wing solutions to the severe economic difficulties of the 1930s. One result of this renewed activity to enforce criminal syndicalism statutes was the case of *De Jonge* v. *Oregon*, which appeared on the U.S. Supreme Court docket on December 9, 1936, with a decision one month later on January 4, 1937.[46] During the early years of the depression, Oregon authorities, particularly in the city of Portland, had been concerned about the Communist party's attempts to organize Unemployed Councils, which besieged local officials with demands for jobs. In March 1930, Portland officials decided to crack down and placed a police spy within the Communist party ranks. In September authorities conducted raids on the party headquarters that produced thirteen indictments under the Oregon Criminal Syndicalism Law of 1919, a typical statute outlawing advocacy of any change in the form of government. The first to be convicted was Ben Boloff, an illiterate Russian immigrant laborer and a Communist party member who denied any advocacy or belief in criminal syndicalism. Boloff was the only person convicted in this series of arrests, and the Oregon Supreme Court upheld his conviction in 1931.

Boloff's conviction, and subsequent death as a result of tuberculosis contracted while in prison, helped to create a movement for the repeal of the Oregon Criminal Syndicalism Law. After a voters' initiative failed to muster enough signatures, State Senator Peter Zimmerman introduced a repeal measure during the 1933 session of the Oregon Legislature. The bill received considerable support from the Grange, the Oregon Federation of Labor, educational institutions, and a number of influential newspapers. Despite the repeal sentiment, in the end the legislature modified the law only slightly by omitting the section that punished a person merely for belonging to a group that advocated syndicalist doctrine.[47]

It was this modified version of the law that the state used in the arrest of Dirk De Jonge, who on July 27, 1934, addressed a Communist party-organized public meeting in Portland. Handbills had advertised the gathering as a "protest against illegal raids on workers' halls and homes and against the shooting of striking longshoremen by Portland police." Most of the 150 to 300 persons who attended this orderly meeting were not Communists, and the speakers adhered to the immediate issues. However, they did encourage people to join the Communist party and to purchase literature available at the meeting. Police raided the meeting and arrested De Jonge and several others. The indictment brought under the Criminal Syndicalism Law charged that he "did then and there...conduct and assist in conducting an assemblage of persons, organization, society and group; to-wit; The Communist Party...which...did then and there...teach and advocate the doctrine of criminal syndicalism and sabotage."[48]

Despite the fact that the state could not demonstrate that any unlawful activity had taken place at the meeting, the jury convicted De Jonge primarily because of his Communist party membership. The prosecution had introduced additional criminal syndicalist literature, attempting to demonstrate the party's adherence to illegal doctrine. When De Jonge appealed his case to the Oregon Supreme Court, his attorneys, led by Osmond Fraenkel, argued that he had been denied due process of law because he had been convicted on a charge not made in the indictment. However, the Oregon justices reasoned differently and held that De Jonge's participation in a meeting called by the Communist party demonstrated his guilt.[49] Neither the content nor the proceedings of the meeting was relevant, according to the state court.

When Osmond Fraenkel argued De Jonge's appeal before the U.S. Supreme Court, he contended that the Oregon Criminal Syndicalism Law violated the due process clause of the Fourteenth Amendment in relation to the First Amendment guarantees of free speech and assembly. He questioned the constitutionality of a statute that "punishes a person for participation in a lawful meeting, called for a lawful purpose, merely because the meeting was called by an organization which, it is charged, advocated prohibited doctrines." He found this policy particularly disturbing since the Communist party had been included on the Oregon ballot in the 1932 election.[50]

On the other side, the state's brief argued that

the State has determined through its legislative body, that to preside at, conduct, or assist in conducting a meeting of an organization which has as its objective the advocacy, teaching or affirmative suggestion of crime, sabotage or violence as a means of affecting a change or revolution in industry or government, involves such dangers to the public peace and the security of the State, that these acts should be penalized in the exercise of its police power.

Oregon revealed even more of its paternalistic nature by stating further:

Laws of this type are founded upon the principle that the moron, especially those [sic] who are class conscious, and who believe that men in high places got there through imposition upon the toilers, are likely to translate into action the words of their voluble leaders. The will of the schemer is often carried out by the acts of the unthinking.[51]

In 1937 the Oregon arguments did not impress the U.S. Supreme Court. By this time the influence of legal realism upon the Hughes Court had created a greater concern for the facts applied as evidence in a case.[52] In a unanimous decision, in which Justice Harlan Fiske Stone did not participate, the High Court, speaking through Chief Justice Charles Evans Hughes, ruled the Oregon Criminal Syndicalism Law to be unconstitutionally broad. The state had sentenced De Jonge to seven years in prison for assisting at a meeting considered unlawful merely because it had been arranged by the Communist party. Hughes countered, "peaceable assembly for lawful discussion cannot be made a crime." As the chief justice saw it, De Jonge's sole offense was his participation in a lawful gathering.[53] Hughes pointed out that the Oregon statute demanded a great curtailment of freedom of speech and assembly. Hughes reiterated what the Court had declared earlier: "Freedom of speech and of the press are fundamental rights which are safeguarded by the due process clause of the Fourteenth Amendment"; then he broadened the concept by stating that the right of assembly was "equally fundamental." In reference to the legislature's concern with state security the Court stated, "legislative intervention can find constitutional justification only by dealing with the abuse. The rights themselves must not be curtailed."[54]

The chief justice went on to make a firm declaration on behalf of the importance of political discussion:

The greater the importance of safeguarding the community from incitements to the overthrow of our institutions by force and violence, the more imperative is the need to preserve inviolate the constitutional rights of free speech, free press and free assembly in order to maintain the opportunity for free political discussion, to the end that government may be responsive to the will of the people and that changes, if desired, may be obtained by peaceful means. Therein lies the security of the Republic, the very foundation of constitutional government.[55]

As a result of this line of reasoning, the Supreme Court declared the Oregon law in conflict with the due process clause of the Fourteenth Amendment, reversed De Jonge's conviction, and remanded the case for further proceedings. Later in 1937, the Oregon Legislature, having already experienced a movement for repeal of the Criminal Syndicalism Statute, removed the law from the books and substituted a simple conspiracy measure. Despite the impetus that the Supreme Court gave to the Oregon Legislature, the *De Jonge* decision left many questions unanswered. A May 1937 article in the *Columbia Law Review* pointed to a few of these: Are communist doctrines seditious? Could party membership be punished? Could the clear and present danger test be applied to criminal syndicalism laws? Did the Communist party possess the unique position of being legal under election laws, but illegal under criminal syndicalism statutes? Even more crucial was the nature of the *De Jonge* precedent: "By choosing to rest its decision on the broad ambit of the Oregon statute, the Court confirmed a previously suspected intent to decide each case on the narrowest possible grounds, rather than articulate criteria of constitutionality for criminal syndicalism laws less sweeping in scope."[56]

From a more positive standpoint the *University of Pennsylvania Law Review* in a case note on *De Jonge* saw a solution for an increasing array of problems based on state security laws: "The increasing prevalence of repressive legislation in recent years points to the desirability of clearly defined limitations upon the power of the states to impair civil liberties."[57] Apparently, this author saw great possibilities for the use of the Fourteenth Amendment and few difficulties within the tiers of the federal system. As subsequent developments would demonstrate, many state courts and legislatures would see the situation differently.

Even though *De Jonge* joined *Fiske* in the line of precedents supporting the protection of political speech, the High Court opinion in the Oregon case was not a sweeping statement. In addition, the *Gilbert-Gitlow-Whitney* holdings remained to support state attempts to continue enforcement of state security statutes. Later in 1937, three months after the *De Jonge* ruling, the Court would provide another interpretation on the subject of political speech and state security statutes.

The case of *Herndon* v. *Lowry*, argued on February 8, 1937, and decided on April 26, 1937, considered the Georgia Anti-Insurrection Law, which had been in effect since 1866.[58] Originally passed as a Reconstruction modification of a regulation designed to prevent slave revolts, the statute read, "Any attempt, by persuasion or otherwise, to induce others to join in any combined resistance to lawful authority of the state shall constitute an attempt to incite insurrection." The act stipulated the death penalty for actual insurrection, but not for an attempt to incite.[59] The statute, which was a mid-nineteenth-century prototype for later state security legislation, also included a clause that would impose a five-to twenty-year sentence for circulating insurrectionary literature, and it was this section that authorities used to arrest Angelo Herndon. Between 1866 and the prosecution of Herndon, Georgia had used the statute only twice. The revival of its application during the early years of the Great Depression was due partly to tremendous fear of communist agitation among blacks and also, as Charles Martin has pointed out in his detailed study of the Herndon case, because the Georgia Legislature had not enacted any subsequent sedition or criminal syndicalism statutes.[60]

In the spring of 1930 concern over what was considered to be a communist threat to Atlanta prompted Fulton County Prosecutor John H. Hudson to begin a series of raids and arrests. As already pointed out in the *De Jonge* discussion, Communists in a number of cities throughout the country had sponsored Unemployed Councils, which had encouraged organized labor activity and had also preached racial equality among workers.[61] The Atlanta of the early thirties was still a very traditional southern city filled with considerable racial friction and suffering severe depression consequences, evidenced by a much-decreased tax base, high unemployment, and exhausted relief funds. Despite all of the evidence of severe social and economic problems, Fulton County Commissioner Walter C. Hendrix commented in June 1932, "I do not believe that there is any vast army of starving in our midst."[62] For those who thought like Hendrix, the logical reason for unrest among the people was the presence of outside—primarily communist—agitators.

Atlanta authorities considered Angelo Herndon to be such an agitator. Born in poverty in Ohio in 1913, Herndon had lived in the South since the early twenties. In 1930 he had responded to an advertisement for a meeting of the Birmingham, Alabama, Unemployed Council. He attended and was swayed by the rhetoric of economic unity of blacks and whites. Shortly after joining the group, he participated in a campaign to organize miners. After an arrest and conviction, later thrown out on appeal, he formally joined the Communist party. In 1932, work with the Unemployed Councils took him to Atlanta where he recruited new members and also campaigned for William Z. Foster for president.[63] Herndon and the Council also began to make plans for a large rally of the jobless to be held at the Fulton County Courthouse on June 30 for the purpose of demonstrating to Commissioner Hendrix the need for poor relief. The night before the rally Herndon and others distributed leaflets advertising this meeting, which took place under Herndon's leadership. As a result, the county commissioners, after conferring with white demonstrators only, promised economic relief for both races. Life in Atlanta quieted down, but the demonstration had reminded the local authorities of the communist presence in town.

As a result, Atlanta police undertook surveillance of the leaders of the Unemployed Council and on July 11, 1932, arrested Angelo Herndon as he collected the Council's mail at a post office box. Herndon went to jail without the court setting bail; and the Fulton County Grand Jury, which met the next day, took no action. Finally, after a *habeas corpus* petition, the grand jury indicted him on July 22, charging the capital crime of an attempt to incite insurrection through meetings and speeches that sought to bring both whites and blacks together into the Communist party with the purpose of inciting riots. The grand jury also charged that Herndon had solicited persons "for the purpose of waging war against the state" by means of the Communist party and that he had circulated pamphlets aimed at insurrection. All of this activity was alleged to have taken place on July 16, a day that Herndon had spent in the Fulton County jail.[64]

At first, Herndon's arrest attracted little notice. Most of the existing national concern about racial injustice was focused on the rape trial of young blacks in Scottsboro, Alabama. However, the Communist-supported International Labor Defense (ILD) dispatched William Patterson to Atlanta. He promptly denounced Herndon's indictment as a frame-up and stated that the literature found in Herndon's room contained statements identical to some of those included in books in the Atlanta Public Library. After some confusion over who was to serve as Herndon's counsel, the ILD retained a young black Harvard Law School graduate, Benjamin J. Davis, Jr., and his black partner, John Geer, as defense attorneys. Herndon's attorneys developed several constitutional points as the basis for the case: the alleged unconstitutionality of the insurrection statute, the systematic exclusion of blacks from the jury, and the First Amendment rights of assembly and petition. They also attempted to deal with other political aspects of the trial, such as economic conditions and white supremacy. Although communist funds supported the ILD, the group had many non-communist members—persons in the forefront of helping blacks; and they saw the Herndon case as an opportunity "for a broad assault on racism and Jim Crow justice."[65]

After numerous unsuccessful attempts by the defense to place blacks on the jury, the Herndon trial began on January 16, 1933. Judge Lee B. Wyatt, presided and promptly threw out a challenge to jury selection on the grounds that there had been no intent to discriminate. Police testified as to the evidence they had collected—Communist party literature mailed from New York and minutes of local Communist party meetings. Since the state could show no secret plans for armed intervention, the prosecution concentrated its attack on the radical views of the defendant. The judge allowed the state's evidence despite the fact that the police had seized the papers without a warrant and had admitted in testimony that they had not actually seen Herndon distributing the pamphlets. The inexperienced Davis had difficulty handling the witness testimony, much of which was filled with racist comments. The judge sustained numerous objections to Davis's questions and often ruled the defense attorney's points immaterial.[66]

Prosecution summation for the jury enhanced the political nature of the trial by playing to white fears. County Prosecutor John H. Hudson announced that the Communist party advocated miscegenation, seizure of white property, and secession from the United States. Since Herndon was a Communist, it could be concluded that he was a serious threat to the security of Georgia. Davis countered with charges of racism, stating that Herndon was on trial because he was black. He commented at one point that the Ku Klux Klan was a far more revolutionary force in Georgia than was the Communist party. Despite the judge's charge that the evidence must show advocation of "immediate serious violence," the jury convicted Herndon. The court sentenced him to eighteen to twenty years.[67]

Reaction to the arrest and conviction demonstrated the traditional lines of conflict in Atlanta. Black leaders and white southerners concerned with civil liberties formed a loosely knit Provisional Committee for the Defense of Angelo Herndon, and the American Civil Liberties Union provided funds and support. During 1933, Judge Wyatt denied a motion for a new trial, but the ILD continued to work for support of Herndon and encountered conflict with the Atlanta National Association for the Advancement of Colored People, which wanted to concentrate on the racial rather than the class struggle issues in the *Herndon* case. Meanwhile, by 1934, Herndon and the impossible conditions in the Fulton County jail had attracted some national attention. In the midst of these developments, on May 24, 1934, the Georgia Supreme Court upheld Herndon's conviction. They ruled that the point regarding the statute's constitutionality had not been raised at the proper time in the proceedings, and they dismissed the objection to illegally seized evidence, "evidence discovered by the search of a person while he was under an illegal arrest, if relevant, is not inadmissible."[68] The decision served only to heighten racial conflict in Georgia. The ILD decided to finance a U.S. Supreme Court appeal and

hired New York attorney Whitney North Seymour, assisted by
Walter Gellhorn and Herbert Wechsler, to complete the task of
appealing the first state security case from a southern state.
White Atlanta attorneys W. A. Sutherland and Elbert Tuttle
replaced Davis and Geer whose sloppy trial work had predetermined
the Supreme Court's six-to-three dismissal of Herndon's arguments on technical grounds on May 30, 1935.[69]

By 1935 the *Herndon* case had generated a sizable sympathy
across the country. Liberal hostility to the ILD and the Communist party was replaced by a united front approach as Americans
reacted to the rise of Hitler in Germany. In September 1935,
liberal and radical groups formed the Joint Committee to Aid the
Herndon Defense. After the U.S. Supreme Court refused a rehearing, the case was returned to Georgia in October 1935, and
Herndon surrendered to Fulton County officials to create the
grounds for a *habeas corpus* proceeding. Late in 1935, Judge Hugh
Dorsey ruled the insurrection law unconstitutional because of
vagueness and lack of "a sufficiently ascertainable standard of
guilt." On June 13, 1936, the Georgia Supreme Court reversed
Judge Dorsey; and Seymour appealed again to the U.S. Supreme
Court, which delayed hearing the case until 1937.[70] As a result of
these delays, the second *Herndon* decision came after the *De
Jonge* ruling and in the midst of the Court-packing controversy.

In the brief presented to the Supreme Court, Seymour argued
two central points: first, that the Georgia statute punished utterances that bore no relation to a clear and present danger and,
second, that the standard of guilt found in the statute and applied
by the Georgia courts was unconstitutionally vague. Counsel
contended that the statute did not condemn the specific doctrine
that Herndon had advocated since the statute had originated in
conditions long since removed from the political scene. Furthermore, the argument continued, "no decision of this Court indicates that a state may constitutionally penalize utterances which
may be deemed to import the use of force only at some indefinite
time in the future."[71] In addition, Seymour distinguished the provisions of the Georgia Penal Code from the statutes sustained in
Gitlow and *Whitney*,[72] a move that contributed to the creation of
dual lines of precedent and to the piecemeal nature of the development of constitutional doctrine in the area of political speech.

On April 26, 1937, the High Court ruled five-to-four that the Georgia Anti-Insurrection Law violated the Fourteenth Amendment because the statute placed restrictions upon speech and because it provided no reasonable standard of guilt. In writing the majority opinion, Justice Owen Roberts declared that the Georgia Supreme Court had erred in not granting Herndon a writ of *habeas corpus* and remanded the case to the lower court, which released Herndon. The opinion concluded that the Georgia statute violated free speech and assembly and was so vague and indefinite as to allow conviction for having membership in the Communist party, for advocating social relief measures not criminal on their face, and for expressing views on racial equality. Roberts noted further that there was no evidence Herndon had distributed the booklets seized as evidence:

The statute, as construed and applied, amounts merely to a dragnet which may enmesh anyone who agitates for a change of government if a jury can be persuaded that he ought to have foreseen his words would have some effect in the future conduct of others. No reasonably ascertainable standard of guilt is prescribed.[73]

Justice Roberts also commented on the state's contention that the *Gitlow* ruling, in regard to accepting the action of the legislature, applied in this case. He reasoned that "the judgment of the legislature is not unfettered. The limitation upon individual liberty must have appropriate relation to the safety of the state."[74] In this sense Roberts reasoned contrary to the *Gitlow* majority and applied a clear and present danger type of test in addition to discarding the standards of guilt employed by the state of Georgia. His opinion added to the *Fiske-De Jonge* line of precedents without overturning any rulings in the *Gilbert-Gitlow-Whitney* progression.

In the dissenting opinion Justice Willis Van Devanter wrote for himself and Justices James McReynolds, George Sutherland, and Pierce Butler. In the last opinion written before his retirement Van Devanter contended that the Georgia standard was reasonable and delivered a lengthy discussion on the need to ensure the security of the state.[75]

By the time of the *De Jonge* and *Herndon* decisions of 1937 the Court had begun to deviate from the stand it had taken on state security legislation during the twenties. The gradual, inch-by-inch development of the judicial doctrine of the nationalization of the First Amendment, demonstrated in the 1931 *Near* and *Stromberg* opinions, added to a body of constitutional interpretation that no longer presumed that actions of state legislatures were to go unquestioned. In addition, the Court had applied a form of clear and present danger test in a number of First Amendment opinions, including *De Jonge* and *Herndon*. Yet the development of judicial doctrine here, as in most areas, was a piecemeal process. Even though the *De Jonge* and *Herndon* decisions ruled against state security statutes, the opinions in those cases did not remove the *Gilbert-Gitlow-Whitney* line of precedent, which still could be applied in future cases decided in state supreme courts. As the nation moved into the era of World War II and the ensuing cold war period, enforcement of state security laws continued to raise important First Amendment considerations, and during those years the questions of preemption and federalism were to receive additional judicial consideration.

NOTES

1. Gilbert v. Minn., 254 U.S. 325 (1920); 41 Sup. Ct. Rep. 125 (1920); and 65 Law. Ed. 287 (1920). The conflict between the League and Minnesota authorities is discussed thoroughly in Carol E. Jenson, "Agrarian Pioneer in Civil Liberties: The Nonpartisan League in Minnesota During World War I" (Ph.D. diss., University of Minnesota, 1968); and in Carol E. Jenson, "Loyalty as a Political Weapon: The 1918 Campaign in Minnesota," *Minnesota History*, 43 (Summer 1972), 42-57. Paul L. Murphy, *World War I and the Origins of Civil Liberties in the United States* (New York: Norton, 1979), explains why and how civil liberties issues began to attract attention during the war years and the early twenties.

2. 1917 Minn. Sess. Law Serv. (West), chp. 463.

3. *Report of the Minnesota Commission of Public Safety* (St. Paul: State of Minnesota, 1919), pp. 9-12. Attorney General Smith's quotation is from Tighe, *The Legal Theory of the Minnesota "Safety Commission" Act*, 3 MINN. L. REV. 10 (1918).

4. The platform plans were explained in a series of articles in the *Nonpartisan Leader*, vols. 1-2 (December-January, 1915-1916). See also Jenson, "Loyalty," p. 44. The statements on the war are listed in *Resolu-*

tions Adopted by the Nonpartisan League Conference, September 18-20, 1917, p. 2, Arthur Le Sueur Papers, Minnesota Historical Society.

5. Jenson,"Loyalty," pp. 55-56. In another League case, Townley v. Minn., 257 U.S. 643 (1921), the U.S. Supreme Court did not grant *certiorari*.

6. JOHN LORD O'BRIAN, "CIVIL LIBERTY IN WARTIME," S. DOC. 434, 65th Cong., 2d Sess. 12 (1918), originally published as a *Report of the New York State Bar Association*, vol. 42.

7. Indictment at 2, State v. Gilbert, 141 Minn. 263 (1918), 169 N.W. 790 (1918).

8. Record at 173, 141 Minn. 263, 169 N.W. 790.

9. Brief for Appellant at 21-22, 141 Minn. 263, 169 N.W. 790.

10. Record at 236, 141 Minn. 263, 169 N.W. 790.

11. 141 Minn. 263, 169 N.W. 790.

12. Brief for Plaintiff in Error at 18-19, 254 U.S. 325 (1920).

13. 254 U.S. 325, 331-333.

14. Ibid. at 334.

15. Ibid. at 334-343, quoted at 343.

16. Zechariah Chafee, Jr., *Free Speech in the United States* (Cambridge, Mass.: Harvard University Press, 1967), p. 295, states that Brandeis's dissent in Gilbert was the first occasion for such a statement. However, Justice John Marshall Harlan had made a similar pronouncement in 1907 in Patterson v. Colo., 205 U.S. 454 (1907).

17. Warren, *The New Liberty Under the Fourteenth Amendment*, 39 HARV. L. REV. 436 (1926).

18. Gitlow v. N. Y., 268 U.S. 652 (1925); 45 Sup. Ct. Rep. 625 (1925); and 69 Law. Ed. 1138 (1925).

19. 1902 N.Y. Laws § 160-166. For a picture of New York during the 1914-1919 Red Scare see Julian F. Jaffe, *Crusade Against Radicalism* (Port Washington, N.Y.: Kennikat Press, 1972); chapter 8, "The Courts: Cases of Criminal Anarchy," discusses the Gitlow case at some length. See also Paul L. Murphy, *The Meaning of Freedom of Speech* (Westport, Conn.: Greenwood Press, 1972), p. 80.

20. Further background on the Gitlow case is discussed in Chafee, *Free Speech*, pp. 318-325 and Samuel J. Konefsky, *The Legacy of Holmes and Brandeis* (New York: Macmillan, 1956), pp. 205-208. Governor Al Smith later granted executive clemency to Gitlow, based on Justice Oliver Wendell Holmes's position that Gitlow had presented no clear and present danger. For additional material on Gitlow see Harold Josephson, "The Dynamics of Repression: New York During the Red Scare," *Mid-America* 59 (October 1977), 131-146, and Matthew Josephson and Hannah Josephson, *Al Smith: Hero of the Cities* (Boston: Houghton Mifflin, 1969), p. 236.

21. People v. Gitlow, 234 N.Y. 132, 158 (1922), 136 N.E. 317, 327 (1922).

22. Paul L. Murphy, *The Constitution in Crisis Times* (New York: Harper & Row, 1972), p. 83. For the comment see Zechariah Chafee, Jr., "Walter Heilprin Pollak," *Nation*, 151 (October 12, 1940), 319.

23. Prudential Ins. Co. v. Cheek, 259 U.S. 530, 539 (1922).

24. Meyer v. Neb., 262 U.S. 390 (1923) and Pierce v. Soc'y of Sisters, 268 U.S. 510 (1925).

25. Brief for Plaintiff in Error at 11, 268 U.S. 652 (1925).

26. 268 U.S. 652, 666, 669.

27. Ibid. at 673. For a thorough discussion of clear and present danger see Martin Shapiro, *Freedom of Speech: The Supreme Court and Judicial Review* (Englewood Cliffs, N.J.: Prentice-Hall, 1966).

28. 268 U.S. 652, 668. Sanford quoted from Great Northern Ry. v. Clara City, 246 U.S. 434, 439 (1918). See also Boudin, *"Seditious Doctrines" and the "Clear and Present Danger" Rule*, 38 VA. L. REV. 161 (1952). References to the significance of Gitlow can be found in Chafee, *Free Speech*; Konefsky, *The Legacy of Holmes*; Murphy, *The Constitution*; and Murphy, *The Meaning of Freedom of Speech*, as well as numerous other works on the First Amendment.

29. Fiske v. Kan., 274 U.S. 380 (1927); 47 Sup. Ct. Rep. 655 (1927); and 71 Law. Ed. 1108 (1927).

30. Brief for Plaintiff in Error at 1-7, 274 U.S. 380 (1927).

31. 274 U.S. 380, 387.

32. For a discussion of the Fiske ruling see Chafee, *Free Speech*, pp. 351-352 and Murphy, *The Constitution*, p. 87.

33. Whitney v. Cal., 274 U.S. 357 (1927); 47 Sup. Ct. Rep. (1927); and 71 Law. Ed. 1095 (1927).

34. Eldridge Dowell, *A History of Criminal Syndicalism Legislation in the United States* (New York: Da Capo Press, 1969), p. 49.

35. CAL. GEN. LAWS ANN. act 8428 (Deering).

36. Chafee, *Free Speech*, p. 327. Dowell, *A History of Criminal Syndicalism Legislation*, p. 122, in note 46, states that by 1932 California had imprisoned 135 people for violations of the Criminal Syndicalism Act.

37. Chafee, *Free Speech*, p. 333 and Dowell, *A History of Criminal Syndicalism Legislation*, pp. 122-124.

38. Brief for Plaintiff in Error at 39, 274 U.S. 357. Background material on Anita Whitney can be found in Murphy, *The Constitution*, p. 85; Murphy, *The Meaning of Freedom of Speech*, pp. 49-50; Boudin, "Seditious Doctrines," p. 163; and Chafee, *Free Speech*, pp. 343-344. Miss Whitney's uncle, David Dudley Field, was well known for his work in

codification of state law. Cyrus Field is remembered as the financier responsible for planning the first transatlantic cable.

39. Brief for Plaintiff in Error at 1-2, 274 U.S. 357.

40. Ibid. at 49. See also People v. Whitney, 57 Cal. App. 449 (1922), 207 p. 698 (1922); Chafee, *Free Speech*, p. 354; and Boudin, *"Seditious Doctrines,"* p. 164.

41. Brief for Plaintiff in Error at 1, 22-23, 84, 274 U.S. 357.

42. 274 U.S. 357, 359-374. The opinion is quoted at 374.

43. Ibid. at 377.

44. Ibid at 379. Brandeis stated, "She claimed below that the statute as applied to her violated the Federal Constitution; but she did not claim that it was void because there was no clear and present danger of serious evil, nor did she request that the existence of these conditions of a valid measure thus restricting the rights of free speech and assembly be passed upon by the court or a jury." See also Chafee, *Free Speech*, p. 353.

45. 76 U. PA. L. REV. 203 (1927).

46. De Jonge v. Or., 299 U.S. 353 (1937); 57 Sup. Ct. Rep. 255 (1937); and 81 Law. Ed. 278 (1937).

47. Dowell, *A History of Criminal Syndicalism Legislation*, pp. 119-122; State v. Boloff, 138 Or. 568 (1931), 4 P. 2d 326 (1931). The Oregon Code of 1930, as amended 1933, read as follows: "Criminal Syndicalism hereby is defined to be the doctrine which advocates crime, physical violence, sabotage or any unlawful acts or methods as a means of accomplishing industrial or political change or revolution" (133 Or. Laws § 14-3110-3112).

48. 299 U.S. 353, 360.

49. Transcript of Record at 1, 299 U.S. 353. See also Chafee, *Free Speech*, p. 385 and 37 COLUM. L. REV. 857-860 (1937).

50. Brief for Appellant at 4-12, 299 U.S. 353; quoted at 7.

51. Appellee's Brief at 28-29, 299 U.S. 353.

52. For an analysis of the development of legal realism during this period see Edward A. Purcell, "American Jurisprudence Between the Wars: Legal Realism and the Crisis of Democratic Theory," *American Historical Review*, 75 (December 1969), 424-446. See also Murphy, *The Constitution*, pp. 104-105.

53. 299 U.S. 353, 365.

54. Ibid. at 364-365.

55. Ibid. at 365.

56. Dowell, *A History of Criminal Syndicalism Legislation*, p. 147, Appendix I and 37 COLUM. L. REV. 858 (1937). See additional law journal reaction in 4 U. CHI. L. REV. 490 (1937); 25 CALIF. L. REV.

499 (1937); and Bloom, *Constitutional Law—Validity of Criminal Syndicalism Statute*, 35 MICH. L. REV. 1171 (1937).

57. 85 U. PA. L. REV. 533 (1937).

58. Herndon v. Lowry, 301 U.S. 242 (1937); 57 Sup. Ct. Rep. 732 (1937); 81 Law. Ed. 1066 (1937). A thorough discussion of the Herndon case can be found in Charles H. Martin, *The Angelo Herndon Case and Southern Justice* (Baton Rouge: Louisiana State University Press, 1976).

59. GA. CODE ANN. §§ 26-901—26-904. The law was passed originally by the Georgia General Assembly, meeting in Milledgeville in November-December 1866.

60. Chafee, *Free Speech*, p. 389; Martin, *The Angelo Herndon Case*, pp. 20-21, quoted at p. 21. The only other prior cases prosecuted under the act were Gibson v. Ga., 38 Ga. 571 (1869), in which the Georgia Supreme Court overturned the conviction because the defendant had only attempted incitement and Carr v. State, 176 Ga. 55 (1932), 166 S.E. 827 (1932), and 176 Ga. 747 (1933), 167 S.E. 103 (1933). In the Gibson case authorities charged a "free person of color" with attempting to plan a jail rescue. Chief Justice Joseph E. Brown, sitting during the period of military Reconstruction, applied a strict rule of construction in the case and declared that the code punished attempts at insurrection but not attempts to incite insurrection, thereby reversing the conviction (38 Ga. 573).

61. Georgia authorities felt that communist infiltration began with the Gastonia strike of 1929. This concern resulted in the reactivation of the Reconstruction Anti-Insurrection Law and led to the Carr arrest in 1930.

62. Martin, pp. 1-20, quoted at p. 4.

63. Ibid., pp. 8-10.

64. Transcript of Record at 6-10, 301 U.S. 242 (1937); quoted at 8.

65. Ibid. at 1-5, and Martin, *The Angelo Herndon Case*, pp. 11-16, quoted at p. 16. For additional material on Davis see an autobiographical account in Benjamin J. Davis, *Communist Councilman from Harlem* (New York: International Publishers, 1969). For a discussion of the South of the thirties from the perspective of a black attorney see William Patterson, *The Man Who Cried Genocide* (New York: International Publishers, 1971).

66. Transcript of record at 9-19, 301 U.S. 242.

67. Ibid. at 33-37.

68. Martin, *The Angelo Herndon Case*, pp. 97-108, Herndon v. State, 178 Ga. 832, 844 (1934), 174 S.E. 597, 604 (1934).

69. Martin, *The Angelo Herndon Case*, pp. 140-146; Herndon v. Georgia, 295 U.S. 441 (1935).

70. Lowry, Sheriff v. Herndon, 182 Ga. 582 (1936), 192 S.E. 397 (1936); Martin, *The Angelo Herndon Case*, pp. 157-170, quoted at p. 164. See also White, *Protection of Freedom of Speech Under the Fourteenth Amendment*, 35 MICH. L. REV. 1373 (1937).

71. Brief for Appellant at 4-13, 301 U.S. 242; quoted at 13.

72. Ibid. at 39.

73. 301 U.S. 241, 263-264.

74. Ibid. at 258. See also 50 HARV. L. REV. 1313 (1937).

75. 301 U.S. 241, 264-278.

3. THE SUPREME COURT AND STATE SECURITY STATUTES, 1940-1970

As the nation moved from the economic and political problems of the thirties into the wartime atmosphere of the early forties, security statutes continued to play a role in legal and constitutional history. In contrast to the circumstances of World War I, authorities made few arrests under state security statutes during World War II. After the German invasion of the Soviet Union in June 1941, the anti-Nazi position of both the United States and the Soviet Union made the prosecution of left-wing radicals for violation of either federal or state law far less an issue than during World War I. The 1941-1945 period produced only one U.S. Supreme Court decision involving a state sedition statute—the case of *Taylor* v. *Mississippi*.[1]

In a burst of early wartime enthusiasm in 1942, Mississippi, along with several other southern states, had seen fit to pass sedition statutes that as construed in state courts made it a "criminal offense to communicate to others views and opinions respecting governmental policies and prophecies concerning the state of this and other nations." Since the law applied regardless of the intent, purpose, or result of the speech involved, a person could be arrested under the act for mere conversational speculation about what might happen during the war. The law also made it a criminal act to encourage "violence, sabotage, or disloyalty to the government of the United States, or to the state of Mississippi."[2] The latter provision in the Mississippi Sedition Law, which was similar to a number of other state statutes, raised the potential question of whether states could constitutionally attempt to limit criticism of the U.S. government or whether Congress had preempted the field, particularly after the passage of the Smith Act. In an earlier case Joseph Gilbert's attorneys had raised this same issue, but in 1920 only the dissenting Chief Justice White had chosen to respond to the point.[3]

The *Taylor* case and its companion *Benoit* and *Cummings* cases originated in 1942 when authorities arrested Betty Taylor and two others for violating the recently passed Sedition Law. The defendants were members of the Jehovah's Witnesses and had circulated a pamphlet advocating that persons not salute the flag. Taylor had also stated, to two women who had lost sons in the war, that it was wrong to send our boys overseas to fight enemies. She had argued that peace would come sooner if people stopped worshipping the flag and the government.[4] After their convictions in the trial court, the defendants appealed to the Mississippi Supreme Court, which in a tie vote on January 25, 1943, upheld the state law as valid "temporary, emergency war legislation." The court cited *Gilbert* v. *Minnesota* to state that free speech was not absolute and the 1940 *Minersville School District* v. *Gobitis* compulsory flag salute precedent to hold that First Amendment religious liberty did not extend to a refusal to recognize the authority of the state.[5] Three Mississippi justices dissented concluding that the circumstances presented a greater damage to free speech than to the war effort. They also referred to *Herndon* precedent, noting that the Mississippi statute did not provide a discernible standard of guilt.[6]

Appellants took their case to the U.S. Supreme Court, which heard argument on April 15 to 16, 1943, and rendered a decision on June 14, 1943. New York attorney Hayden C. Covington argued on behalf of the Witnesses that the statute violated freedom of speech, press, and religion and denied due process and equal protection. He also cited *Herndon* precedent to charge that the statute was vague and uncertain and failed to "furnish an ascertainable standard of guilt." Covington contended that the law appeared to be directed at Jehovah's Witnesses since members of this group were the only individuals arrested, and arrested in great numbers, because they refused to stop preaching their pacifist doctrines.[7]

Mississippi's attorney general countered with an argument, based upon the 1940 *Gobitis* opinion, that the statute prevented the use of religious liberty as a pretext for unpatriotic statements. The brief contended that the state was attempting to instill patriotism by requiring flag salutes and other activities. The American Civil Liberties Union filed an *amicus* brief on behalf of the appellants, declaring that the Mississippi law was unconstitutional on its face on grounds of vagueness and overbreadth since it provided no definition of disloyalty and included no clear and present danger test.[8]

On the same day that the Supreme Court delivered the better-known opinion in *West Virginia State Board of Education* v. *Barnette*, reversing the *Gobitis* flag salute position, the justices also reversed the state court judgment in the *Taylor* case. In an unanimous opinion written by Justice Owen Roberts the majority held that the Mississippi Jehovah's Witnesses were communicating beliefs and ideas and "under our decisions criminal sanctions cannot be imposed for such communication." In Roberts's opinion the Mississippi statute denied the liberty of the Fourteenth Amendment and lacked a necessary test of clear and present danger.[9]

Despite the similarity between the Mississippi law of 1942 and the Minnesota Sedition Act of 1917 the Court did not overturn *Gilbert* v. *Minnesota*. Lawyers for Taylor successfully challenged the Mississippi statute primarily on First Amendment grounds of free exercise of religion. Covington did not present congressional preemption arguments in his brief, and therefore *Taylor* provided no opportunity for the Court to rule on that point. The focus on the freedom of religion issue also presented circumstances that provided little opportunity for adjustment of the *Gilbert* ruling, and that case remained as part of the line of precedent upholding state restriction of speech. The question of federal preemption and supersession in the sedition field would receive full consideration in the well-publicized case of *Pennsylvania* v. *Nelson*, a decision that generated severe reaction within the federal system.[10]

During the post-World War II period, which produced the security emphasis of the cold war and the intense suspicions of the McCarthy era, Congress and state legislatures extended the network of control with additional statutes. Passage of additional legislation at both the federal and state levels of government produced numerous questions regarding relationships within the federal system. Despite Chief Justice White's 1920 dissenting view that security matters were "within the exclusive legislative power of Congress," the Court majority in *Gilbert* had seen the Minnesota Sedition Law as a local police measure.[11] The possibility for federal preemption of the security area had appeared again in 1941 in *Hines* v. *Davidowitz*, a case in which the Supreme Court did rule that Congress had preempted the field of alien registration. Justice Hugo Black wrote that Congress under the exercise of its power over foreign affairs had provided a thorough security system in passing the Alien Registration Act of 1940: "When it made this addition to its uniform naturalization and immigration laws, it plainly manifested a purpose to do so in such a way as to protect the personal liberties of law-abiding aliens through one uniform rational registration system."[12] Strong commerce power preemption rulings by the early Roosevelt Court had helped to pave the way for the opinion in *Hines*, which was the first time the Court applied the congressional preemption concept outside the commerce area. During the early postwar period the Court in a 1947 commerce ruling, *Rice* v. *Santa Fe Elevator Corporation*, provided further guidance in the preemption area by holding that once Congress had acted in a legislative area—in this case the regulation of agricultural warehouses—then state regulations on those points no longer applied. In the majority opinion, Justice William O. Douglas concluded that the Court would have to consider other "asserted conflicts between the State and Federal Acts when and if they arise."[13]

In the early fifties as cold war concerns dominated much of American politics, many questions about preemption and supersession remained unanswered. Many authorities viewed two levels of security statutes as complementary and argued that Congress had intended no exclusion of state action. On the other hand, concern over national security problems and their relationship to international politics and foreign policy prompted arguments for one uniform national system of regulation. In 1955 in an article in the *Michigan Law Review*, Alan Reeve Hunt considered the current area of conflict. He appreciated the difficulty of determining any foolproof and precise test that would distinguish areas of state and federal action since Congress had never been precise on this point in the wording of national security statutes: "Congressional intent, it must be concluded, has been an unsatisfactory guide for decision, much having been presumed or inferred which may or may not be warranted in actual fact." Hunt also made a perceptive observation of the whole preemption picture:

In. . .fields where questions of federal preemption arise it is obvious from a reading of the opinions that a judge's determination on the issue of pre-emption is profoundly influenced by his view as to the wisdom or the constitutionality on other grounds of the act in question.[14]

Hunt considered the point regarding application of commerce power precedent to security statutes and pointed to the hazy nature of the security area as compared with the commerce clause's "bulwark of federal power;" and he acknowledged that security statute cases had civil liberties considerations while most commerce power rulings did not. He concluded:

In formulating conclusions as to the probable impact of supersedure doctrines on state anti-subversive legislation, perhaps the most that can be said is that there exists a firm though not unassailable basis for invalidating many of these state laws. Invalidation may proceed not so much on the ground of exclusive federal power or direct conflict with federal law as on the ground of obstruction of congressional purpose or invasion of a federally-occupied field.[15]

Pennsylvania v. *Nelson* appeared on the U.S. Supreme Court docket in the midst of the conflict of political and legal opinion over these issues of federalism and during a period of continued strong anti-communist feeling. After a long and controversial trial the Court of Quarter Sessions of Allegheny County had convicted Steve Nelson, an acknowledged member of the Communist party, for violating the Pennsylvania Sedition Act of 1919. The indictment had charged that Nelson had encouraged persons unknown "to take certain measures and engage in certain conduct with a view of overthrowing and destroying by force" the governments of both Pennsylvania and the United States. Furthermore, according to the indictment, Nelson had incited persons unknown to commit overt acts "with a view to bringing the Government of this State and of the United States into hatred and contempt."[16]

The Pennsylvania Supreme Court reversed a Superior Court affirmation of the trial court, overturned Nelson's conviction for sedition against the federal government, and ruled that Congress had preempted the field of sedition legislation. Therefore, state law could not apply in this case.[17] The Commonwealth of Pennsylvania appealed to the U.S. Supreme Court, and for the first time the preemption issue became the focal point in a state security case before the Supreme Court.

In presenting their argument, lawyers for Pennsylvania contended that a state could punish acts that advocated forceful overthrow of the U.S. Government, that it was Pennsylvania's duty under the police power to suppress insurrection without the necessity of depending upon the federal government. Attorneys for the state claimed that if Congress had wished to keep states out of the sedition field, it would have said so; and they pointed to *Gilbert* v. *Minnesota* as an example of Court approval of cooperative federalism in the security legislation field.[18]

Herbert Thatcher and Victor Rabinowitz, attorneys for Nelson, argued that once Congress had passed a sedition law, as it had done in 1940, that action preempted and superseded parallel state legislation. They reasoned that the sedition field was not an area for concurrent jurisdiction since if both laws were permitted to stand, it would create the issue of double punishment, which had already developed in Steve Nelson's case.

The fact that the state might have a deep interest in suppressing sedition against the United States does not confer jurisdiction on the state to make the federal crime its own any more than would a similar interest confer jurisdiction on the state to declare war because hostile activities of a foreign nation threatens [sic] the lives and property of its citizens.[19]

In their brief Rabinowitz and Thatcher also attempted to avoid conflict with one of the dual lines of security statute precedent and distinguished the *Nelson* case from the *Gilbert* ruling, relied on so heavily in Pennsylvania's argument. They argued that the Minnesota statute "was construed to have as its purpose the prevention of breaches of the peace" and that the majority of the Court had not considered the preemption issue. They also distinguished *Nelson* from *Gitlow* and *Whitney* on grounds that the statutes in those cases did not involve subversion of the U.S. Government and because there was no federal sedition statute in effect at the time of those rulings.[20]

One demonstration of the national legal interest focused on the *Nelson* case can be seen in the large number of *amicus curiae* briefs filed. U.S. Solicitor General Simon Sobeloff argued on behalf of the Justice Department that the Smith Act had not precluded enforcement of state sedition statutes. Texas, Massachusetts, and Illinois filed petitions on behalf of Pennsylvania. New Hampshire Attorney General Louis Wyman, well known for security prosecutions in his own state, filed a brief joined by the attorneys general of twenty-four additional states.[21] The American Civil Liberties Union, represented by Osmond Fraenkel, Herbert Levy, and Julian Goldberg, presented an *amicus* argument that state sedition statutes threatened the freedoms of the First Amendment; and the Philadelphia yearly meeting of the Society of Friends contended that federal statutes had preempted the field. They also pointed out the disparate penalties that existed under the vast variety of state statutes. In addition, a number of individuals who had been indicted or interrogated under sedition laws in other states and whose lives were affected seriously by the *Nelson* proceedings presented an *amicus* petition.[22]

On April 2, 1956, the High Court ruled six-to-three to uphold the Pennsylvania Supreme Court's reversal of Nelson's conviction. Chief Justice Earl Warren wrote the opinion of the Court, which followed the direction of the respondent's brief and avoided First Amendment civil liberties considerations to deal solely with the narrow issue of whether or not the Smith Act superseded Pennsylvania law. Warren explained that although the Pennsylvania Supreme Court had resolved the situation by declaring that the *Nelson* case involved only sedition against the United States, the U.S. Supreme Court had granted *certiorari* "because of the important question of federal-state relationship involved."[23] This ruling was not to affect the state's right to enforce security legislation when Congress had not occupied the field. The chief justice distinguished *Nelson* from earlier decisions such as *Gitlow* and *Whitney*, where he said supersession had not been an issue, and from *Gilbert*, where he argued that the state had prosecuted an offense under the police power.[24]

The majority reasoned that the *Nelson* case met the tests of supersession because they concluded that federal regulation under the Smith Act, the Internal Security Act of 1950, and the Communist Control Act of 1954 was pervasive and left no room for state action:

the conclusion is inescapable that Congress has intended to occupy the field of sedition. Taken as a whole, they evince a congressional plan which makes it reasonable to determine that no room has been left for the States to supplement it. Therefore, a state sedition statute is superseded regardless of whether it purports to supplement the federal law.[25]

The majority also denied arguments for concurrent jurisdiction by claiming federal interest to be so dominant as "to preclude enforcement of state laws on the same subject," a precedent achieved in *Rice* v. *Santa Fe Elevator Corporation*. Furthermore, the six-man majority held that state and federal enforcement of sedition legislation led to confusion and lack of uniformity and that utilization of the Federal Bureau of Investigation was necessary to effective law enforcement in these matters.[26] Also, the Pennsylvania statute allowed for the initiation of a sedition indictment "upon an information made by a private individual." Consequently, "the opportunity... present for the indulgence of personal spite and hatred or for furthering some selfish advantage or ambition need only be mentioned to be appreciated." The High Court upheld the Pennsylvania Supreme Court as "unassailable"; state statutes were not to be concerned with sedition against the United States.[27] Despite these rulings, the *Gilbert* lines of precedent remained intact, and the use of state police power to restrict political speech remained a viable probability.

Justice Stanley Reed wrote a dissent in which Justices Harold Burton and Sherman Minton joined. They felt the Pennsylvania law should stand because Congress had not specifically barred the exercise of state power in the security field. Congress had been well aware of state security legislation but had made no attempt to void it, and the Court should not do so without a clear mandate from Congress. The dissenting justices relied heavily upon the *Gilbert* precedent that states and Congress "may enact criminal statutes for mutual protection unless Congress has otherwise provided." In addition, Reed referred to a section of the Smith Act that stated, "Nothing in this title shall be held to take away or impair the jurisdiction of the several states under the laws thereof."[28]

In many respects the Court ruling in *Pennsylvania* v. *Nelson* and subsequent use of the opinion as a precedent created a set of circumstances in which state security interpretation turned more and more upon procedural points. No case better demonstrates the procedural difficulties involved within the federal system than *Dombrowski* v. *Pfister*, delivered by the High Court in April 1965.[29] It was a case that originated in the heat of the civil rights struggles of the mid-sixties and created a jungle of procedural overtones concerning the issues involved with the relationships within the federal system.

James A. Dombrowski served as executive director of the Southern Conference Educational Fund (SCEF), a civil rights organization dating back to the thirties and one often accused of left-wing connections. He had petitioned the United States District Court for the Eastern District of Louisiana seeking injunctive and declaratory relief against threat of prosecution under Louisiana's Subversive Activities Control Law and Communist Propaganda Law.[30] In October 1963, during a period when national attention focused on civil rights work and when an interracial lawyer's conference was meeting in New Orleans, Louisiana authorities had at gunpoint raided the homes of Dombrowski, SCEF Treasurer Benjamin Smith, and SCEF Attorney Bruce Waltzer. In addition to arresting the three men and charging them with violation of the security statutes, authorities also ransacked SCEF offices and seized the organization's files, confiscated books in Dombrowski's personal home library, and seized files at Smith's and Waltzer's law offices. All of these activities were carried out at gunpoint and were defended by James Pfister, Chairman of the Louisiana Joint Legislative Committee on Un-American Activities, as part of an attempt to prevent "racial agitation."[31]

Later in the month Judge J. Bernard Cooke of the Criminal Court for the Parish of Orleans summarily vacated the arrest warrants for the SCEF leaders on grounds of a lack of probable cause. The judge also suppressed the seized evidence because of what he termed the illegal nature of the raid. However, the authorities continued to threaten prosecution, and the Joint Legislative Committee investigated SCEF during November 1963 and designated the organization as a communist front.[32]

Confiscation of the files virtually destroyed SCEF's functional capacity, and the charges of communist activity frightened prospective members and contributors.[33] In early November 1963, Dombrowski, Smith, and Waltzer sought relief in the United States District Court on the basis of Section 1983, Title 42, of the United States Code, which provides federal court access to:

every person who, under color of any statute, ordinance, regulation, custom, or usage, of any State or Territory subjects, or causes to be subjected, any citizen of the United States or other person within the jurisdiction thereof to the deprivation of any rights, privileges, or immunities secured by the Constitution and laws, shall be liable to the party injured in an action at law, suit in equity, or other proper proceeding for redress.[34]

The three SCEF officials argued that the Louisiana security statutes violated First and Fourteenth Amendment freedom of expression rights, that the laws were excessively broad and vague, and that authorities applied the provisions to interfere with civil rights activities rather than to secure a conviction. Consequently, Dombrowski and the others concluded that the raids and arrests and threat of possible indictment constituted acts of bad faith on the part of the state.[35]

On February 20, 1964, a three-judge district court panel ruled two-to-one to dismiss the complaint "for failure to state a claim upon which court relief could be granted" and because the judges saw no "case of threatened irreparable injury to federal rights." The two judges in the majority hoped that a state court might narrow the statutory construction and thereby avoid constitutional questions.[36]

However, dissenting Judge John Minor Wisdom saw harassment of a civil rights organization and chided his two colleagues for reaching a decision that appeared "to rest on a sort of visceral feeling that somehow, if relief were granted, the Court would be impinging on States' Rights." Wisdom saw no barring of federal court relief since the circumstances involved "a civil action which was brought *before* any criminal proceeding was begun in the state courts." Furthermore, he argued, "this Court knows from other litigation... that the Louisiana legislature regards the movement to increase Negro voting in the state as part of the Communist conspiracy."[37]

Shortly after announcement of the three-judge panel's decision, the Orleans Parish Grand Jury indicted Dombrowski and Smith for membership and leadership in SCEF and indicted Smith and Waltzer for their membership in the National Lawyers Guild.[38] Dombrowski and the others then decided to appeal the three-judge panel decision to the U.S. Supreme Court. Attorneys Leon Hubert and Arthur Kinoy argued for the appellants; and William Kunstler, Michael Kunstler, and A. P. Tureaud assisted. The NAACP Legal Defense and Education Fund, the American Civil Liberties Union, and the National Lawyers Guild each submitted an *amicus* brief on behalf of Dombrowski. Attorneys argued that the Louisiana Subversive Activities Law was so vague that it failed "to meet the most minimal standards of the First and Fourteenth Amendments" and that the vagueness and overbreadth "lends itself to selective enforcement against locally unpopular causes," particularly those seeking equal rights for blacks. They argued further that this appeal demonstrated "the importance of the doctrine of preemption to the preservation of the concept of a Federal Union."[39]

On April 26, 1965, Justice William Brennan delivered the opinion of the court in *Dombrowski* v. *Pfister*. A five-man majority of seven participating justices reversed the lower court and declared that the Louisiana practices "suggest that a substantial loss of impairment of freedoms of expression will occur if appellants must await the state court's disposition and ultimate review in this Court of any adverse determination. These allegations, if true, clearly show irreparable injury." Brennan went on to state that "because of the sensitive nature of constitutionally protected expression, we have not required that all of those subject to overbroad regulations risk prosecution to test their rights."[40] In the majority view "a series of state criminal prosecutions will not provide satisfactory resolution of constitutional issues," and the district court had erred in not considering the freedom of expression issue. If the state used the statute to harass the SCEF, then the state interpretation of the law "is irrelevant." In many ways the Court was saying that much of the harm in the *Dombrowski* situation was the bad faith and harassment that constituted the nature of the prosecution as well as the question of the statute's constitutionality.[41] Brennan also pointed out that "the denial of injunctive relief may well result in the denial of any effective safeguards against the loss of protected freedom of expression, and cannot be justified."[42]

The Court ruled as well on the indictment of the SCEF officials for failure to register as members of an organization designated by Louisiana as a communist front. Here, the justices held the statute invalid for being overly broad and threw out the registration because it included groups not on the U.S. Attorney General's list. The Court ordered the district court to conduct further hearings to determine the extent of injunctive relief but indicated that a limiting construction of the statute must be made: "The record suffices, however, to permit this Court to hold that, without the benefit of limiting construction, the statutory provisions on which the indictments are founded are void on their face." The Court also ordered a halt to any further state action to enforce the Subversive Activities Law and requested the return of SCEF papers and files.[43]

Justices John Marshall Harlan and Tom Clark dissented. Harlan wrote the opinion and saw premature federal interference in state affairs: "This decision abolishes the doctrine of federal judicial abstention in all suits attacking state criminal statutes for vagueness on First-Fourteenth Amendment grounds."[44] The dissenters also felt the decision disturbed the balance of federal-state constitutional relations and interfered too much with state criminal procedures.

In essence the effect of the *Dombrowski* ruling was to order lower federal courts to consider the use of declaratory and injunctive relief against state criminal proceedings involving free speech where an applied statute appeared "vague and overbroad on its face" or where there were charges of prosecution in bad faith. According to the Supreme Court in *Dombrowski*, state activity of either type had a chilling effect upon free expression of ideas. However, many states saw such action by lower federal courts as a direct interference with federalism's traditions of comity, and the Supreme Court had held in earlier cases that federal courts should abstain from intervention of this type.[45] On the other hand, as one commentator has pointed out, comity has been a judge-fashioned device; and "considerations of comity have never included allowing a bad faith prosecution to proceed unimpeded," for the very concept of comity assumes that state courts act in good faith.[46] In terms of the vagueness point, constitutionality of a statute became a crucial question. As Brennan stated, "abstention is at war with the purposes of the vagueness doctrine, which demands appropriate federal relief regardless of the prospects for expeditious determination of state criminal prosecutions."[47] Brennan's words offered hope that the federal courts could be relied upon for judicial protection of First Amendment free speech rights.

Some law journal commentators optimistically saw *Dombrowski* as an "effective weapon for social change" because "the availability of such relief in the federal courts redressed the balance between those seeking to achieve social change and those using their control of the organs of governmental power to resist it."[48] Subsequent Court determination at both the state and federal levels, however, quickly eroded those hopes. The complicated structure of the opinion, the state wrath incurred over the abstention and comity issues, and the apparent loophole that would allow an indictment to turn bad faith into good faith transformed the application of *Dombrowski* precedent into a procedural jungle. Other post-*Dombrowski* developments affected the efficacy of a precedent protecting individual rights—including political speech. In the late sixties much of the nature of protest litigation changed. In a number of cities black power confrontations, sometimes leading to violence, replaced sit-ins, peaceful demonstrations, and what had become traditional civil rights forms of protest. In addition, the anti-Viet Nam War movement began to challenge numerous aspects of U.S. political and military policy. These confrontations of the late sixties took place at scattered points throughout the country, involved issues broader than black-white relations, and were no longer confined to the southern racial context. Furthermore, change in Supreme Court personnel, beginning with Nixon's first appointment in 1969, brought a new chief justice who was concerned with what he saw as an overloaded federal docket. These factors cannot be overlooked in attempting to explore the post-*Dombrowski* maze.[49]

The *Dombrowski* case had developed in circumstances surrounding the work of an organization active in the civil rights field for a number of years. However, application of *Dombrowski* precedent came in a number of cases involving the more recently organized movements for social change during the late sixties. One situation involving the latter category of social protest developed in the case of *Epton* v. *New York*, in which the 1968 U.S. Supreme Court in a *per curiam* ruling denied *certiorari* for want of a federal question.[50] Even though the High Court did not agree to hear this case, *Epton* constituted a significant development in the history of state security statutes because its circumstances very much reflected the racial turmoil of the late sixties and because it involved the same Criminal Anarchy Act used to convict Benjamin Gitlow. The Court refused to grant *certiorari*, but Justice Potter Stewart wrote a concurring opinion and Justice William Douglas a dissent, thus providing some reflection of how the justices viewed an old state security law applied to new forms of social protest.

William Epton, the principal in the case, was an avowed Marxist and a member of the Harlem Club of the Progressive Labor Movement. Beginning in May 1964, Epton had become active in recruiting a rather small cadre of followers, organized with block captains. When the 1964 Harlem Riots began on the evening of July 18, the police focused attention on Epton and his followers and arrested him and a number of others. Authorities charged Epton and his co-conspirators with using the organization to seek armed revolt against the police, with advocating criminal anarchy, and with conspiring to engage in such advocacy.[51] It was the first time the state had applied the Criminal Anarchy Act since it had been used against Gitlow in the early twenties.[52]

Epton's trial, held in Supreme Court, New York County, later dismissed a fourth count of substantive riot, but convicted Epton of each of the other three charges and sentenced him to serve three concurrent one-year terms. During the proceedings Epton's attorneys argued that the conditions that caused the 1964 riot were present long before Epton began his organizational activities and that there was no evidence connecting him to the actual circumstances of the 1964 violence in Harlem. In the subsequent appeals Epton's counsel also presented the constitutional arguments that the New York Criminal Anarchy Law was an unconstitutional restraint upon free speech and since the trial court had based much of Epton's conviction upon what he had said, that conviction could not stand. His attorneys also argued that the federal Smith Act, supported by the rulings in the *Nelson* opinion, superseded the New York state security statute.[53]

When the New York Court of Appeals delivered its opinion on May 16, 1967, the judges upheld Epton's conviction on a five-to-one vote. Judge John Scileppi refused to discard the Appeals Court's twenty-five-year-old ruling in *Gitlow* despite the court's admission that there was no evidence that Epton had any substantial following in the Harlem community.

. . . one gets the distinct impression on reading the record that, had it not been for the apparently spontaneous buildup of pressure within the Negro ghettoes of New York City in the summer of 1964, following the killing of a 15-year-old Negro boy by an off-duty police lieutenant, Epton and his group might well have continued little noticed and of scant significance to anyone but themselves.

Judge Scileppi went on to state the court's opinion that there was no evidence that Epton's group had caused the riots that had begun on July 18, 1964; but Scileppi did note that it was in May of that year "when tensions in Harlem had already heightened over the issue of police brutality, that Epton and the others seized upon the notion that this unrest in the community might be utilized by them in developing a mass following."[54] According to the court, just prior to the riots Epton had begun preaching organized resistance to the police, exclaiming that the police had "declared war on us and we should declare war on them and every time they kill one of us damn it, we'll kill one of them." Epton had then advocated setting up his own state and his own army and weapons system to carry out his plan for what he called ultimate freedom. When between 100 and 150 persons attended a rally Epton had scheduled, he cancelled a demonstration planned for police precinct headquarters but promised future protests.[55]

Despite the fact that the New York Court of Appeals did not apply cause-and-effect reasoning in the *Epton* case, the court did read into the application of the Criminal Anarchy Act new procedural guidelines that advocacy must be accompanied by intent and that there must be a clear and present danger that the act will succeed. The court concluded that the condition for application of these tests had been met and that Epton had violated both of them. The judges made this adaptation of the original *Gitlow* ruling because they reasoned that Holmes's and Brandeis's dissenting opinion in the case more closely represented the law of the mid-1960s. However, the New York court opinion still clung to the *Gitlow* procedural ruling that courts must presume that the legislature intended to enact a constitutional statute.[56]

Judge Adrian Burke dissented in part in the *Epton* case, pointing out that in his judgment the Appeals Court's 1922 ruling in *Gitlow* was no longer considered good law. He referred to Holmes's and Brandeis's *Gitlow* dissent as the currently acceptable part of the 1925 U.S. Supreme Court ruling because he saw the Criminal Anarchy Statute to be in conflict with the First and Fourteenth Amendments on grounds of vagueness and indefiniteness. He would have dismissed the count of criminal anarchy as unconstitutional because it was too broad and because he felt his colleagues were engaging in judicial legislation: "Over and above the impropriety of such judicial legislation, however, is the more serious problem of the Court's allowing an apparently moribund statute, whose previous authoritative construction would today clearly be held unconstitutional, to be invoked as a means of punishing speech."[57]

In contrast to the action taken by the New York Court of Appeals, during the late sixties several federal courts ruling in civil rights cases held state security statutes similar to those of New York to be unconstitutional. In February 1967, in *Ware* v.

Nichols a three-judge panel in the Fifth Circuit held the Mississippi Criminal Syndicalism Law to be unconstitutionally vague
and overly broad. In March 1967 in *Carmichael* v. *Allen* another
three-judge panel ruled in similar fashion regarding the Georgia
Anti-Insurrection Statute, which had already been thrown out in
Herndon v. *Lowry*, but which Georgia had continued to apply. In
McSurely v. *Ratliff* in September 1967, the Sixth Circuit Court of
Appeals threw out the Kentucky Criminal Syndicalism Statute;
and in March 1968, another three-judge panel in the Ninth Circuit
discarded the California Criminal Syndicalism Law for being "on
its face unconstitutionally vague and overbroad."[58]

When the *Epton* case reached the U.S. Supreme Court in 1968,
a majority of the justices felt the riot issue contained no federal
question because they concluded that Epton's activity was not
protected by the First Amendment.[59] However, Justice Stewart
indicated in his concurring opinion that he felt the constitutionality
of the Criminal Anarchy Act should be reconsidered but that the
issue had not been presented properly in this case.[60]

Justice Douglas also saw a need to reconsider *Gitlow* and the
New York law in the light of several decades of constitutional
development. Douglas voted to grant *certiorari* and dissented from
the *per curiam* opinion because he saw a substantial federal First
Amendment question in the fact that Epton had given speeches and
distributed leaflets. Since New York had convicted Epton of an
overt act of organizing against the state, he felt the issue of "whether
the overt act required to convict a defendant for conspiracy must be
shown to be constitutionally unprotected presents an important
question." Douglas relied on his own and Hugo Black's concurring
opinion in *Yates* v. *United States* as a precedent for his view: "The
issue, then, is whether Epton's speeches and his participation in
the preparation and distribution of leaflets can be used as overt acts
in a conspiracy charge, without a requirement that they must first
be found constitutionally unprotected." Douglas felt the *Epton* case
should be reviewed on procedural grounds and on what he considered
to be a lack of proper instructions to the jury regarding the line to
be drawn between protected and unprotected speech.[61]

Another case reflecting the political speech issues of the late
sixties emerged in *Brandenburg* v. *Ohio*, argued February 27,

1969, and decided June 9 of that year.[62] The circumstances had involved a speech given by a Ku Klux Klan leader at a Cincinnati-area gathering of the organization that had included a cross burning and the presence of a number of armed persons. Klan members had worn the standard garb including hoods, and the speaker had made anti-black and anti-Semitic statements, such as "I believe the nigger should be returned to Africa, the Jew returned to Israel." The Klan had conducted the so-called rally under rather unusual circumstances with only news reporters and participants in attendance. Local television stations and the networks had filmed the event, and the prosecution later relied on those films as well as the statements of television reporter Harold Alan Leonard and two policemen who testified at the trial that they recognized Clarence Brandenburg's voice and wristwatch from the film.[63]

Authorities arrested the speaker, Brandenburg, under the 1919 Ohio Criminal Syndicalism Act, a statute similar to the California law discussed in conjunction with the *Whitney* case.[64] The indictment against Brandenburg included two counts: unlawfully advocating terrorism as a means of political reform and assembling a group to advocate criminal syndicalism. After his conviction in the trial court Brandenburg sought a ruling from the Court of Appeals of Hamilton County challenging the Criminal Syndicalism Law on First and Fourteenth Amendment grounds, but the Appeals Court affirmed the decision of the trial court. Later, the Ohio Supreme Court dismissed the suit for lack of a constitutional question. Only once before had the Ohio Supreme Court considered the Criminal Syndicalism Act, in *State* v. *Kassay* in 1932; and then the court had upheld the law as an exercise of the state police power.[65]

Arguments before the U.S. Supreme Court regarding jurisdiction in the Brandenburg case demonstrate quite pointedly the existence of dual lines of High Court precedent on the subject of political speech. Ohio continued to argue a police power justification for the Criminal Syndicalism Law and relied on *Gitlow* and *Whitney* precedent, all in an attempt to persuade the Supreme Court to deny *certiorari*.[66] However, attorneys for Brandenburg contended that the "facts surrounding appellant's conviction render[ed] it unconstitutional under any standard put forth by this Court." They applied arguments based upon the *Fiske* and *De*

Jonge opinions.[67] In the appellant's brief Brandenburg's counsel argued that the Ohio statute was unconstitutional on its face and suffered from "vagueness and overbreadth" in punishing speech protected by the First and Fourteenth Amendments. They cited the recent Supreme Court decision in *Keyishian* v. *Board of Regents*, which had declared loyalty oath provisions required of New York school teachers to be invalid on the grounds of "impermissible overbreadth."[68] In addition, attorneys for Brandenburg contended that according to *Nelson* and other rulings federal law superseded state law on matters regarding statements against the U.S. Government and also that Ohio authorities had denied Brandenburg's due process rights in failing "to meet the most minimal evidential standards."[69]

The U.S. Supreme Court responded in an unanimous *per curiam* decision reversing the Ohio Supreme Court and also overturning the 1927 precedent in *Whitney* v. *California*, long discredited by subsequent Supreme Court rulings. The Court held that the state could prevent advocacy only when the prevention was directed at lawless action. On the contrary, the Ohio law punished mere advocacy and therefore was unconstitutional on its face because it violated the First and Fourteenth Amendments for failure to distinguish mere advocacy from "incitement to imminent lawless action."[70] Justices Black and Douglas each wrote separate concurring opinions, both of which agreed with their colleagues in regard to the unconstitutionality of the Ohio statute and the overruling of *Whitney*. However, the two opinions expressed disapproval of the clear and present danger test that the majority essentially applied in *Brandenburg*. Douglas reasoned that all speech was protected, that "the quality of advocacy turns on the depth of the conviction; and government has no power to invade that sanctuary of belief and conscience."[71]

In considering the *Taylor, Nelson, Dombrowski*, and *Brandenburg* cases in the years between 1940 and 1970, the Court dealt with a number of circumstances reflecting the struggle between the desire for the protection of political speech and the desire of many states to continue prosecutions under state security statutes. In *Taylor* the justices applied freedom of religious expression guarantees and clear and present danger reasoning to discard the

Mississippi Sedition Act. In *Nelson* the Court attempted to clarify the question of congressional preemption. In *Dombrowski* the justices undertook to protect First Amendment freedoms from the chilling effect of state laws and officials. Finally, in *Brandenburg* they voided a criminal syndicalism statute on grounds of vagueness and the lack of a clear and present danger application and overturned the forty-two-year-old *Whitney* precedent. These four decisions combined with *Fiske*, *De Jonge*, and *Herndon* precedents might seem on first glance to indicate that the process of nationalization of the First Amendment protection of political speech was a matter of judicial certainty. However, the history of the security statute rulings of many state appellate courts during these same years demonstrated a resistance to applying Supreme Court rulings that relied upon First Amendment principles to restrict state action.

NOTES

1. Taylor v. Miss. 319 U.S. 583 (1943); 63 Sup. Ct. Rep. 1200 (1943); and 87 Law. Ed. 1600 (1943). See also Emerson, *Freedom of Expression in Wartime*, 116 U. PA. L. REV. 985 (1968). The Supreme Court heard Taylor along with two companion cases—Benoit v. Miss. and Cummings v. Miss. A firsthand account of Justice Department treatment of both left- and right-wing radicals during the prewar and war period can be found in Francis Biddle, *In Brief Authority* (Westport, Conn.: Greenwood Press, 1976). The wartime attorney general discussed the situation in chapter 15 on "Seditionists, Father Coughlin, and the Chicago *Tribune*."

2. See Headnote, 87 Law. Ed. 1600, 1601 and 1942 Miss. Laws, chp. 178.

3. Brief of Plaintiff in Error at 5, 18-19, Gilbert v. Minn., 254 U.S. 325 (1920). For Chief Justice White's dissent see 254 U.S. 325, 334.

4. Transcript and Record at 5, 70, 141, 319 U.S. 583.

5. Taylor v. State, 194 Miss. 1 (1943), quoted at 41, 11 So. 2d 663 (1943), quoted at 676; Cummings v. State, 194 Miss. 59 (1943), 11 So. 2d 683 (1943); and Benoit v. State, 194 Miss. 74 (1943), 11 So. 2d 689 (1943). The Mississippi court considered Gilbert, 254 U.S. 325 and Minersville School Dist. v. Gobitis 310 U.S. 586 (1940) as pertinent precedents. Minersville involved a family of Jehovah's Witness children who had been expelled from a Pennsylvania public school for refusing to participate in a daily flag salute exercise required by the local school board. The Witnesses

contended that such a ceremony demonstrated a recognition of the authority of the state, a position contrary to Witness acceptance of God as the sole authority. The Supreme Court in an opinion written by Justice Felix Frankfurter upheld the action of the board, reasoning that the requirement of this daily exercise was geared to building national unity and patriotism. The decision contributed to an atmosphere that produced a wealth of state legislation directed against the Witnesses, of which the Mississippi Sedition Law was an example.

6. 194 Miss. 1, 41-59; 11 So. 2d 663, 676-683.

7. Appellants' Brief at 16-17, 90, 319 U.S. 583.

8. Brief for State of Mississippi at 52, 319 U.S. 583 and Brief for the American Civil Liberties Union, *amicus curiae*, at 9-10, 25, 319 U.S. 583.

9. 319 U.S. 583, 590. In W. Va. State Bd. of Educ. v. Barnette, 319 U.S. 628 (1943), the Supreme Court applied a clear and present danger test to overturn the three-year-old Gobitis ruling and declared such flag salute requirements unconstitutional.

10. Pa. v. Nelson, 350 U.S. 497 (1956); 76 Sup. Ct. Rep. 477 (1956); and 100 Law. Ed. 640 (1956).

11. 254 U.S. 325, 334.

12. Hines v. Davidowitz, 312 U.S. 52, 74 (1941). See also Zechariah Chafee, Jr., *Free Speech in the United States* (Cambridge: Harvard University Press, 1967), pp. 295-296.

13. Bratton, *The Preemption Doctrine: Shifting Perspectives on Federalism and the Burger Court*, 75 COLUM. L. REV. 634 (1975) and Rice v. Santa Fe Elevator Corp., 331 U.S. 218, 237 (1947).

14. Hunt, *Federal Supremacy and State Anti-Subversive Legislation*, 53 MICH. L. REV. 422, 424 (1955).

15. Ibid. at 428 and 438.

16. Transcript of Record at 9-10, 350 U.S. 497. The trial was long and drawn out with numerous delays and continuances, and the Transcript of Record totaled 1,421 pages. After much haggling over representation, Nelson conducted his own defense. For an autobiographical account see Steve Nelson, *The 13th Juror* (New York: Masses and Mainstream, 1955).

17. Commonwealth v. Nelson, 377 Pa. 58 (1954), 104 A. 2d 133 (1954).

18. Reply Brief for Petitioner at 14, 350 U.S. 497.

19. Brief for Respondent at 11-13, 47, 350 U.S. 497; quoted at 13. Nelson was also tried in the U.S. District Court for the Western District of Pennsylvania for violation of the Smith Act. See Brief for Respondent at 8, 350 U.S. 497.

20. Ibid. at 13-14.

21. Brief for the United States as *amicus curiae*; Brief of the Commonwealth of Massachusetts as *amicus curiae*; Brief of the State of Texas as *amicus curiae*; Brief of *amicus curiae*, Latham Castle, Attorney General of the State of Illinois; Brief of the State of New Hampshire as *amicus curiae* in support of the Petition for Writ of *Certiorari* to the Supreme Court of Pennsylvania, 350 U.S. 497. The American Legion also filed a brief on behalf of Pennsylvania. The list of states joining in the New Hampshire *amicus* petition included Arizona, Connecticut, Florida, Georgia, Indiana, Kansas, Louisiana, Maine, Maryland, Massachusetts, Michigan, Mississippi, Montana, Nebraska, Nevada, New Mexico, New York, North Carolina, Ohio, South Carolina, Tennessee, Virginia, Washington, and Wisconsin.

22. Brief for the American Civil Liberties Union as *amicus curiae*; Brief for the Civil Liberties Committee of the Philadelphia Yearly Meeting of the Religious Society of Friends, *amicus curiae*; and Brief of Individual *amici curiae*, 350 U.S. 497. The list of individuals included Carl Braden in Kentucky, Dirk Struik in Massachusetts, William Uphaus in New Hampshire, and fourteen persons in Florida.

23. 350 U.S. 497, 499.

24. Ibid. at 500.

25. Ibid. at 504.

26. Ibid. at 504-505.

27. Ibid. at 507, 509. Warren quoted the Pennsylvania Supreme Court on the matter of the indictment procedures. See 377 Pa. 58 at 74-75, 104 A. 2d 133 at 141.

28. Ibid. quoted at 517, 519. Even though the Nelson case reached the Supreme Court as the second Red Scare was beginning to decline, the immediate impact of the decision was considerable and primarily negative. After the Supreme Court refused to rehear the case on May 14, 1956, the Justice Department, speaking through Deputy Attorney General William P. Rogers, wrote to Mississippi Senator James Eastland, Chairman of the Senate Judiciary Committee. The Justice Department recommended that state and national governments work to "supplement each other." On May 23, the National Association of Attorneys General, meeting in convention, passed a resolution favoring congressional legislation allowing states to prosecute sedition against the United States. Actually, Senator John McClellan and Representative Howard Smith, in anticipation of the Nelson decision, earlier had introduced far-reaching proposals declaring that Congress alone had the power to determine preemption. After the Supreme Court decision these bills were voted out of committee, but neither passed during the 84th Congress.

Additional congressional reaction was prompted by the fact that the network of forty-two state sedition statutes, along with a number of other related laws, was at stake; and the Nelson ruling had prompted questions as to the validity of any state security legislation. On June 5, 1956, the Senate reported the first of several bills aimed at clarifying the role of the states on the subject of security laws. Although committees in both houses passed versions of this legislation, neither house approved the McClellan and Bridges bills or the Smith and Walter proposals during 1956. These bills were reintroduced during the next session, but only the Smith bill passed and only in the House. Debate of these proposals was extremely heated and often produced severe diatribes against the Supreme Court. However, despite severe negative congressional reaction against the Nelson opinion, strong disagreement over the extent to which Congress might curtail its own power of preemption and supersession resulted in failure of passage of any bill supporting concurrent state and federal action. See Campbell, *Supremacy Clause and Preemption— Pennsylvania Sedition Act Declared Invalid*, 30 SO. CALIF. L. REV. 106 (1956); Cramton, *Pennsylvania v. Nelson: A Case Study in Federal Preemption*, 26 U. CHI. L. REV. 85 (1958-1959); Shenas, *Doctrines of Pre-emption: State Sedition Act Superseded by Federal Smith Act*, 4 UCLA L. REV. 118 (1956); Rogge, *State Power Over Sedition, Obscenity and Picketing*, 34 N.Y.U. L. REV. 857 (1959); and Paul L. Murphy, *The Constitution in Crisis Times* (New York: Harper & Row, 1972), p. 322.

29. Dombrowski v. Pfister, 380 U.S. 479 (1965); 85 Sup. Ct. Rep. 1116 (1965); and 14 Law. Ed. 22 (1965).

30. The Southern Conference Education Fund was founded in 1938 and maintained headquarters in Louisville (Margaret Fish, ed., *Encyclopedia of Associations*, 11th ed. [Detroit: Gale Research, 1978], 701). See LA. REV. STAT. ANN. §§ 358-388, 390-390.5 (West). In State v. Jenkins, 236 La. 300 (1958), 107 So. 2d 648 (1958), in the wake of the Supreme Court's Nelson ruling, the Louisiana Supreme Court had declared an earlier version of the law superseded by federal legislation. In 1960 after Uphaus appeared to narrow the Nelson precedent, the Louisiana Legislature created the Joint Committee on Un-American Activities and in 1962 reinstated the Subversive Activities Control Law in a slightly different form. See Brief for Appellants and Appellants-Intervenors at 23-24 and Jurisdictional Statement at 7, 26, 380 U.S. 479.

31. Transcript of Record at 1-3, 25-26, 380 U.S. 479. The Joint Legislative Committee had determined that since segregation was considered a way of life in Louisiana, any attempt to further the cause of civil rights was to be considered subversive and subject to the vague provisions of the

Subversive Activities Control Law. At one point the Joint Legislative Committee also declared that the Southern Christian Leadership Conference, Student Nonviolent Coordinating Committee, and Southern Conference Education Fund were under communist control. See Brief for Appellants and Appellants-Intervenors at 27, 31, 380 U.S. 479.

32. Transcript of Record at 4 and Brief for Appellants and Appellants-Intervenors at 7, 380 U.S. 479.

33. 380 U.S. 479, 487.

34. 42 U.S.C. § 1983 (1976). This provision was included in the Civil Rights Act of 1866.

35. Transcript of Record at 75, 380 U.S. 479.

36. Dombrowski v. Pfister, 227 F. Supp. 556, 564 (E.D. La. 1964).

37. Ibid. at 572.

38. Jurisdictional Statement at 9-10, 380 U.S. 479.

39. Brief for Appellants and Appellants-Intervenors quoted at 12-13, 78, 380 U.S. 470. See also Briefs for *amicus curiae*, 380 U.S. 479.

40. 380 U.S. 479, 486.

41. Ibid. at 489-490. See also Stickgold, *Variations on a Theme of Dombrowski v. Pfister: Federal Intervention in State Criminal Proceedings Affecting First Amendment Rights*, 1968 WIS. L. REV. 369.

42. 380 U.S. 479, 492.

43. Ibid. at 493-497, quoted at 497.

44. Ibid. at 498.

45. See R.R. Comm'n. v. Pullman Co., 312 U.S. 496 (1941), and Douglas v. City of Jeanette, 319 U.S. 157 (1943). It should be pointed out that the section of the U.S. Code under which the Supreme Court took jurisdiction in Dombrowski was passed in 1948, after the Railroad Commission and Douglas decisions. See 28 U.S.C. § 2281 (1964).

46. Stickgold, *Variations on Dombrowski v. Pfister*, pp. 369-370.

47. 380 U.S. 479, 492.

48. Sedler, *Dombrowski in the Wake of Younger: The View from Without and Within*, 1972 WIS. L. REV. 1.

49. These developments are discussed in Sedler, *Dombrowski*, p. 8. See also Fiss, *Dombrowski*, 86 YALE L. J. 1117 (1977).

50. Epton v. N.Y., 390 U.S. 29 (1968); 88 Sup. Ct. Rep. 824 (1968); and 19 Law. Ed. 2d 808 (1968).

51. People v. Epton, 19 N.Y. 2d 496, 496-497 (1967), 227 N.E. 2d 829, 831-832 (1967), and Respondent's Brief in Opposition to Writ of *Certiorari* at 1-3, 390 U.S. 29. New York charged and later convicted Epton of violating Section 16a of the New York penal law, which defines criminal anarchy as "the doctrine that organized government should be over-

thrown by force or violence or by assassination of the executive head or of any of the executive officials of government, or by any unlawful means."

52. Harris, *Black Power Advocacy: Criminal Anarchy or Free Speech,* 56 CALIF. L. REV. 717 (1968).

53. 19 N.Y. 2d 496, 502, 504, 507 (1967); 227 N.E. 2d 829, 832, 834 (1967). On December 8, 1966, the New York Supreme Court, Appellate Division, First Judicial Department, unanimously affirmed the trial court judgment. See 276 N.Y.S. 2d 847 (1966).

54. 19 N.Y. 2d 496, 501; 227 N.E. 2d 829, 832.

55. Ibid. and Respondent's Brief at 10-11, 390 U.S. 29.

56. 19 N.Y. 2d 496, 506-507; 227 N.E. 2d 829, 834-835.

57. 19 N.Y. 2d 496, 511; 227 N.E. 2d 829, 838.

58. Harris, *Black Power Advocacy,* p. 719, discusses this group of cases. Ware v. Nichols, 266 F. Supp. 546 (N.D. Miss. 1967); Carmichael v. Allen, 267 F. Supp. 985 (N.D. Ga. 1967); McSurely v. Ratliff 282 F. Supp. 848 (E.D. Ky. 1967); and Harris v. Younger, 281 F. Supp. 507 (C.D. Cal. 1968). Each of these cases involved civil rights workers. A full discussion of McSurely v. Ratliff can be found in Richard Harris, *Freedom Spent* (Boston: Little, Brown, 1976). The U.S. Supreme Court in Younger v. Harris, 401 U.S. 37 (1971), overturned the ruling in the California case.

59. 390 U.S. 29.

60. Ibid. at 30.

61. Ibid. at 30-35, quoted at 31, 32, 33.

62. Brandenburg v. Ohio, 395 U.S. 444 (1969); 89 Sup. Ct. Rep. 1827 (1969); and 23 Law. Ed. 2d 430 (1960).

63. Transcript of Proceedings at 7-13, 40-44, 295 U.S. 444; quoted at 24.

64. OHIO REV. CODE ANN. § 2923.13 (Page). The Ohio Legislature removed the criminal syndicalism provision from the code after the Supreme Court's Brandenburg ruling. During the early stages of the proceedings, Brandenburg's attorney argued that the Smith Act had preempted the security field and that the Ohio criminal syndicalism provision did not apply. See Transcript at 1, 395 U.S. 444.

65. Brief for Appellant at 11, 395 U.S. 444. See State v. Kassay, 126 Ohio St. 177 (1932), 184 N.E. 521 (1932).

66. Brief of Appellees in Opposition to Jurisdiction at 3-10, 395 U.S. 444.

67. Jurisdictional Statement at 16-18, 395 U.S. 444; quoted at 15.

68. Brief for Appellant at 9-16, 395 U.S. 444. See Keyishian v. Bd. of Regents of the Univ. of the State of N.Y., 385 U.S. 589 (1967).

69. Brief for Appellant at 27-32, 395 U.S. 444; quoted at 32.

70. 395 U.S. 444, 449.

71. Ibid. at 457. See also Linde, *"Clear and Present Danger" Reexamined: Dissonance in the* Brandenburg *Concerto*, 22 STAN. L. REV. 1163 (1970), and Strong, *Fifty Years of "Clear and Present Danger": From Schenck to Brandenburg—and Beyond*, 1969 SUP. CT. REV. 41.

4. STATE COURTS AND DUAL LINES OF PRECEDENT

As state high courts applied the Supreme Court rulings in state security cases, the effect of the dual lines of precedent became apparent. Dual lines of Supreme Court reasoning provided the basis for dual lines of application. These applications constructed a contradictory progression of state court rulings that detracted from what might appear to have been a protected-speech doctrine promulgated by the High Court. In addition, these state court rulings reflected the piecemeal development of the whole body of First Amendment case law. In turn, the contradictory lines of precedent and the gradual development of free speech doctrine contributed to the building of the state networks of control.

The dual lines of Supreme Court precedent developed in state security statute cases are summarized in table 1. The *Gilbert-Gitlow-Whitney* rulings all declared that free speech was not an absolute right and provided state courts with a basis to uphold state security statutes as police power regulations without the use of any type of clear and present danger test.[1] In addition, *Gilbert* held that the Fifth Amendment double jeopardy protection did not remove the concept of concurrent jurisdiction; and the *Gitlow* justices ruled that courts were to presume that state statutes were valid and designated the states as the primary judges of the validity. In *Whitney* the Court decided that states could classify and categorize despite the equal protection restrictions of the Fourteenth Amendment. With this battery of rulings at their disposal, state courts found many opportunities to uphold state

TABLE 1 FIRST AMENDMENT APPLICATIONS DEVELOPED IN STATE SECURITY STATUTE CASES BEFORE THE U.S. SUPREME COURT

CASE	FIRST AMENDMENT APPLICATION
Gilbert v. *Minnesota* 7-2, 1920	Police power used to preserve peace Free speech not absolute
Gitlow v. *New York* 7-2, 1925	Free speech not absolute Can restrict if bad tendency 14th Amendment applies 1st Amendment to states
Whitney v. *California* unanimous, 1927	Free speech not absolute California law not in violation of 1st Amendment despite lack of clear and present danger test
Fiske v. *Kansas* unanimous, 1927	Kansas law unconstitutionally applied to Fiske
De Jonge v. *Oregon* unanimous, 1937	Statute violated 1st Amendment Peaceful assembly not a crime Assembly as fundamental as speech and press
Herndon v. *Lowry* 5-4, 1937	Statute violated 1st Amendment Statute restricted free speech
Taylor v. *Mississippi* unanimous, 1943	Statute violated 1st Amendment Freedom of religion, free exercise No clear and present danger test in statute
Pennsylvania v. *Nelson* 6-3, 1956	No 1st Amendment ruling
Dombrowski v. *Pfister* 5-2, 1965	Without limiting construction Statute violated 1st Amendment Unconstitutional on its face
Brandenburg v. *Ohio* unanimous, 1969	Statute violated 1st Amendment Overturned *Whitney* precedent Clear and present danger rule applied

security laws and other statutes that built the state networks of control.

In 1922 the Illinois Supreme Court applied what was to become typical *Gilbert* police-power reasoning to uphold the conviction of thirty-nine Communist Labor party members charged with insurrection and sedition. Despite a challenge that the case involved a matter of federal law the Illinois court insisted, "There is nothing in the federal Constitution in any way granting to the federal government the exclusive right to punish disloyalty." In 1927 the Supreme Court of North Carolina used both *Gitlow* and *Whitney* precedents to sustain a libel conviction of the *Raleigh Times*; and in 1929 the Pennsylvania Supreme Court applied similar police power reasoning to uphold that state's Criminal Syndicalism Law.

In contrast, the twenties produced one notable exception to the state high court policy of applying *Gilbert* to reinforce state police power in the security area. In November 1921 the New Mexico Supreme Court reversed the conviction of an IWW organizer and declared the state's insurrection and sedition statute in violation of the New Mexico Constitution. Justice Frank Parker maintained, "Under its terms no distinction is made between the man who advocates a change in the form of our government by constitutional means...and the man who advocates the overthrow of our government by armed revolution or other forms of force and violence."[2] This distinction, which resembled Justice Holmes's clear and present danger test, became an important element in U.S. Supreme Court interpretation in state security rulings by the end of the thirties. However, in state court application the New Mexico Supreme Court ruling remained an exception well into the sixties.

After the *Gitlow* and *Whitney* rulings supplemented *Gilbert* in defense of state attempts to curb certain political speech, state courts applied one or more of these precedents to curtail political activity related to the economic plight and desperate conditions brought on by the Great Depression. In 1932 in *Carr* v. *State*, the Georgia Supreme Court applied *Gilbert* in upholding the state's Anti-Insurrection Act, and in 1934 it repeated the ruling in *Herndon* v. *State*, citing *Gitlow* and *Whitney*. In 1931 the Pennsylvania Superior Court in a case involving a Communist party member, used the *Gitlow* bad-tendency application to uphold that state's

1919 Sedition Law and to reject application of the clear and present danger test where the "legislative body itself has previously determined the danger of substantive evils arising from utterances of a specific character." Twice—in 1931 and again in 1936—*Gitlow* and *Whitney* provided crucial precedents for the Oregon Supreme Court in upholding that state's Criminal Syndicalism Law, which was later discarded by the U.S. Supreme Court in *De Jonge*.[3]

By the late thirties the *De Jonge* and *Herndon* rulings discarding state security statutes joined the rejection of the application of the Kansas Criminal Syndicalism Law in *Fiske* as an alternative to the *Gilbert-Gitlow-Whitney* line of precedents.[4] In response, state attorneys and state courts utilized the distinguishing technique to separate an instant case from the High Court precedents that had ruled in favor of the First Amendment. In 1937, a few months following the *De Jonge* and *Herndon* rulings, the California Court of Appeals for the Third District relied very heavily upon *Gitlow* and *Whitney* to distinguish a criminal syndicalism case from *De Jonge* and *Herndon*. The California court drew a fine line between mere advocacy and the so-called overt acts of organizations, and the judges utilized arguments that the state must take steps to preserve itself. Despite this stance on behalf of the police power, the court then reversed the conviction on grounds of a confused and inconsistent jury decision.[5]

A number of other state courts also found reason to distinguish their cases from what they regarded as irrelevant precedents. In June 1937 the Alabama Supreme Court did so in *Patterson* v. *State*, one of the much-publicized Scottsboro cases, on grounds that the *De Jonge* due process ruling had no bearing on the *Patterson* rulings excluding evidence of alleged bias on the part of witnesses.[6] In 1938, in a Jersey City case involving the denial of a speaking permit to Socialist leader Norman Thomas, the New Jersey Supreme Court distinguished the case at bar from the *De Jonge* position that assembly was a cognate right protected from state encroachment. The New Jersey court quoted Chief Justice Hughes's *De Jonge* opinion: "The greater the importance of safeguarding the community from incitements to the overthrow of our institutions by force and violence, the more imperative is the need to preserve inviolate the constitutional rights of free speech, free press and free assembly." However, Justice Joseph Bodine insisted: "It should be noted that the Supreme Court in that [*De Jonge*] case was not dealing with an application for a permit to hold a public meeting in the public streets of a municipality, but was dealing with the constitutionality of a law of the State of Oregon relating to criminal syndicalism." The New Jersey court relied heavily on Oliver Wendell Holmes's Massachusetts precedent in *Commonwealth* v. *Davis* and justified its position further on grounds that "when opposition to a speaker's views runs high, no reason exists for subjecting the speaker and innocent bystanders to dangers of assault."[7] Several citizens' groups and veterans' organizations had protested against allowing Thomas to speak, and the court reasoned that these circumstances increased the likelihood of disturbance.

In another case in the late thirties the Supreme Judicial Court of Massachusetts, Worcester, upheld restrictions on handbill distribution and littering and cited *De Jonge* and other civil liberties precedents on grounds that freedom of the press was "subject to reasonable rules formulated to serve the public interest." In 1939, in the *Meadowmoor Dairies* case, the Illinois Supreme Court granted a permanent injunction against picketing and distinguished the case from *De Jonge*, as well as *Lovell, Grosjean,* and *Near*: "All of these cases involved legislation attempting to suppress or limit free speech by criminal process or by way of injunction. They did not involve the construction to be given in case of conflicting constitutional rights." The Illinois court saw a conflict between speech rights and property rights and opted for property rights.[8] In 1939 the Washington Supreme Court granted a permanent antipicketing injunction on the same grounds. However, the Appellate Department of the Los Angeles County Superior Court in two separate 1939 decisions reversed trial court judgments against pickets; and the California Supreme Court the next year affirmed the protection of free speech under the First Amendment. These divergent state court opinions on the question of applying *De Jonge* and other First Amendment rulings in picketing circumstances helped to demonstrate the need for a U.S. Supreme Court clarification on the subject, a ruling that came in *Thornhill* v. *Alabama* in 1940.[9]

However, even after the *Thornhill* judgment appeared, *De Jonge* continued to provide guidance in labor relations cases. In 1944 the Colorado Supreme Court considered in a declaratory judgment the confusing provisions of the state's Labor Peace Act. The court discarded the entire statute for infringing on the jurisdiction of the National Labor Relations Act. In so ruling, the court contributed to the federalism questions based upon the commerce power, and this reasoning foreshadowed the preemption issues raised in many state security cases of the fifties. However, the Colorado judges also ruled certain sections of the law unconstitutional on civil liberties grounds. Citing *De Jonge* and other cases, they reasoned, "we think the decisions indicate that the constitutional guarantee of assembly to the people is not restricted to the literal right of meeting together 'to petition the Government for a redress of grievances.' "[10]

Despite the application of *De Jonge* precedent in the Colorado case, the early forties was a period in which state courts were also relying on the *Gilbert-Gitlow-Whitney* line. In 1941, two East Coast state supreme courts applied the precedents in a manner that demonstrated the pick-and-choose nature of state court application of security statute rulings. In *State* v. *Klapprott* the New Jersey Supreme Court considered the conviction of persons whose anti-Semitic comments were found in violation of a group libel law. Chief Justice Thomas J. Brogan reasoned that the statute's references to terms of "hatred," "abuse," and "hostility" were "abstract and indefinite admits of no contradiction"; and speech could not be prohibited by such a vague definition that bore no relation to violence or breaches of the peace. The court applied *Near* and *Cantwell* prior-restraint rulings as major precedents but also pointed to the *Gitlow* nationalization concept and to *De Jonge* as support for discarding the New Jersey statute.[11]

The contrasting position developed in *State* v. *Chaplinsky*, considered by the Supreme Court of New Hampshire, Strafford. Authorities had arrested Walter Chaplinsky for calling the City Marshal of Rochester "a damned fascist" and a "goddamned racketeer." The arrest had occurred after repeated warnings had been given and while authorities were protecting Chaplinsky from a crowd that over the course of an afternoon had reacted increasingly more negatively to his distribution of Jehovah's Witness materials. The New Hampshire court upheld the conviction under a law that prohibited "any offensive, derisive or annoying word" to any person in a public place. The court held that the statute met the *Herndon* and *Stromberg* vagueness tests and reasoned that Chaplinsky had attempted to inflame others with his "classical fighting words," not protected under *De Jonge* and other Supreme Court rulings. Justice Elwin L. Page cited *De Jonge*—"These rights may be abused by using speech or press or assembly in order to incite to violence or crime"—and *Herndon*—"The limitation upon individual liberty must have appropriate relation to the safety of the state." The New Hampshire court regarded Chaplinsky's statements as an abuse of basic constitutional rights and considered the state to be in a position to restrict him. The U.S. Supreme Court later agreed, adding further confusion to the issue of what speech was protected and what was not.[12]

During the early forties both the *De Jonge* and *Herndon* rulings as well as *Gilbert* served as precedents in several Jehovah's Witness cases. The Criminal Court of Appeals of Oklahoma and the Superior Court of Pennsylvania both dealt with cases involving the sect and the unlicensed street distribution of reading materials. Citing *De Jonge*, *Near*, and *Grosjean*, the courts reversed convictions of the distributors. In early 1943 the Mississippi Supreme Court applied *Gilbert* as a principal precedent in upholding the conviction in the *Taylor* case. The U.S. Supreme Court later reversed that ruling, but it did not consider overturning *Gilbert*. Although the High Court declared the Mississippi Sedition Law unconstitutional for failing to provide a clear and present danger test, the facts of the case limited the application of the ruling primarily to cases involving the Witnesses. In 1944 the Colorado Supreme Court ruled in a Witness flag-salute case considering a school board action that had made the ceremony mandatory. The Colorado court ruled for the reinstatement of the students, an action in keeping with the Supreme Court's *Barnette* decision of 1943. The court also quoted Justice Roberts's *Herndon* admonition regarding the relationship between the liberty of the individual and the safety of the state.[13]

The *De Jonge-Herndon* line of precedent also appeared in cases that did not involve freedom of religion. A 1946 California Supreme Court case illustrated in its majority and dissenting opinions the applications of the same *De Jonge* precedent in contrasting judicial arguments. *Danskin* v. *San Diego Unified School District* involved a challenge to a section of the California Civic Center Act, which required an affidavit of loyalty from groups requesting use of school auditorium facilities if those groups were thought to advocate overthrow of the government. The San Diego Chapter of the American Civil Liberties Union brought suit when they were asked to sign the affidavit as a condition for using the facilities for a program on the Bill of Rights in postwar America. Justice Roger Traynor cited *De Jonge, Herndon,* and a number of other First Amendment opinions as a basis for discarding that section of the act. He saw a "close analogy between the present case and the suppression of a public meeting by criminal prosecution held invalid in *De Jonge* v. *Oregon.*" He also relied on the Court reasoning in *Bridges* v. *California*:

When the United States Supreme Court held in *Bridges* v. *California*...that the suppression of freedom of speech in the absence of a clear and present danger of substantive evils is a violation of the constitutional guaranty of free speech, it adopted the views of Mr. Justice Holmes and Mr. Justice Brandeis in their minority opinion in *Gitlow* v. *New York*...and *Whitney* v. *California*...and other cases.[14]

In other words Traynor reasoned that *Bridges*, which fell within the *De Jonge-Herndon* line of reasoning, really rendered the *Gilbert-Gitlow-Whitney* precedents obsolete. However, the Supreme Court had chosen not to overturn those precedents, and they remained applicable for state court use. In contrast to Traynor's reasoning Justice Homer Spence's dissent contended that the law could be upheld on application of *De Jonge* precedent since in his analysis the Oregon opinion cited *Gitlow* and *Whitney* with approval in relation to the idea that some political speech could be restricted.[15] Spence's argument was another variation of the position that speech is not absolute.

During the period of postwar strikes and labor unrest in the late forties several state supreme courts ruled against attempts to restrict picketing and other union activity, but they still clung to state authority by insisting that free speech was not an absolute and that the abuse might be punished. As the postwar Red Scare began to take hold, a number of appellate tribunals reached conflicting conclusions on the question of loyalty oaths and applied *Whitney* as precedent. For example, the Superior Court of New Jersey, Appellate Division, discarded a loyalty oath required of candidates for public office and referred to *Whitney* along with *Stromberg, Thornhill, Barnette,* and *Thomas* v. *Collins* as precedents supporting the concept of freedom of thought. On the other hand, the Second District Court of Appeals in California upheld a loyalty oath for employees of Los Angeles County and cited *Whitney, Stromberg,* and *De Jonge.* The California Supreme Court later threw out the loyalty oath requirement but not until 1967. The contradictory use of precedents in these two cases again points up the complexity of the issue of free speech and demonstrates how state courts often arbitrarily chose those precedents. The repeated statement that free speech was not an absolute made *Whitney* a precedent for upholding the loyalty oath, whereas other statements on the importance of free thought, along with Brandeis's concurring opinion, served as a basis to discard the New Jersey oath and other restrictions.[16]

A classic example of application of the nationalization principle appeared in *Commonwealth* v. *Gilfedder* in 1947. The Supreme Judicial Court of Massachusetts, Suffolk, considered the recurring question of a permit requirement for speech and assembly. In July 1946, members of the Socialist party of Massachusetts and the Socialist Labor party of America had spoken on Boston Common without having secured the permit stipulated in the General Rules of Park Commissioners. The gatherings had been peaceful, and the Socialists had distributed pamphlets that contained neither improper language nor advocacy of overthrow of the government. The Massachusetts high court speaking through Justice Stanley Elroy Qua sustained the exceptions sought by the defendants and declared these park regulations to be: "on their faces in conflict with the rights of freedom of speech, of the press, and of assembly guaranteed by the First Amendment to the Constitution of the United States made applicable to the states by § 1 of the Fourteenth Amendment." He based his reasoning on *De Jonge, Schnei-*

der v. *State,* and a litany of cases headed by *Hague* v. *CIO* that provided much of the basis for the contrast between this decision and the one rendered by the New Jersey Supreme Court in the 1938 Norman Thomas case.[17]

The security scare of the cold war period provided ample opportunity for state court application of the *Gilbert-Gitlow-Whitney* line of precedent in security cases. In 1950, *Gilbert* and *Gitlow* served as a basis for the New York Court of Appeals' upholding the constitutionality of the Feinberg Law, which required removal of school employees "for the utterance of any treasonable or seditious word or words or the doing of any treasonable or seditious act or acts while holding such a position." In citing *Gilbert,* the New York judges decided the concept of freedom of speech did not protect words that authorities felt would imperil the government. The next year the New Jersey Supreme Court applied *Gilbert* in much the same manner to uphold the conviction of a man charged with interfering with enlistment. Also in 1951 in the *Beauharnais* group libel case, the Illinois Supreme Court relied upon the *Gitlow* precedents that presumption of a statute's constitutionality had to be made in favor of the state and that free speech was not an absolute right. A different twist on the security issue developed in a ruling by the Appellate Department of the Los Angeles County Superior Court in 1951. The judges declared invalid a county ordinance requiring members of the Communist party to register because "compliance with the ordinance would amount to a virtual confession that the registrant had violated the so-called Criminal Syndicalism Act," which *Whitney* and subsequent rulings had held to be constitutional.[18]

During the mid-fifties state court application of the dual lines of precedent was complicated further by increased judicial consideration of the federalism preemption question. In what later became the well-known *Commonwealth* v. *Nelson* decision the Pennsylvania Supreme Court in an April 1954 opinion ruled out state attempts to control Communist party activity directed against the U.S. Government. The justices distinguished the case from *Gilbert* and dismissed application of the Minnesota case as one dealing with a "local police measure, aimed to suppress a species of seditious speech which the Legislature of the State [had] found objectionable." However, dissenting Justice John Bell saw the *Gilbert* police power issue to be analogous to *Nelson*. Three days after the Pennsylvania ruling the New Hampshire Supreme Court at Hillsborough unanimously upheld the state attorney general's investigating powers under the New Hampshire Subversive Activities Act. The state supreme court, in upholding a law that made the attorney general both the investigator and the prosecutor, quoted from *Gilbert*: "The State is not inhibited from making the national purposes its own purposes." The New Hampshire justices went on to reject the ruling of their Pennsylvania brethren: "Insofar as *Commonwealth of Pennsylvania* v. *Nelson*...gives support to the position that it does [prohibit such activity], we do not adopt it."[19]

After the U.S. Supreme Court in 1956 upheld the Pennsylvania high court's action in declaring that Congress had preempted the field of protecting the U.S. Government, many states resisted the decision. Since twenty-four state attorneys general intent upon hunting subversives had joined New Hampshire's Louis Wyman in an *amicus* brief arguing against congressional preemption of the sedition field, this resistance was not unexpected.[20] New Hampshire voiced opposition almost immediately and continued its recalcitrance by pursuing several cases. In a June 8, 1956, decision the New Hampshire Supreme Court, Merrimack, concluded in a *per curiam* opinion:

While it is not clear what a state legislative investigation of subversive activites may accomplish at the present time, we are not satisfied that the *Nelson* case, *supra*, purports to preclude such an investigation. If state investigation of subversive activities is to be prohibited, a declaration to that effect must come from higher authority than this court.[21]

During the next year state supreme courts handled a rash of cases related to the issues of *Nelson*. On February 28, the New Hampshire Supreme Court, Merrimack, spoke again on the subject of the attorney general's investigations. In *Wyman* v. *Uphaus* the court held that the legislature was entitled to know the names of those registered at a summer resort operated by the New Hampshire World Fellowship Center, Incorporated. Therefore,

Uphaus was to be held in contempt for refusing to divulge information. The New Hampshire court distinguished this case from *Commonwealth of Pennsylvania* v. *Nelson* by deciding simply that the New Hampshire circumstances fell outside the scope of the earlier opinion. In 1959 the U.S. Supreme Court also upheld Wyman's investigations as valid state activity and repeated that *Nelson* precedent applied only to state attempts to control sedition against the United States. Like *Nelson*, *Uphaus* also left many unanswered questions and confused the issues of federalism still further.[22]

In contrast to those judges who found reason to distinguish cases from *Nelson* precedent, several state supreme courts followed the Supreme Court's directive on the preemption question. On May 3, 1956, the Supreme Judicial Court of Massachusetts, Middlesex, declared in *Commonwealth* v. *Gilbert* that U.S. statutes "exclusively preempted" the case. At this time Massachusetts state courts also quashed indictments against other persons accused of violating the state's sedition law. On May 14, the Michigan Supreme Court ruled unconstitutional five sections of that state's sedition statute, known as the Trucks Act. However, the Michigan court applied the *Nelson* ruling in the narrowest sense, relying solely upon the issue of supersession. On June 22, 1956, the Kentucky Court of Appeals dismissed a state sedition statute indictment against civil rights worker Carl Braden of the Southern Conference Education Fund. However, the Kentucky court did not discard the statute, leaving it available for use during the intense civil rights struggles of the sixties.[23]

The post-*Nelson* state court reaction provided a dramatic example of state courts' picking and choosing from the two lines of precedents, and the dichotomy continued until the end of the decade. During December 1958 the high courts of both Louisiana and Florida dealt with sedition matters. In Louisiana the court interpreted the *Nelson* ruling to apply to the entire field of subversive activity and pronounced the state statutes on the subject to be unenforceable because, as Justice E. Howard noted, the Louisiana law was very similar to Pennsylvania's. The Florida Supreme Court, in a ruling later overturned by the U.S. Supreme Court, dealt with the circumstances of a legislative committee that compelled witnesses to answer questions regarding possible Communist party activity among civil rights groups and ordered them to produce membership lists of the National Association for the Advancement of Colored People (NAACP). The Florida court ruled that Congress had preempted only the field of sedition committed against the federal government and held that the Florida laws prohibiting subversion against the state continued to be valid.[24]

In another 1958 case involving the NAACP the Arkansas Supreme Court ruled that the association would have to disclose its membership lists in order to enjoy tax-immunity status since in the court's opinion the civil liberties protections outlined in *De Jonge* and other opinions applied only to persons and not to organizations. In another civil rights-related case three years later, the Georgia appellate bench first acknowledged the *Herndon* clear and present danger test, twenty-four years after the Supreme Court pronouncement. The Georgia Court of Appeals declared unconstitutional on free speech grounds an Albany ordinance requiring that those licensed to solicit for dues-paying memberships had to demonstrate good moral character and provide evidence they had not belonged to any organization holding communist beliefs.[25]

Thousands of miles away, the Washington Supreme Court in the late fifties also demonstrated the dichotomy in the application of Supreme Court precedents. In 1958 the justices discarded the censorship provisions of the state's Comic Book Act on *Herndon* void-for-vagueness grounds as well as equal-protection reasoning. However, the next year the court demonstrated the apparent ease by which state courts might distinguish a case at bar from the *Nelson* precedent in an appeal; it involved a group of professors seeking a declaratory judgment that the Washington Subversive Activities Law of 1955 violated state and federal constitutions. The Washington court ruled that the use of an executive order to place subversive organizations on an attorney general's list was an unconstitutional denial of due process, but the court upheld other sections. The justices held that the *Nelson* precedent did not involve acts of sedition against the state, nor did it deny to states the power to set prerequisites for public employment or to control public institutions.[26]

After the U.S. Supreme Court's *Uphaus* v. *Wyman* opinion in 1959 confused the preemption issue still further, state applications of *Nelson* precedent in security cases declined. In November 1960 the Florida Supreme Court upheld a loyalty oath for teachers on grounds that the requirement did not infringe unconstitutionally upon speech and press guarantees. The court expressed dissatisfaction with repeated challenges of this type: "We think the time is now passed when statutes of this type are subject to question because of alleged preemption of the field of subversive control by the Federal Government." In *State* v. *Levitt* in January 1965 the Indiana Supreme Court held that the state's anti-communist statute did not conflict with the Smith Act. The Indiana justices relied on the dissenting opinion in *Nelson*, which said Congress had indicated in the legislation that it had not preempted the field with the Smith Act.[27]

Although by the advent of the sixties a number of state supreme courts were applying the nationalization concept in what had become traditional areas, state courts were reluctant to relinquish state authority in a number of cases that developed from events of the civil rights movement and thereby skirted the application of the Bill of Rights via the Fourteenth Amendment. In 1963 in what became a well-known set of Louisiana cases involving a courthouse civil rights demonstration, the Louisiana Supreme Court upheld the conviction of the Reverend B. Elton Cox for obstructing a public passage and disturbing the peace even though it recognized *De Jonge* precedent for applying the Bill of Rights to the states. In a Louisiana case involving the Black Muslims the state's Criminal Anarchy Statute withstood a challenge on grounds that it was overly vague and infringed on the First Amendment. However, the decision also reversed the conviction and remanded for a new trial based on the failure of the state to establish guilt.[28]

A 1964 Georgia Supreme Court ruling also reflected the conflict between state law and the civil rights movement. In a case involving a conviction for a violation of an antitrespass ordinance—a person had been arrested for failure to leave a privately owned restaurant—the court held there was no state action involved in the failure of police to enforce a statute concerned with the duty of an innkeeper to receive guests. The Georgia court chose to ignore the U.S. Supreme Court's *Peterson* v. *Greenville* decision of 1963. The opinion cited *Herndon* on the confusing point that, even though a law may be constitutional on its face, it may not be applied legally in such a way to interfere with any person's rights under the Constitution of Georgia or of the United States. In another civil rights decision the Alabama Court of Appeals in 1965 held invalid as a form of prior restraint a Birmingham ordinance requiring parade permits. The case involved a peaceful and unobstructing Good Friday march led by the Reverend Fred Shuttlesworth. The court ruled the ordinance unconstitutional on *De Jonge* grounds of failing to meet "ascertainable constitutional standards." Two years later the Alabama Supreme Court, applying a very narrow construction, upheld the conviction that the U.S. Supreme Court reversed in 1969.[29]

During the politically turbulent second half of the sixties, state supreme courts continued to use *Nelson* precedent selectively, especially in cases involving security questions. In *People* v. *Epton* in 1967, the New York Court of Appeals upheld a conviction of a black power activist arrested under the Criminal Anarchy Act, the same statute involved in the *Gitlow* case more than forty years earlier. The New York court discarded the *Nelson* preemption precedent and relied heavily upon the 1925 upholding of the statute in *Gitlow*, seeming to ignore more than forty years of constitutional development. However, in another 1967 case the same New York court ruled that revocation of a longshoreman's registration because of deceitful testimony regarding subversive activity at age fifteen or sixteen was too severe. Here, in a case less controversial than Epton's, the court recognized a long line of free speech precedents as well as the *Nelson* preemption concept.[30]

By the second half of the sixties the "chilling effect" ruling in *Dombrowski* v. *Pfister* was available to state courts that chose to render decisions applying the *De Jonge-Herndon* line of precedent. In 1966 the Alaska Supreme Court distinguished a case at bar from *Dombrowski* and ruled that Seward teachers possessed free speech rights, but could be subject to nonretention if they exercised them. It reasoned that the act of making allegedly false statements about the superintendent of schools did not enjoy constitutional protection. In December 1967 the New York Court of Appeals quoted *Dombrowski* in affirming an extortion conviction in which a wiretap had been issued upon probable cause: "The State must, if it is to invoke the statutes after injunctive relief has been sought, assume the burden of obtaining a permissible narrow construction in a noncriminal proceeding before it may seek modification of the injunction to permit future prosecutions." The majority upheld the conviction over the strong objection of Judge Stanley Fuld, who dissented to hold for a new trial and who argued that the majority could not use *Dombrowski* precedent as the basis for its decision to uphold the use of the wiretap and at the same time ignore the corollary to the exclusionary rule very recently established in *Berger* v. *New York*: "I have come on no case, and none has been called to our attention, in which a State court has presumed to resuscitate a statute by a retroactive reinterpretation after the United States Supreme Court had (as it has done here) declared it constitutionally dead."[31]

Defendants at times attempted to employ the *Dombrowski* void-for-vagueness rule to escape application of a particular statute to a particular circumstance. In January 1969 the New Jersey Supreme Court held that questions asked of applicants for a firearms purchaser identification card, which required the applicant to list organizational memberships, were "clear and understandable, and may be answered negatively, affirmatively or qualifiedly. Whatever the answer it merely serves as a basis for any needed further inquiry." Anti-Viet Nam War student demonstrators arrested in the 1967 University of Wisconsin protest against the Dow Chemical Company's defense contracts contended that the state disorderly conduct statute was overly broad enough to be unconstitutional on its face, according to *Dombrowski* standards. However, in February 1969 the Wisconsin Supreme Court ruled the statute to be constitutional in relation to the First Amendment. Basing much of his reasoning on *Chaplinsky*, Justice Connor Hansen held: "Constitutionally protected rights, such as freedom of speech and peaceable assembly are not the be all and end all. They are not an absolute touchstone. The United States Constitution is not unmindful of other equally important interests such as public order."[32]

In another university-related case of 1969, the New York Court of Appeals ruled that professors at the State University of New

York at Stony Brook could be compelled to appear before a Suffolk County Grand Jury investigating drug abuse. The appeals bench held that First Amendment rights did not preclude an appearance before a grand jury. The court found great difference between these circumstances and the *Keyishian* and *Dombrowski* precedents cited by the defendants.

We have no statutes attempting to proscribe conduct in this case. Rather, the specious argument made here is that teachers will be intimidated in their lectures merely because of the potential threat of being compelled to appear before a Grand Jury inquiry. If this allegation is true, the intimidation is attributable to something other than a violation of constitutional rights. *Keyishian* and *Pfister* are clearly inapplicable.[33]

Claim to strict use of *Dombrowski* procedural precedent in these three cases would seem to be misplaced since no defendant sought a federal court injunction, but the chilling effect argument would still apply.

New Jersey's appellate courts on two occasions in 1969 and 1970 dealt with application of *Dombrowski* in the case of *Anderson* v. *Sills*, which had originated in the summer of 1967, during the same period as the Newark riots, and involved student protests at Saint Peter's College in Jersey City. The NAACP sought a declaratory judgment and injunctive relief against a reporting system used by local and county officials to gather material on potential and actual civil disorders. In July 1969 the Superior Court, Chancery Division, applied *Dombrowski* to rule that a directive by Attorney General Arthur J. Sills requesting submission of this information to the state police violated the First Amendment. The judges based their decision on *Dombrowski* and other recent U.S. Supreme Court decisions that had discarded forms of government activity found to be in contradiction with the exercise of First Amendment rights. In June 1970 the New Jersey Supreme Court reversed this ruling because of lack of evidence of either a "deterrent effect" or an "intent to inhibit exercise of First Amendment rights and no evidence as to relevance of information sought to police obligation with respect to civil disorders." Chief Justice Joseph Weintraub distinguished the Anderson case from

Dombrowski, U.S. v. *Robel, NAACP* v. *Button, Watkins* v. *U.S.*, and others because the New Jersey system "imposes no liability or obligation or restriction whatever upon the citizen. . . . It is no more than a communication to law enforcement agencies about their respective powers and duties."[34]

In the first of a series of cases related to freedom of assembly the Pennsylvania Superior Court in a *per curiam* opinion in November 1969 upheld the loitering and prowling conviction and the sentencing that followed the revocation of an original probation ruling. Judge J. Sydney Hoffman in dissent felt the *Dombrowski* void-for-vagueness rule should apply, especially since the probation was revoked upon the sole testimony of the probation officer. In January 1970 the Supreme Court of California ruled that a statute prohibiting the disturbance of a lawful meeting must be construed in such a way that it not conflict with the First Amendment. The court applied the *Dombrowski* concept of chilling effect in ruling against the "threat of sanctions" in a case involving a group of farm workers attending a meeting in a public park at which the local congressman spoke. Later in 1970 the New Jersey Superior Court, Law Division, held that an antiloitering ordinance was not unconstitutional because it was specific, defined the acts in detail, and provided a warning before an arrest could be made. The California Supreme Court in another 1970 case ruled that the state law did not preempt the San Rafael trespass ordinance because of overbreadth or vagueness. Even though the court distinguished the California case from *Dombrowski*, the judges admitted: "We do, of course, realize the chilling effect that prosecution might exert in deterring petitioners and other individuals from exercising their fundamental rights." However, in the *habeas corpus* proceeding they felt they could not determine "in absence of established facts, whether petitioner's conduct is protected by the First Amendment."[35]

In 1970 certain state courts were still distinguishing cases from the *Nelson* preemption precedent, and in two double-jeopardy opinions delivered that year two courts reached opposite conclusions, once again reflecting the persistence of the dual lines of precedent. The Wisconsin Supreme Court upheld the theft, burglary, and arson convictions of a group of antiwar protestors who had burned draft records. The court in applying *Gilbert* and denying the *Nelson* type of preemption doctrine ruled, "We can only say that our law has not yet concluded that punishment by separate sovereignties for the same act constitutes double jeopardy." In contrast, the Ohio Court of Appeals, Cuyahoga County, ruled to quash a bank robbery indictment on the grounds that both federal and state constitutional provisions barred state prosecution of defendants tried by federal courts for the same act. The judges relied upon *Nelson* to make their point regarding preemption. Also in 1970 the Maryland Court of Special Appeals considered the well-known case of the Catonsville Nine, which involved the Fathers Berrigan and others accused of seizing draft records in an anti-Viet Nam War protest. The Maryland court denied that the *Nelson* rules for supersession applied to selective service files. The Maryland judges saw no conflict with federal law enforcement jurisdiction because "the conduct prohibited by the two sovereigns is not identical nor does it concern the same subject." Again, a state court applied a federalism-based argument to distinguish the case before it from the restrictions imposed by the *Nelson* ruling.[36]

The 1969 decision in *Brandenburg* v. *Ohio*, which removed the *Whitney* precedent, left the *Gilbert* and *Gitlow* rulings unscathed. *Brandenburg* took its place in the *De Jonge-Herndon-Dombrowski* lineup; and although certain state courts found reason to distinguish their cases from the new ruling, many others did apply the *Brandenburg* line of reasoning. In September 1970 the Washington Supreme Court reversed a conviction and remanded for a new trial in a case involving the state's Uniform Flag Law. During an antiwar protest the defendant had held the flag while another had set it afire. The Washington court held that in order to sustain the conviction the act must have been done knowingly and with intent of defiling and desecrating. Therefore, the trial court's instruction that the defendant was guilty regardless of intent was erroneous. In reference to *Brandenburg* the court said, "The offense does not, therefore, include conduct amounting to provocation or incitement to or advocacy of crime, violence, riot or public disorder." On September 18, the Superior Court of Pennsylvania delivered a *per curiam* opinion upholding a riot conviction. Judge Theodore

Spaulding dissented and called for a new trial. Citing *Stromberg*, *Herndon*, and *Brandenburg*, he reasoned:

The jury should have been instructed that they could not find the conduct of this incident unlawful unless they found that it was conducted in a violent and turbulent manner, or for the purpose of arousing the crowd to violent and turbulent behavior, or with reckless disregard of the likelihood of such arousal. . . . Since the jury may have convicted the appellants for constitutionally protected activity, the court below incorrectly upheld the verdict.[37]

Several California appellate courts also utilized the *Brandenburg* precedent during 1969-1970. On October 8, 1969, the Court of Appeals, First District, ruled that distribution of leaflets publicizing high school student strikes as a protest against the Viet Nam War did not violate a vagrancy statute. To have upheld the vagrancy application, the court reasoned, would have punished mere advocacy of an idea. In February 1970, Judge Delbert Wong of the Appellate Division of the Los Angeles County Superior Court dissented on *Brandenburg* grounds in a case involving persons who had refused to disperse from the place of an allegedly unlawful assembly. The trial court and the appellate division majority ruled the assembly unlawful because they saw it as having been called for purposes of violence. In another case in the same court on May 21, 1970, the majority of judges upheld the conviction of demonstrators who temporarily stopped cars at the entrance to a college campus and then allowed them to proceed after distributing anti-Viet Nam War literature. Again Judge Wong dissented, emphasizing the preferred position of First Amendment rights put forth in the Brandeis's *Whitney* statement and in the *Brandenburg* opinion. He also felt the jury should have been asked to determine whether the obstruction was reasonable or unreasonable.[38]

The application of the *Brandenburg* ruling made it appear as though the course of development in state security cases had gone full circle. The U.S. Supreme Court had applied a clear and present danger test in a criminal syndicalism statute case, and some courts began to follow suit. In overturning *Whitney* v. *California*, the Supreme Court had removed a precedent for upholding state security legislation. But had free speech really achieved a new level of protection against state encroachment? Or was the apparent reason for optimism premature in 1970? The answer lies primarily in events that have occurred since 1970 and will not be covered here.

However, it is essential to point out that the tandem operation of the piecemeal nature of the process of judicial review and the development of Supreme Court First Amendment doctrine, together with the evolution of dual lines of precedent, served to provide a basis for the reinforcement of state networks of control. Once the Court had delivered the *Gilbert*, *Gitlow*, and *Whitney* opinions, attorneys representing those arrested for security statute violations either argued to distinguish their cases from the precedents or emphasized client circumstances that differed from those in the precedents. The nature of the process added to the piecemeal development and also provided little occasion for the Supreme Court to overturn earlier pro-police-power rulings even though the justices were in the process of developing First Amendment doctrine that protected political speech. The presence of the resulting dual lines of precedent provided opportunity for state courts that did not accept the Supreme Court doctrine of protected political speech to select the alternate line of precedents. The dichotomy, which has been traced here through five decades of state court application of U.S. Supreme Court precedent, testifies to the tenacity of the conflicting lines of judicial reasoning that have reinforced the maintenance of state networks of control.

NOTES

1. Gilbert v. Minn., 254 U.S. 325 (1920); Gitlow v. N.Y., 268 U.S. 652 (1925); and Whitney v. Cal., 274 U.S. 357 (1927).

2. People v. Lloyd, 304 Ill. 23, 33, (1922), 136 N.E. 505, 511 (1922); Pentuff v. Park, 194 N.C. 146 (1927), 138 S.E. 616 (1927); Commonwealth v. Widovich, 295 Pa. 311 (1929), 145 A. 295 (1929); and State v. Diamond, 27 N.M. 477, 479 (1921), 202 P. 988, 989 (1921).

3. Carr v. State, 176 Ga. 55 (1932), 166 S.E. 827 (1932); Herndon v. State, 178 Ga. 832 (1934), 174 S.E. 597 (1934), and 179 Ga. 603 (1934), 176

S.E. 620 (1934); Commonwealth v. Lazar, 103 Pa. Super. Ct. 417, 423 (1931), 157 A. 701, 703 (1931); State v. Boloff, 138 Or. 568 (1931), 4 P. 2d 326 (1931); State v. Denny, 152 Or. 541 (1936), 53 P. 2d 713 (1936). Boloff is discussed in Eldridge Dowell, *A History of Criminal Syndicalism Legislation in the United States* (New York: Da Capo Press, 1969), p. 120.

4. De Jonge v. Or., 299 U.S. 353 (1937); Herndon v. Lowry, 301 U.S. 242 (1937); and Fiske v. Kan., 274 U.S. 380 (1927).

5. People v. Chambers, 22 Cal. App. 2d 687 (1937), 72 P. 2d 746 (1937).

6. Patterson v. State, 234 Ala. 342 (1937), 175 So. 371 (1937). Haywood Patterson was one of the defendants in the well-known Scottsboro cases, which involved the hurried trial of nine young black men arrested on rape charges. Eventually, the U.S. Supreme Court ruled that counsel had to be provided in all state cases involving capital offenses and that blacks were not to be excluded systematically from the jury selection process. See Powell v. Ala., 287 U.S. 45 (1932), and Norris v. Ala., 294 U.S. 587 (1935).

7. Thomas v. Casey, 121 N.J.L. 185, 189, 190, 192 (1938), 1 A. 2d 866, 869, 871 (1938); and De Jonge, quoted at 299 U.S. 353, 365. The year following the New Jersey Supreme Court's decision in the Norman Thomas case, the U.S. Supreme Court also dealt with the question of Jersey City's speaking permit requirements. In Hague v. CIO, 307 U.S. 496 (1939), the High Court found unconstitutional the ordinance that granted the police chief control over speaking permits and literature distribution. The CIO case reached the Supreme Court via the Federal District Court for New Jersey and the Court of Appeals for the Third Circuit, 25 F. Supp. 127 (D. N.J. 1938) and 101 F. 2d 774 (1939). The Supreme Court's decision essentially overturned Commonwealth v. Davis, 162 Mass. 510 (1895), 39 N.E. 113 (1895). In his Davis opinion Justice Holmes had provided an often-quoted guideline, "For the Legislature absolutely or conditionally to forbid public speaking in a highway or public park is no more an infringement of the rights of a member of the public than for the owner of a private house to forbid it in his house." The U.S. Supreme Court upheld the decision in 176 U.S. 43 (1896).

8. Commonwealth v. Nichols, 301 Mass. 584, 586 (1938), 18 N.E. 2d 166, 167 (1938); and Meadowmoor Dairies, Inc. v. Milk Wagon Drivers' Union of Chicago, 371 Ill. 377, 393 (1939), 21 N.E. 2d 308, 316 (1939). These state courts considered De Jonge, 299 U.S. 353, as well as the prior restraint rulings in Near v. Minn., 283 U.S. 697 (1931); Grosjean v. Am. Press Co., 297 U.S. 233 (1936); and Lovell v. Griffin, 303 U.S. 444 (1938). In Near, Chief Justice Charles Evans Hughes wrote for a 5-4 majority, declaring that the Fourteenth and First Amendments prevented states

from engaging in prior restraint of printed materials. In Grosjean the Court further nationalized freedom of the press by striking down a tax that Huey Long's government had imposed upon any Louisiana newspaper with a circulation of more than 20,000 per week. In Lovell, an early Jehovah's Witness case, the Supreme Court unanimously discarded a Griffin, Georgia, ordinance that required the city manager's written permission for literature distribution.

9. Fornili v. Auto Mechanics' Union Local No. 297 of Int'l. Ass'n. of Machinists, 200 Wash. 283 (1939), 93 P. 2d 422 (1939); People v. Garcia, 37 Cal. App. 2d Supp. 753 (1939), 98 P. 2d 265 (1939); People v. Gidaly, 35 Cal. App. 2d Supp. 758 (1939), 93 P. 2d 660 (1939); and McKay v. Retail Auto. Salesmen's Local No. 1067, 16 Cal. 2d 311 (1940), 106 P. 2d 373 (1940). See Thornhill v. Ala., 310 U.S. 88 (1940), in which the Supreme Court held an Alabama antipicketing statute unconstitutional on first Amendment grounds.

10. AFL v. Reilly, 113 Colo. 90, 98 (1944), 155 P. 2d 145, 148-149 (1944).

11. State v. Klapprott, 127 N.J.L. 395, 402 (1941), 22 A. 2d 877, 881 (1941).

12. State v. Chaplinsky, 91 N.H. 310, 317 (1941), 18 A. 2d 754 (1941). See also Chaplinsky v. N.H., 315 U.S. 568 (1942).

13. Ex parte Walrod, 78 Okla. Crim. 299 (1941), 120 P. 2d 783 (1941); Emch v. City of Guymon, 75 Okla. Crim. 1 (1942); Commonwealth v. Reid, 144 Pa. Super. Ct. 569 (1941), 20 A. 2d 841 (1941); Taylor v. State, 194 Miss. 1 (1943), 11 So. 2d 663 (1943); and Zavilla v. Masse, 112 Colo. 183 (1944), 147 P. 2d 823 (1944).

14. Danskin v. San Diego Unified School Dist., 28 Cal. 2d 536, 543 (1946), 171 P. 2d 885, 889-890 (1946). See Bridges v. Cal., 314 U.S. 252 (1941), in which Justice Hugo Black added the words *substantial* and *serious* to the clear and present danger doctrine. The Supreme Court held that published comments regarding labor leaders involved in pending litigation had not created any serious danger or evil.

15. 28 Cal. 2d 536, 543; 171 P. 2d 885, 889-890.

16. Imbrie v. Marsh, 3 N.J. 578 (1949), 68 A. 2d 761 (1949), and Steiner v. Darby, 88 Cal. App. 2d 481 (1949), 199 P. 2d 429 (1949). Two decades later the California Supreme Court discarded the Los Angeles County loyalty oath in Vogel v. County of Los Angeles, 68 Cal. 2d 18 (1967), 434 P. 2d 961 (1967). These cases of the late forties also considered the precedents in Stromberg v. Cal., 283 U.S. 359 (1931); Thornhill v. Ala., 310 U.S. 88; W. Va. State Bd. of Educ. v. Barnette, 319 U.S. 628 (1943); Thomas v. Collins, 323 U.S. 516 (1945); and De Jonge, 299 U.S. 353. In

Thomas v. Collins the Supreme Court overturned a contempt citation of a CIO organizer who had failed to register with Texas officials before soliciting union memberships.

17. Commonwealth v. Gilfedder, 321 Mass. 335, 339 (1947), 73 N.E. 2d 241, 243 (1947). The Massachusetts court considered De Jonge, 299 U.S. 353; Schneider v. Irvington, 308 U.S. 147 (1939), which struck down city ordinances attempting to control literature distribution; and Hague v. CIO, 307 U.S. 496 (1939).

18. Thompson v. Wallin, 301 N.Y. 476, 485 (1950), 95 N.E. 2d 806, 809 (1950); State v. De Fillipis, 15 N.J. Super. 7 (1951), 83 A. 2d 16 (1951); People v. Beauharnais, 408 Ill. 512 (1951), 97 N.E. 2d 343 (1951); and People v. McCormick and People v. Steinberg, 102 Cal.App. 2d Supp. 954, 962 (1951), 228 P. 2d 349, 354 (1951). In Keyishian v. Bd. of Regents of the Univ. of the State of N.Y., 385 U.S. 589 (1967), the Supreme Court reversed a lower federal court decision that had upheld the Feinberg Law. The High Court cited Herndon as well as Yates v. U.S., 355 U.S. 66 (1957); Noto v. U.S., 367 U.S. 290 (1961); Scales v. U.S., 367 U.S. 302 (1961); and Sweezy v. N.H., 354 U.S. 234 (1957), all cases that drew lines between advocacy of subversive action and advocacy of ideas. In 1954 the Supreme Court upheld the constitutionality of the Illinois group libel law in Beauharnais v. Ill., 343 U.S. 250 (1952).

19. Commonwealth v. Nelson, 377 Pa. 58, 72 (1954), 104 A. 2d 133, 140 (1954), and Nelson v. Wyman, 99 N.H. 33, 49 (1954), 105 A. 2d 756, 769 (1954).

20. Brief for the State of New Hampshire *amicus curiae* in Support of the Petition for Writ of *Certiorari* to the Supreme Court of Pennsylvania, Pa. v. Nelson, 350 U.S. 497 (1956). See also note 21, chapter 3.

21. Kahn v. Wyman, 100 N.H. 245, 246 (1956), 123 A. 2d 166, 167 (1956).

22. Wyman v. Uphaus, 100 N.H. 436 (1957), 130 A. 2d 278 (1957); and Uphaus v. Wyman, 360 U.S. 72 (1959). See also Zifkin, *Federal Preemption of State Sedition Laws*, 33 SO. CALIF. L. REV. 94 (1959).

23. Commonwealth v. Gilbert, 334 Mass. 71 (1956), 134 N.E. 2d 13 (1956); Albertson v. Millard, 354 Mich. 519 (1956), 77 N.W. 2d 104 (1956); and Braden v. Commonwealth, 291 S.W. 2d 843 (1956). The Kentucky struggle is discussed in Richard Harris, *Freedom Spent* (Boston: Little, Brown, 1976).

24. State v. Jenkins, 236 La. 300 (1958), 107 So. 2d 648 (1958); Gibson v. Florida Legislative Investigating Comm., 108 So. 2d 729 (1958). The U.S. Supreme Court overturned the Gibson decision in 372 U.S. 539 (1963).

25. Bates v. City of Little Rock, 229 Ark. 819 (1958), 319 S.W. 2d 37 (1958); and Wolfe v.City of Albany, 104 Ga. App. 264 (1961), 121 S.E. 2d 331 (1961).

26. Adams v. Hinkle, 51 Wash. 2d 763 (1958), 322 P. 2d 844 (1958); and Nostrand v. Balmer, 53 Wash. 2d 460 (1959), 335 P. 2d 10 (1959).

27. 360 U.S. 72; Cramp v. Bd. of Pub. Instruction of Orange County, 125 So. 2d 554, 557 (1960); and State v. Levitt, 246 Ind. 275 (1965), 203 N.E. 2d 821 (1965). The U.S. Supreme Court overturned the Florida ruling in 368 U.S. 278 (1961).

28. State v. Cox, 244 La. 1087 (1963), 156 So. 2d 453 (1963); and State v. Cade, 244 La. 534 (1963), 153 So. 2d 382 (1963). The U.S. Supreme Court later overturned the Cox conviction. See Cox v. La., 379 U.S. 559 (1965), and Kalven, *The Concept of the Public Forum: Cox v. Louisiana,* 1965 SUP. CT. REV. 1.

29. Walker v. State, 220 Ga. App. 415 (1964), 139 S.E. 2d 278 (1964); and Shuttlesworth v. City of Birmingham, 43 Ala. App. 68 (1965), 180 So. 2d 114 (1965); 281 Ala. 542 (1967), 206 So. 2d 348 (1967); and 394 U.S. 147 (1969).

30. People v. Epton, 19 N.Y. 2d 496 (1967), 227 N.E. 2d 829 (1967); and Bell v. Waterfront Comm'n. of N.Y. Harbor, 20 N.Y. 2d 54 (1967), 228 N.E. 2d 756 (1967).

31. Watts v. Seward School Bd., 421 P. 2d 586 (1966); and People v. Kaiser, 21 N.Y. 2d 86, 104, 109 (1967), 223 N.E. 2d 818, 829, 832 (1967). See also Berger v. N.Y., 388 U.S. 41 (1967), in which the Supreme Court declared the New York eavesdropping law unconstitutional and held that electronic surveillance conducted by states had to meet Fourth Amendment standards.

32. Application of Walter Marvin, Jr., 53 N.J. 147, 150 (1969), 249 A. 2d 377, 378 (1969); and State v. Zwicker, 41 Wis. 2d 497, 509 (1969), 164 N.W. 2d 512, 518 (1969).

33. Boikess v. Aspland, 24 N.Y. 2d 136, 142 (1969), 247 N.E. 2d 135, 138, (1969). In addition to seeing the instant case in a different light from Dombrowski, the New York court also distinguished it from Keyishian, 385 U.S. 589.

34. Anderson v. Sills, 106 N.J. Super. 545 (1969), 256 A. 2d 298 (1969) and 56 N.J. 210, 211, 221 (1970), 265 A. 2d 678, 679, 684 (1970). See also Watkins v. U.S., 354 U.S. 178 (1957), and U.S. v. Robel, 371 U.S. 415 (1963). In Watkins the Warren Court overturned the contempt conviction of a House Un-American Activities Committee (HUAC) witness who had refused on First Amendment grounds to answer questions. Chief Justice Warren's opinion turned on the point of the vagueness involved in the

resolutions that had created HUAC and in the committee's investigating policies. In Robel the Court invalidated the McCarran Act provision that banned from employment in defense plants persons holding membership in groups registered with the Subversive Activities Control Board. The five-to-two majority held that a distinction must be made between sensitive and nonsensitive jobs and that the quality and degree of membership had to be considered before dismissing employees.

35. Commonwealth v. Watson and Russell, 215 Pa. Super. Ct. 499 (1969), 258 A. 2d 541 (1969); In re Kay, 1 Cal. 3d 930 (1970), 464 P. 2d 142 (1970); Camarco v. City of Orange, 111 N.J. Super. 400 (1970), 268 A. 2d 354 (1970); and In re Cox, 3 Cal. 3d 205, 224 (1970), 474 P. 2d 992, 1004 (1970). The first Cox quotation is from note 23 on the pages indicated.

36. State ex rel. Cullen v. Ceci, 45 Wis. 2d 432, 457 (1970), 173 N.W. 2d 175, 187 (1970); State v. Fletcher, 22 Ohio App. 2d 83 (1970), 259 N.E. 2d 146 (1970); and Melville v. State, 10 Md. App. 118, 124 (1970), 268 A. 2d 497, 500 (1970).

37. State v. Turner, 78 Wash. 2d 276, 281 (1970), 474 P. 2d 91, 95 (1970); and Commonwealth v. Belgrave, 217 Pa. Super. Ct. 297, 303-304 (1970), 269 A. 2d 317, 320 (1970).

38. Mandel v. Mun. Court for Oakland-Piedmont Judicial Dist., 276 Cal. App. 2d 649 (1969), 81 Cal. Rptr. 173 (1969); People v. Uptgraft, 8 Cal. App. 3d Supp. 1 (1970), 87 Cal. Rptr. 459 (1970); and People v. Horton, 9 Cal. App. 3d Supp. 1 (1970), 87 Cal. Rptr. 818, 830 (1970).

5. THE FREE SPEECH APPLICATION LAG

Supreme Court pronouncement of dual lines of precedent and the corresponding development of dual lines of state court application have been only two of the discernible features involved in building the network of control. During the fifty-year period under consideration state courts and at times state legislatures have interwoven a number of techniques that have created what can be termed a free speech application lag, which has contributed further to the discrepancy between U.S. Supreme Court First Amendment interpretation and state court opinions.

The free speech application lag can be explained by placing developments into four categories for more detailed analysis. Although many courts have been reluctant to discard state law outright, there have been occasions on which state courts have engaged in a sidestep action by overturning the application of a statute in a particular case. This first category might appear to have involved civil liberties victories, but it has also included court action that has prevented the appeal of cases to higher courts. Second, state authorities have often exercised selective enforcement of state security statutes, applying them rarely and usually only in times of severe political and economic disagreement. Third, state courts have been very reluctant to transfer First Amendment speech protection from one set of historical circumstances to another, a practice that has forced civil liberties defenders to return to square one in their attempts to establish protection each time a newly developed area of political speech has been challenged. Finally, certain state legislatures have been persistent in refusing to remove from the statute books the type of laws that the Supreme Court has declared unconstitutional. Other legislatures have modified state regulations in minor, technical ways in order to comply with High Court rulings. All of these developments, which crisscross and overlap one another, have served to enlarge the discrepancy between U.S. Supreme Court and state supreme court interpretation and have thereby contributed to the weaving of the network of control.

In the first category, state court sidestep, judges have discarded the application of a law in a particular case, but have retained the statute, thereby providing at best a narrow free speech precedent. In so doing, state courts have followed an example provided by the Supreme Court in 1927 in *Fiske* v. *Kansas*. In that case justices ruled unanimously that the Kansas Criminal Syndicalism Law could not be applied to Harold Fiske primarily because the prosecution had not provided evidence that either Fiske or his organization, the Industrial Workers of the World, had violated the statute: "Thus applied the act is an arbitrary and unreasonable exercise of the police power of the State, unwarrantably infringing the liberty of the defendant in violation of the due process clause of the Fourteenth Amendment."[1]

In providing a sidestep example for state courts to follow, this ruling set a narrow precedent and left opportunity for courts to distinguish from *Fiske* on grounds that the ruling was limited solely to application in that case alone. The Ohio Supreme Court was among the first to follow this line of reasoning in *State* v. *Kassay* in 1932 when it upheld that state's Criminal Syndicalism Law and its application on grounds that free speech was fundamental, but not absolute. The case involved a man who had said he would blow up the airship on which he was working. Justice Florence Allen, soon to be distinguished as the first woman appointed to a U.S. Court of Appeals, dissented on grounds that the Ohio law should be discarded because it was of an even more sweeping nature than those laws or applications held unconstitutional in *Fiske*, *Stromberg*, and *Near*.[2]

A number of state courts applied the *Fiske* type of sidestep during the late thirties and early forties, again in the mid-fifties shortly after the Supreme Court ruling in *Pennsylvania* v. *Nel-*

son, and during the sixties. Each of these periods was a time of intense political or economic criticism and conflict. In *People* v. *Chambers* in 1938 the California Third District Court of Appeals reversed a criminal syndicalism conviction on procedural grounds, but made no criticism of the California statute, the same law that had been at issue in the *Whitney* case. The California judges decided that since the jury had acquitted the seventeen defendants of the charges of teaching or abetting criminal syndicalism, it would have been impossible for them to have committed the act of organizing such illegal activity, despite the fact that the jury had convicted them of the organizing charge.[3] In *State* v. *Sentner* in 1941 the Iowa Supreme Court ruled on circumstances involving a labor dispute typical of the era. William Sentner represented the United Electrical, Radio, and Machine Workers of America, the union that employees at the Maytag plant at Newton had selected as their agent under the stipulations of the National Labor Relations Act. During a contract renewal discussion in June 1939, Sentner made a speech reflecting his opinion that Maytag employees were not paid properly; and he called on citizens and civic organizations for support. Two days later the company imposed an immediate wage cut and threatened to fire those who did not accept it. Many workers left the plant, formed picket lines, and faced a back-to-work movement organized by nonunion employees.[4] The company sought an injunction, opposed by Sentner in another speech; and authorities arrested him for violating the Iowa Criminal Syndicalism Law, the first prosecution under that statute since its passage in 1919. After consideration of a long assignment of errors, the Iowa high court threw out Sentner's conviction on grounds that the prosecution had presented no evidence that he had ever advocated criminal syndicalism. However, the court upheld the law, applying *Gitlow-Whitney* precedent.[5] State supreme court action of this type prevented a possible appeal to the U.S. Supreme Court, which, considering the unanimous *De Jonge* opinion of 1937 and the appointments to the Roosevelt Court, was not likely to rule in favor of a state criminal syndicalism law.

Two years after *Sentner*, in 1943, the Oklahoma Criminal Court of Appeals dealt with two cases applying this sidestep technique.

In *Shaw* v. *State* in February the court reversed the conviction of a Communist party member, but left the state's Criminal Syndicalism Law intact. The court rejected the concept of guilt by association, declaring, "If this court were to sustain the conviction, it could only be because there is a popular demand for it and this in effect would mean a substitution of mob rule for that of courts of law." However, the judges applied *Gitlow* precedent to uphold the statute and repeated this action in *Wood* v. *State* in September, since the court agreed that the disposition in *Shaw* controlled in *Wood*.[6]

Over ten years later the Supreme Court ruling in *Nelson* prompted two state appellate benches to rule quickly on pending cases involving state security statutes. On May 3, 1956, one month after *Nelson*, the Supreme Judicial Court of Massachusetts, Middlesex, ruled that the two cases involving Margaret Gilbert's criticism of the U.S. Government fell into areas "exclusively pre-empted" by U.S. statutes, and the court quashed the indictments against her. The Massachusetts Sedition Law remained intact because the court did not "wish to be understood as saying that there can never be an instance of any kind of sedition directed so exclusively against the State as to fall outside the sweep of *Commonwealth of Pennsylvania* v. *Nelson*."[7]

In the second post-*Nelson* reaction of this type the Court of Appeals of Kentucky in June 1956 reversed the conviction of Carl Braden with instructions to dismiss indictments against him. Braden's civil rights activities in Louisville had resulted in his conviction under the Kentucky Sedition Law. The Kentucky court saw the Braden case as one that had developed under a sedition statute similar to Pennsylvania's. Yet the judges chose not to void the state law on preemption grounds: "It will suffice to say that we are compelled to follow the result reached by it [Nelson], since there is no logical way to distinguish the instant case from the Nelson case as decided by the United States Supreme Court."[8] The Kentucky security statute remained, along with those of Ohio, California, Iowa, Massachusetts, and a number of other states, to be applied in additional cases during the more intense civil rights and antiwar activities of the sixties.

An example of the sidestep application during the decade of the sixties took place in *State* v. *Cade*, a Louisiana case in which the state prosecuted a group of Black Muslims under a criminal anarchy statute. The Louisiana Supreme Court reversed the conviction and remanded the case for retrial on grounds that the trial court had failed to establish any evidence of advocacy of subversion by violence. At the same time the Louisiana court upheld the law on *Gitlow-Whitney* grounds as a "reasonable and constitutional exercise by the state of its police power."[9] The court did not find the statute to be overly vague or an infringement of the First Amendment. In this case, as in *Sentner*, the *Gitlow-Whitney* line of precedent served as a basis for a judicial sidestep that kept the state security statute intact but declined to apply it in a particular circumstance, a move that hardly provided a broad precedent for the future protection of political speech.

A second feature of the free speech application lag has been the selective enforcement process, by which state security statutes have remained dormant, sometimes for decades, and then have been activated during periods of intense conflict. One of the oldest state security statutes, the Georgia Anti-Insurrection Act of 1866, passed by a Reconstruction legislature attempting to reinstate a defunct slave code, was applied only once between 1866 and 1930. In 1869 in *Gibson* v. *State* the Georgia Supreme Court overturned that conviction.[10] During the early thirties authorities revived use of the statute since the legislature had not passed either a criminal syndicalism or a sedition statute to apply to critics of the state and local authorities. In 1932 in *Carr et al.* v. *State* the Georgia Supreme Court, applying *Gilbert-Gitlow-Whitney* precedent, affirmed the denial of a demurrer challenging the constitutionality of the statute on First and Fourteenth Amendment grounds. A year later the Georgia high court upheld Carr's conviction.[11] Authorities employed the statute again in 1932 to arrest Angelo Herndon for his work with the Unemployed Councils.

In 1936 when arguments on Herndon's behalf were presented to the Supreme Court for the second time, Whitney North Seymour attempted to distinguish Herndon's case from *Gitlow* and *Whitney* on the basis of the difference between the Georgia statute and the New York and California laws. He contended that the New York Criminal Anarchy Act and the California Criminal Syndicalism Law involved references to specific doctrine "explicitly stated and condemned by the statute," whereas the Georgia law was vague and referred only to the incitement of insurrection. He referred to the dormant-active policy when he argued further that the conditions involved in the *Gitlow* and *Whitney* cases did not "differ essentially from those at the time of the statute's enactment." However, Seymour contended that the 1866 Georgia law, based on slave codes dating back to 1804, aimed at conditions that "disappeared soon after the end of the war."[12] Seymour's success in convincing five members of the Supreme Court that the Georgia law violated the First and Fourteenth Amendments because of the lack of a clear and present danger test and the use of vague standards of guilt was based in part on his distinguishing the Herndon circumstances and the Georgia statute from the specifics of *Gitlow* and *Whitney*. This legal tactic proved to be a successful strategy in this case, but it also helped to contribute to the creation of dual lines of precedent. Seymour's contention that the authorities were applying Georgia law in circumstances not related to the original purpose for passing the statute is a point that can be made in analyzing the application of a number of the state security statutes and a development that is very much a part of the dormant-active aspect of the free speech application lag. Since the statutes often went unused for a number of years, the issues and the political groups changed by the time the authorities revived application of the law.

Although Herndon's attorneys convinced five Supreme Court justices that the Georgia Anti-Insurrection Statute violated the Bill of Rights, Georgia officials did not agree, and they waited until 1939 to drop charges against seventeen other persons similarly indicted under the law.[13] The state retained the statute on the books, and it was applied in civil rights cases during the 1960s. On November 1, 1963, one-time *Herndon* defense attorney Elbert Tuttle, then a judge of the Court of Appeals for the Fifth Circuit, headed a three-judge panel considering a case involving civil rights workers in Americus, Georgia; and a federal court again declared the 1866 statute unconstitutional. According to *Herndon* historian Charles Martin, "This ruling was significant because it marked the first time that a federal court had intervened in a civil rights case at the request of a private party to halt a state court proceeding," demonstration of an important development in federalism.

Georgia authorities clung to their states' rights position and persisted in applying the old law. In 1966, Atlanta police arrested black power advocate Stokely Carmichael for violating the statute's provisions, but the federal district court later dismissed the case.[14] The judicial history of this Georgia statute not only reflects the dormant-active technique employed by some states, but also reveals a staunch resistance of state officials to pronouncements by the federal bench, two central factors in the maintenance of the network of control.

Another dramatic example of the dormant-active component in the selective enforcement of state security statutes can be found in the history of the New York Criminal Anarchy Law applied in the well-known prosecution of Benjamin Gitlow for his activities in the Left Wing faction of the Socialist party. The act, passed in 1902 in the uproar over President McKinley's assassination, went unused until the arrest of Gitlow in 1919. After Gitlow's conviction and the subsequent Supreme Court ruling upholding the statute's constitutionality, the law remained dormant until authorities revived it in 1964 to arrest William Epton, a leader of a group known as the Progressive Labor Movement; it comprised a total of six members, including Epton, his wife, and Adolph Hart, an undercover agent of the New York Police Department's Bureau of Special Services.[15]

Authorities charged Epton and the group with violation of the Criminal Anarchy Statute because of months of alleged "advocating and preparing for violence against existing government authority" through plans for a block-by-block organization. When tension reached a high point in Harlem in July 1964, following the death of a fifteen-year-old black youth shot by an off-duty white police lieutenant, Epton used the occasion to attempt to organize a mass demonstration against the police. Later, after the planned demonstration was cancelled because of a lack of interest, rioting broke out in Harlem. Epton continued in attempts to organize against the police and prepared for another march and rally. After repeatedly warning Epton to cease his activities, police arrested him. Since the New York Court of Appeals upheld his conviction and the Supreme Court refused to grant *certiorari*, the statute remained in effect although the New York Court of Appeals wrote a clear and present danger test into their interpretation of the statute in the case. In his dissent Court of Appeals Judge Adrian Burke acknowledged the active-dormant factor in his reference to the use of "an apparently moribund statute...as a means of punishing speech."[16]

Additional states have also practiced this type of selective, dormant-active law enforcement. Iowa authorities did not use that state's 1919 Criminal Syndicalism Law for nearly twenty years until the arrest of Sentner for activities in the 1938 Maytag strike.[17] *De Jonge* precedent influenced the Iowa Supreme Court's opinion in overturning Sentner's conviction; but the law remained as an example of a criminal syndicalism statute never applied, in a reported case, to the group it was intended to police—the Industrial Workers of the World. Similarly, the Ohio Criminal Syndicalism Act, discussed in connection with the *Fiske* application in *State* v. *Kassay*, was considered by a state appellate tribunal only twice in the years while it was in effect. The Ohio Supreme Court upheld the law in 1932, and authorities reactivated it in 1964 to arrest Ku Klux Klan leader Clarence Brandenburg, who successfully sought a Supreme Court ruling of unconstitutionality on First Amendment grounds.[18] Neither Kassay nor Brandenburg was associated with the IWW or any syndicalist group. The Iowa and Ohio cases—together with the circumstances of the Whitney and De Jonge arrests under California and Oregon criminal syndicalism provisions as well as the Gitlow and Epton trials under the New York Criminal Anarchy Law—demonstrated the readiness with which state authorities transferred a statute designated to restrict one group to a situation involving another organization. This transference, which was also demonstrated in relation to the Georgia Anti-Insurrection Act, has served as a corollary to the selective enforcement aspect of the free speech application gap.

Even though state authorities have found a number of occasions to transfer application of a security statute from one group voicing criticism to another, state courts often have been reluctant to transfer First Amendment protection secured in one area of political speech to speech involved in later developments of political and social protest. The first U.S. Supreme Court applications of the First Amendment to the states via the vehicle of the Fourteenth

Amendment came in cases involving what by the late twenties and thirties had become familiar examples of left-wing protest—socialist and communist organizations and the Industrial Workers of the World. Harold Fiske was associated with the IWW. Dirk De Jonge and Angelo Herndon both had Communist party connections and were involved with programs responding to the needs of the most desperate victims of the Great Depression. The stand that the Supreme Court took in both *De Jonge* and *Herndon* regarding the need for a clear and present danger application and for the necessity for statutes to establish reasonable standards of guilt did not deter state authorities and state courts from applying security laws and other restrictions in the numerous labor relations cases and other political speech issues that appeared in the late thirties and early forties.

In *Thomas* v. *Casey*, a case discussed in chapter 4, the New Jersey Supreme Court in 1938 upheld a Jersey City refusal to issue a meeting permit to Socialist leader Norman Thomas. In distinguishing the case at bar from the cognate rights doctrine of *De Jonge*, the court chose not to see a correlation between assembly and speech infringements imposed by the Oregon Criminal Syndicalism Statute and those restrictions employed in Jersey City. Instead, the New Jersey justices emphasized a point made by the Supreme Court in *De Jonge* regarding legislatures possessing authority to correct abuses of free speech. As a result, the New Jersey court concluded that to have allowed Thomas the permit and the subsequent speech most likely would have resulted in a protest and disturbance. In the court's view this would have constituted an abuse of the First Amendment rights and would have interfered as well with public "freedom of movement" in the park. In this case a circumstantial contrast involving buildings, parks, and permits provided an opportunity for the state court to maintain the network and avoid transferring the concept of the protection of freedom of speech and assembly from one type of gathering to another. The year after the Thomas case the Supreme Court declared the Jersey City ordinance unconstitutional in *Hague* v. *CIO*. As a result, some state courts in subsequent rulings did discard similar permit requirements for left-wing groups, but they did not do so until the U.S. Supreme Court had provided a directive and usually only in cases that corresponded to *Hague* on numerous technical as well as substantive points.[19]

During the period of the late thirties and early forties, state courts provided other examples of reluctance to transfer *De Jonge* application to other areas of political speech. In *Commonwealth* v. *Nichols* in 1938 the Supreme Judicial Court of Massachusetts, Worcester, upheld the regulation of the distribution of handbills because such activity was to be "subject to reasonable rules formulated to serve the public interest," in this situation to protect the public against annoyance. The court cited *De Jonge* along with *Whitney* and *Gitlow* as well as *Lovell* v. *Griffin,* a unanimous Supreme Court opinion that had invalidated a similar ordinance but in a case involving Jehovah's Witnesses, who were not involved in the Massachusetts case. The Massachusetts court not only relied on the abuse reference in *De Jonge,* as the New Jersey court had done in *Thomas* v. *Casey,* but also chose to view the even more pertinent *Lovell* v. *Griffin* precedent in a very narrow light that applied only when freedom of religion was also involved.[20]

In the area of labor relations, a very vital issue of the period, state authorities were also very slow to transfer *De Jonge, Stromberg,* and other protective First Amendment precedents to picketing and other types of union activity. The Iowa case of *Sentner* presented one example although the state supreme court did reverse his conviction. In *Meadowmoor Dairies* the Illinois Supreme Court, like a number of other state benches, found no basis for application of First Amendment protection to picketing activity, which the Illinois court perceived as a conspiracy against business. However, after the Supreme Court provided a precedent in *Thornhill* v. *Alabama* in 1940, a case that dealt specifically with picketing, certain state courts were able to sustain protection of this form of political speech; one example was a Colorado case involving the so-called Labor Peace Act, which the state supreme court invalidated on First Amendment precedents and on grounds that it was preempted by the National Labor Relations Act. However, at this time the protection of picketing was not to extend beyond sign carrying. In 1942 the California Supreme Court, speaking through Justice Roger Traynor, upheld convictions of fruit workers arrested for loitering and stopping automobiles during picketing activity, which in itself was held to be protected speech.[21]

During the post-World War II era the central issue related to state security statutes centered on the cold war fears of subversive activity and on loyalty programs in particular. Although the California Supreme Court in 1946 had discarded a loyalty oath statute for lack of a clear and present danger test,[22] most state authorities and courts became increasingly occupied with security issues and did not transfer the Supreme Court protection of the clear and present danger application from the thirties type of political speech cases to the loyalty-related First Amendment issues of the cold war era. In 1949 the Second District Court of Appeals in California, in a typical opinion of the period, upheld loyalty affidavits required of Los Angeles County employees and cited *De Jonge* and *Stromberg* as well as *Whitney* precedents regarding clear and present danger and the police power. Applying much the same free-speech-is-not-absolute line of reasoning, the Court of Appeals of Maryland discarded a taxpayer suit brought against the state Subversive Activities Act; and the Superior Court of New Jersey, Appellate Division, upheld the conviction of a man charged with interfering with enlistment. In 1950 the New York Court of Appeals upheld the constitutionality of the state's Feinberg Law, which required public school and college teachers to swear a loyalty oath as well as an affidavit of nonmembership in a list of organizations to be determined by the Board of Regents. The court of appeals held that the circumstances did create a clear and present danger. In these cases courts applied Holmes's clear and present danger test with a broad definition of danger that left numerous groups outside First Amendment protection.[23]

During the cold war scare of the fifties, developments in the state of New Hampshire also provided a dramatic example of the action of a state government in the security field. State Attorney General Louis Wyman vigorously sought to apply the state's Subversive Activities Act to groups who allegedly desired overthrow of the government. Wyman as attorney general and the state's chief prosecutor also possessed considerable investigatory powers over those thought to violate the state statute. In a number of cases, the first decided in 1954 three days after the preemption ruling of the Pennsylvania Supreme Court in *Commonwealth* v. *Nelson*, the Supreme Court of New Hampshire continued to uphold the statute and Wyman's investigations. Two months after the U.S. Supreme Court voiced its agreement with the Pennsylvania high bench, the New Hampshire court concluded in a *per curiam* opinion that it was "not satisfied that the *Nelson* case...purports to preclude such an investigation." In 1957 the New Hampshire court continued to support Wyman. In the *Wyman* v. *Uphaus* decision, which the U.S. Supreme Court later supported, the New Hampshire justices distinguished Uphaus's case from *Nelson* on grounds that there were types of sedition directed "so exclusively against the state as to fall outside the sweep of Commonwealth of Pennsylvania v. Nelson [*sic*]."[24]

Although Louis Wyman and the New Hampshire Supreme Court chose to distinguish the enforcement of their Subversive Activities Act from *Nelson* precedent, several state courts chose to apply *Nelson* to discard either a security statute or its application. The *Gilbert* decision of the Massachusetts Supreme Court and the *Braden* decision of the Kentucky Court of Appeals both denied application of their state security statutes on grounds of federal statutes preempting the field. It is important to note that neither the U.S. Supreme Court nor the Massachusetts and Kentucky courts made any transference of First Amendment argument in these cases. The constitutional protection found in the *De Jonge* cognate rights doctrine and the *De Jonge* and *Herndon* clear and present danger application was very susceptible to arguments charging that the activities of protest groups of the cold war period fell into the category of the abuse of speech, thereby creating a danger to society. As a result, courts that did discard security statutes or their application relied on the more technical and procedural preemption argument.[25]

During the post-*Nelson* period, two other state appellate courts declared state security provisions unconstitutional but again on preemption grounds, not on First Amendment precedent. In *Albertson* v. *Millard*, decided within one month of *Nelson*, the Michigan Supreme Court discarded several sections of the state's 1948 Trucks Act "on the narrow issue of supersession of the state law by the Federal Smith Act." In 1958 the Louisiana Supreme

Court threw out that state's Subversive Activities and Communist Control Law on supersession and preemption grounds.[26] Since forty-two states had security statutes subject to the *Nelson* ruling, the fact that only four state court systems applied the Supreme Court ruling within a two-year period indicates the recalcitrance of many states on this matter. After 1959 and the Supreme Court ruling in *Uphaus* v. *Wyman,* holding that *Nelson* precedent applied only to state laws aimed to curb sedition against the U.S. Government, numerous state authorities and state courts found additional incentive to circumvent *Nelson* and distinguish their cases.[27]

During the late fifties and into the decade of the sixties the focus of the exercise of political speech gradually moved into the field of civil rights. Again, state courts were reluctant to apply the First Amendment protections directed by the Supreme Court in earlier cases. Not only did a number of state courts distinguish or ignore precedents like *De Jonge, Herndon,* and *Stromberg,* they also chose not to apply *Thornhill, Hague,* and other opinions that had confirmed a constitutional basis for picketing and public gatherings. As a result, those persons seeking Fourteenth Amendment protection for First Amendment freedoms associated with the crusade for racial equality were forced to fight a new battle to secure favorable U.S. Supreme Court precedents in cases reflecting the confrontations of the era. The recalcitrance of state courts in failing to transfer the Supreme Court free speech precedents from one set of circumstances to another led many political and social critics to seek redress in the federal court system, as demonstrated in *Dombrowski* v. *Pfister.* This approach raised additional questions regarding the operations of the courts within a federal system.

In 1958 the Florida Supreme Court demonstrated the process of distinguishing from *Nelson* precedent in a case involving the state's Legislative Investigating Committee, which was attempting to determine Communist party infiltration of civil rights organizations. The supreme court upheld a Dade County Circuit Court, which had ordered witnesses to answer questions related to this issue on grounds that Congress had preempted the field of sedition against only the federal government and not the state. The

Florida case provided a typical example of southern state officials placing civil rights organizations within the domain of security statutes. Another civil rights-related development in Arkansas revealed even more precisely the unwillingness of state courts to transfer constitutional protection from one circumstance to another. The Arkansas Supreme Court in late 1958 upheld an ordinance that required disclosure of the NAACP's membership lists if the organization were to enjoy tax immunity. The court recited the litany of precedents including *De Jonge*, which the NAACP had argued protected the concept of freedom of assembly; but the justices ruled that this protection applied only to persons, not to organizations.[28]

As the civil rights movement began a more vigorous campaign in the early sixties, it encountered considerable opposition on First Amendment issues related to solicitation, public gatherings, and demonstrations. In the summer of 1961 a Georgia court convicted a defendant under an Albany city ordinance that required persons licensed for solicitation to show good moral character and evidence they had never belonged to organizations holding communist beliefs. In its first application of *Herndon* precedent in a reported case the Georgia Court of Appeals reversed the conviction on grounds that the statute bore no relation to the safety of the state. Another civil rights case in 1964 brought a different outcome when the Georgia Supreme Court upheld the trespass conviction of a person who had refused to leave a privately operated public restaurant when ordered to do so by police. The court avoided the state action ruling in *Peterson* v. *Greenville* by holding that no state action was involved in the case despite the presence of a statute on the duty of an innkeeper to receive guests.[29]

Developments in other state courts also reflected this dichotomy in reasoning. In 1963 the Louisiana Supreme Court, citing *Gitlow* and *Whitney*, upheld the conviction of the Reverend B. Elton Cox for obstructing a public passage for breach of the peace during a civil rights demonstration that had blocked the sidewalk. The Louisiana justices declared that the First Amendment free speech clause did not protect such activity, a decision that the U.S. Supreme Court later overturned in a confusing set of opinions.[30] In 1964 the Mississippi Supreme Court upheld the disorderly conduct conviction of a black freedom rider who refused to move from a white waiting room in a bus station. Interpreting the freedom rider's sit-in as a form of speech, the Mississippi court applied *Whitney* precedent stating that speech was not absolute, but was subject to state police power restrictions. The continued presence of *Gitlow-Whitney* precedent affirming that speech is not absolute provided ample opportunity for state courts to limit expression and distinguish between what some judges and analysts have termed *speech pure* and *speech plus*. In contrast, in 1965 the Court of Appeals of Alabama ruled against a Birmingham ordinance that required a parade permit for demonstrations. Civil rights leader Fred Shuttlesworth had conducted a Good Friday march that had not obstructed traffic, and the court found the ordinance invalid as a form of prior restraint and for a lack of ascertainable constitutional standards. The court relied not only on *Herndon* vagueness principle but also on *De Jonge* cognate rights doctrine as developed further in *Thomas* v. *Collins* in regard to prior restraint. It appears that in civil rights cases state courts were more likely to protect speech activity if it could be linked very specifically to the circumstances of earlier symbolic speech rulings associated with picketing and other activities of labor unions.[31]

Later in the sixties, political protest increasingly reflected student unrest, criticism of the draft, and other forms of opposition to the Viet Nam War. Again, state courts appeared unwilling to apply previously determined First Amendment protection in relation to new issues of political speech; and the issues of violence and destruction of property complicated the picture still further. In 1969 the Wisconsin Supreme Court upheld the convictions of University of Wisconsin students who had participated in the anti-Viet Nam Dow Chemical protest in Madison. Defendants had blocked doorways, spoken into bullhorns inside buildings, and struck at officers. The students' attorneys contended that the disorderly conduct statute under which they had been arrested was overly broad and violated the First Amendment along *Dombrowski* lines. The Wisconsin justices opted for public order, holding that "constitutionally protected rights, such as freedom of speech and peaceable assembly, are not the be all and end all." The following year the Wisconsin Supreme Court delivered another opinion on the subject of political protest, this time involved with the burning of draft records. Appellants had relied on *Nelson* precedent to argue preemption, but the Wisconsin tribunal disagreed. Justice Nathan Heffernan wrote, "We can only say that our law has not concluded that punishment by separate sovereignties for the same act constitutes double jeopardy."[32]

In another draft records destruction case also decided in 1970 the Court of Special Appeals of Maryland upheld the Baltimore County Circuit Court conviction of the Catonsville Nine protestors, a group that included the Fathers Berrigan. The Maryland judges also denied federal preemption and ruled that *Nelson* preemption precedent did not apply here: "the conduct prohibited by the two sovereignties is not identical nor does it concern the same subject."[33] In these three anti-war cases state courts dealt with circumstances involving either violence or the destruction of property and as a result excluded this type of protest from First Amendment protection on police power grounds.

California courts also dealt with the problem of protest during this period. The Appellate Department of the Superior Court for Los Angeles County considered two cases in the spring of 1970, both of which involved demonstrating college students in nonviolent circumstances. At San Fernando State College nine students had been prosecuted for remaining at a place of alleged unlawful assembly after having been warned to disperse. The court upheld the unlawful assembly charge, contending that the arrests had been made to avoid violence. The college president had outlawed all public gatherings and thereby created a form of prior restraint, an action that placed this case in a position very parallel to many labor cases of the early forties. Yet the court held that constitutional rights had not been curtailed. Judge Delbert Wong dissented, quoting Brandeis's concurrence in *Whitney*: "The fact that speech is likely to result in some violence or in destruction of property is not enough to justify its suppression." The same court delivered a similar opinion in a case involving a demonstration at Southwest College that had stopped automobiles but had not prevented anyone from entering the campus. Judge Wong voiced the same dissent as in the earlier case.[34]

Another issue of student protest resulted in an Iowa Supreme Court opinion in 1970. A group of Grinnell College students disrobed at a public meeting of a sex education class to protest the alleged exploitation of women in *Playboy* magazine. Authorities arrested the students for indecent exposure, and the Iowa Supreme Court upheld the convictions, declaring such activity outside the protected exercise of free speech. In the opinion of the justices, disrobing was a nonspeech activity.[35]

Cases discussed here illustrate the point that as the substance of political speech changed over the decades, state courts found it difficult to transfer application from one substantive issue to another and consequently provided an additional web for the network of control. The presence of violence and destruction of property provided judges with a justification for denial of First Amendment protection in a number of the antiwar protest cases. However, state courts also chose not to make transfer of First Amendment doctrine in situations of student protest that were in many ways parallel to earlier labor and civil rights campaigns that had resulted in Supreme Court extension of First Amendment protection. A change in historical circumstances and a change in the substance of the issues provided a pretext for nontransference of First Amendment protection even when the nonviolent protests resembled those of earlier eras. In this sense the technique of nontransference of precedent often resembled the distinguishing process discussed in chapter 4.

The fourth component in the free speech lag focused on the recalcitrance of state legislatures in resistance to Supreme Court rulings or in modification of statutes to comply technically with a precedent favorable to civil liberties. The persistence of dual lines of Supreme Court precedent has undoubtedly provided part of the incentive for the resilience of state security statutes, but certain states have demonstrated particular defiance of federal court rulings.

Georgia has provided the most direct and blatant defiance of a Supreme Court ruling. After the 1937 *Herndon* ruling the state waited two years before dropping charges against others indicted under the Anti-Insurrection Act at the same time as Herndon. A Georgia apellate court did not apply *Herndon* precedent in a reported case until 1961, twenty-four years after the Supreme Court opinion. The Georgia Anti-Insurrection Law remained on the books throughout the period, and authorities resurrected it to arrest civil rights workers during the sixties. In November 1963, a three-judge federal court panel in Atlanta declared the statute unconstitutional for the second time. Yet Georgia officials persisted in applying the old law; and in 1966 Atlanta police employed it to arrest black power advocate Stokely Carmichael. The federal district court later dismissed the case. The 1866 statute is no longer included in the Georgia Code and has been replaced by a 1968 revision.[36]

California has provided two examples of persistent resistance to Supreme Court directives, and the circumstances also demonstrate the confusion that can develop within a dual system of state and national courts. California enforced its 1919 Criminal Syndicalism Law very vigorously during the twenties with the *Whitney* case and subsequent Supreme Court decision emerging as the most celebrated example. Authorities revived the statute during the unrest of the sixties and applied it in the arrest of John Harris, Jr., for distributing leaflets advocating change in industrial ownership via the political process. In March 1968 a three-judge panel of the Federal Court for the Central District of California declared the California Criminal Syndicalism Statute unconstitutional on vagueness and overbreadth grounds. Even after the Supreme Court overruled *Whitney* in *Brandenburg*, the California statute remained on the books, and in 1971 the Supreme Court upheld Harris's conviction in the interests of comity and federalism, a definite backing away from the *Dombrowski* ruling of 1965. In 1976 the California Legislature modified the Criminal Syndicalism Law but changed only the provision relating to the sentence imposed by the statute. Despite a negative U.S. Supreme Court ruling the California Criminal Syndicalism Law remains on the books, sustained in part by the tension between federal and state court systems.[37]

Another California example of legislative maneuvering in response to court rulings involved the Civic Center Act already discussed in regard to the 1946 *Danskin* case. In that opinion Justice Roger Traynor discarded, as an intrusion of free speech and denial of equal protection, that section of the act that required loyalty oaths of groups who were judged to be advocates of overthrow of the government and who sought to use school auditorium facilities. The California Legislature revised the statute to require the loyalty oath of all groups requesting use of facilities, and in 1961 the state supreme court declared this modification unconstitutional. The legislature responded again, making the law more specific and requiring applications desiring to use school auditoriums to sign a statement swearing that they did not advocate criminal syndicalism or breaking of the law. In 1963 the supreme court upheld this modification on the grounds that the state's Criminal Syndicalism Statute had been upheld by the U.S. Supreme Court in *Whitney*.[38]

State judicial and legislative reaction to the 1956 *Nelson* preemption ruling provided another set of examples of state recalcitrance. Shortly after the *Nelson* decision, the Michigan Supreme Court and the Louisiana Supreme Court declared parts of their state security laws unconstitutional, and the Supreme Judicial Court of Massachusetts and the Kentucky Court of Appeals discarded the application of their state statutes in the *Gilbert* and *Braden* cases. However, courts in the other thirty-eight states that maintained security statutes similar to Pennsylvania's did not follow suit; and in some, particularly New Hampshire, authorities seemed to defy *Nelson* precedent. Even though these states may not have had security cases pending, the involvement of twenty-seven states in *amicus* briefs on behalf of Pennsylvania in the *Nelson* case plus inaction on the part of legislatures throughout the remainder of the decade revealed much about state attitudes on this question. For example, after the Louisiana Supreme Court discarded the state's first Subversive Activities Law in the 1958 *Jenkins* case, the legislature repassed the statute in 1960 after the U.S. Supreme Court's *Uphaus* ruling. Two years later the legislature supplemented the law, making it so broad that any civil rights activity could be interpreted to fall within its scope, circumstances directly related to the events of the *Dombrowski* case. The U.S. Supreme Court voided the second version of the statute in *Dombrowski*, but the statute remains on the books in Louisiana.[39]

Most state legislatures have responded to the Supreme Court directives with silence and inaction.[40] However, there have been several exceptions, the most notable being Oregon's repeal of its Criminal Syndicalism Law in 1937 shortly after the *De Jonge* ruling. The legislature then replaced the unconstitutional provision with a conspiracy statute. In 1963 under the leadership of Attorney General Walter Mondale the Minnesota Legislature made an attempt to revise and update its statutes in line with federal court decisions. Lawmakers repealed the Sedition Act of 1917, at issue in *Gilbert*, but retained the state's Criminal Syndicalism Law, which remains despite *Brandenburg*. In 1967 the New York Legislature, eleven years after the *Nelson* ruling, revised the Criminal Anarchy Act, applied in *Gitlow* and *Epton*, to apply to sedition directed against the state of New York rather than at activities critical of all organized governments, as stipulated in the 1902 statute. Following the Supreme Court's *Brandenburg* decision of 1969, the Ohio legislature repealed that state's Criminal Syndicalism Law. The actions of the Oregon, Minnesota, New York, and Ohio Legislatures have been exceptions to the resistance demonstrated by other states, and several of these exceptions have not moved to modify state security statutes to any great degree. The new states of Alaska and Hawaii, which entered the Union in 1959, did not follow closely the examples set by older states with their proliferation of security statutes. Originally, Alaska adopted a criminal syndicalism statute but repealed it in 1978. Hawaii originally devised a procedural treason provision identical to the one in the U. S. Constitution and a statute outlawing subversive activity. In 1972 the Hawaii Legislature repealed those provisions, replacing them with a section on loyalty.[41]

The four components of the free speech application lag have crisscrossed throughout the fifty-year period under discussion, weaving a nationwide network of state legislation and state court interpretation that has attempted to control and restrict groups critical of governmental activities. At times the components of the lag have been woven so tightly that it is difficult to unravel them for purposes of analysis. Often these threads have been tied closely to other components of the network, especially to the dual lines of precedent provided by the U.S. Supreme Court. In the process of applying dual lines of precedent and contributing to the free speech application lag, state appeals courts, aided by state legislatures, have extended the security statute restrictions on political speech to additional areas of judicial interpretation. This process has expanded and tightened the comprehensive network of control, constituted by the various state networks.

NOTES

1. Fiske v. Kan., 274 U.S. 380, 387 (1927).

2. State v. Kassay, 126 Ohio St. 177, 193 (1932), 184 N.E. 521, 527 (1932). Franklin Roosevelt appointed Florence Allen to the federal appeals bench in 1934. "Florence Ellinwood Allen," *Who Was Who in America* (Chicago: Marquis Who's Who, Inc., 1968), vol. 4, p. 22. See also Stromberg v.Cal., 283 U.S. 359 (1931), explained in note 17, chapter 1, and Near v. Minn., 283 U.S. 697 (1931), explained in note 8, chapter 4.

3. People v. Chambers, 22 Cal. App. 2d 687, 726 (1937), 72 P. 746, 763 (1938).

4. State v. Sentner, 230 Iowa 590, 595-596 (1941), 298 N.W. 813, 814 (1941).

5. 230 Iowa 590, 599-601, 621; and 298 N.W. 813, 816, 824.

6. Shaw v. State, 76 Okla. Crim. 271, 313 (1943), 134 P. 2d 999, 1020 (1943); and Wood v.State, 76 Okla, Crim. 89 (1943), 141 P. 2d 309 (1943).

7. Commonwealth v. Gilbert, 334 Mass. 71, 75 (1956), 134 N.E. 2d 13, 16 (1956).

8. Braden v. Commonwealth, 291 S.W. 2d 843, 844 (1956). See also Brief of Individual *amici curiae*, Pa. v. Nelson, 350 U.S. 497 (1956).

9. State v. Cade, 244 La. 534, 545 (1963), 153 So. 2d 382, 386 (1963).

10. GA. CODE ANN. §§ 26-901—26-904; Gibson v. Ga., 38 Ga. 571 (1869); and Charles H. Martin, *The Angelo Herndon Case and Southern Justice* (Baton Rouge: Louisiana State University Press, 1976), p. 21.

11. Carr v. State, 176 Ga. 55 (1932), 166 S.E. 827 (1932) and 176 Ga. 747 (1933), 167 S.E. 103 (1933).

12. Brief for Appellant at 42-43, Herndon v. Lowry, 301 U.S. 242 (1937).

13. Martin, *The Angelo Herndon Case*, pp. 211-212.

14. Ibid., pp. 214-215. Harris v. Fred Chappell, Sheriff, Harris v. Pace, Aelony v. Pace, 8 RACE REL. L. REP. 1355 (1963). Carmichael v. Allen, 267 F.Supp. 985 (N.D. Ga. 1967).

15. 1902 N.Y. Laws §§ 160-166; Gitlow v. N.Y., 268 U.S. 652 (1925); Epton v. N.Y., 390 U.S. 29 (1968); Respondent's Brief in Opposition to Petition for Writ of *Certiorari* at 5-18, 390 U.S. 29; and Harris, *Black Power Advocacy: Criminal Anarchy or Free Speech*, 56 CALIF. L. REV. 717 (1968).

16. N.Y. PENAL LAW § 240.15 (McKinney); Respondent's Brief in Opposition to Writ of *Certiorari* at 9, 12-18, 390 U.S. 29; and People v. Epton, 19 N.Y. 2d 496, 511 (1967), 227 N.E. 2d 829, 838 (1967).

17. 230 Iowa 590 (1941), 298 N.W. 813 (1941).

18. Brief for Appellant at 11, Brandenburg v. Ohio, 395 U.S. 444 (1969).

19. Thomas v. Casey, 121 N.J.L. 185, 190 (1938), 1 A. 2d 866, 869 (1938). See also Hague v. CIO, 307 U.S. 496 (1939); and Commonwealth v. Gilfedder, 321 Mass. 335 (1947), 73 N.E. 2d 241 (1947). Hague is discussed in note 7, chapter 4.

20. Commonwealth v. Nichols, 301 Mass. 584, 586 (1938). See also Lovell v. Griffin, 303 U.S. 444 (1938).

21. 230 Iowa 590, 298 N.W. 813; Meadowmoor Dairies, Inc. v. Milk Wagon Drivers' Union of Chicago, 371 Ill. 377, 389 (1939), 21 N.E. 2d 308, 310 (1939); Thornhill v. Alabama, 310 U.S. 88 (1940); AFL v. Reilly, 113 Colo. 90 (1944), 155 P. 2d 145 (1944); and Ex parte Bell, 19 Cal. 2d 488 (1942), 122 P. 2d 22 (1942).

When the U.S. Supreme Court ruled in the Meadowmoor case, the majority—speaking through Justice Felix Frankfurter—held that state courts could enjoin picketing accompanied by violence and threats to property (312 U.S. 287 [1941]).

22. Danskin v. San Diego Unified School Dist., 28 Cal. 2d 536 (1946), 171 P. 2d 885 (1946), discarded a loyalty oath provision in the Civic Center Act. In a similar example in Imbrie v. Marsh, 3 N.J. 578 (1949), 68 A. 2d 761 (1949), the New Jersey Supreme Court, Appellate Division, threw out a requirement of denial of belief in violence, which was a prerequisite for candidacy for the state legislature.

23. Steiner v. Darby, 88 Cal. App. 2d 481 (1949), 199 P. 2d 429 (1949); Hammond v. Lancaster, 194 Md. 462 (1950), 71 A. 2d 483 (1950); State v. De Fillipis, 15 N.J. Super. 7 (1951), 83 A. 2d 16 (1951); and Thompson v. Wallin, 301 N.Y. 476 (1950), 95 N.E. 2d 806 (1950).

24. Nelson v. Wyman, 99 N.H. 33 (1954), 105 A. 2d 756 (1954); Kahn v. Wyman, 100 N.H. 245, 246 (1956), 123 A. 2d 166 (1956); and Wyman v. Uphaus, 100 N.H. 436, 441 (1957), 130 A. 2d 278, 282 (1957). See also Wyman v. De Gregory, 100 N.H. 163 (1957), 137 A. 2d 512 (1957). Attorney General Wyman's activities are discussed in David Caute, *The Great Fear* (New York: Simon and Schuster, 1978).

25. 334 Mass. 71 (1956), 134 N.E. 2d 13 (1956); and 291 S.W. 2d 843 (1956).

26. Albertson v. Millard, 345 Mich. 519, 522 (1956), 77 N.W. 2d 104, 105 (1956); and State v. Jenkins, 236 La. 300 (1958), 107 So. 2d 648 (1958).

27. See First Unitarian Church v. County of Los Angeles, 48 Cal. 2d 419 (1957), 311 P. 2d 508 (1957); Norstrand v. Balmer, 53 Wash. 2d 460 (1959), 335 P. 2d 10 (1950); Cramp v. Bd. of Pub. Instruction of Orange County, 125 So. 2d 554, 557 (1961), which relied on the Supreme Court's Uphaus ruling in 360 U.S. 72 (1959); and State v. Levitt, 246 Ind. 275 (1965), 203 N.E. 2d 821 (1965). The Supreme Court later discarded the Florida teachers' loyalty oath on due process grounds (368 U.S. 278 [1961]).

28. Gibson v. Fla. Legislative Investigating Comm., 108 So. 2d 729 (1958); and Bates v. City of Little Rock, 229 Ark. 819 (1958), 319 S.W. 2d 37 (1958). In 372 U.S. 539 (1963) the Supreme Court applied the First and Fourteenth Amendments to reverse the judgment of the Florida court.

29. Wolfe v. City of Albany, 104 Ga. App. 264 (1961), 121 S.E. 2d 331 (1961); and Walker v.State, 220 Ga. App. 415 (1964), 139 S.E. 2d 278 (1964).

30. State v. Cox, 244 La. 1087 (1963), 156 So. 2d 453 (1963); and Cox v. La., 379 U.S. 536 and 379 U.S. 559 (1965). See also Kalven, *The Concept of the Public Forum*: Cox v. Louisiana, 1965 SUP. CT. REV. 1.

31. Thomas v. State, 160 So. 2d 657 (1964); and Shuttlesworth v. City of Birmingham, 43 Ala. App. 68 (1956), 180 So. 2d 114 (1965). The Alabama Supreme Court upheld the law in 281 Ala. 542 (1967), 206 So. 2d 348 (1967). Thomas v. Collins, 323 U.S. 516 (1945), is explained in note 16, chapter 4. Kalven, *The Concept of the Public Forum*, comments critically on the pure and plus distinction that emerged from Cox, 379 U.S. 559; Edwards v. S.C., 372 U.S. 229 (1963); and other Supreme Court opinions.

32. State v. Zwicker, 41 Wis. 2d 497, 509 (1969), 164 N.W. 2d 512, 518 (1969); and State ex rel. Cullen v. Ceci, 45 Wis. 2d 432, 457 (1970), 173 N.W. 2d 175, 187 (1970).

33. Melville v. State, 10 Md. App. 118 (1970), 268 A. 2d 497 (1970).

34. People v. Uptgraft, 8 Cal. App. 3d Supp. 1, 16 (1970), 87 Cal. Rptr.459, 468 (1970); and People v. Horton, 9 Cal. App. 3d Supp. 1 (1970), 87 Cal. Rptr. 818 (1970).

35. State v. Nelson, 178 N.W. 2d 434 (1970).

36. Martin, *The Angelo Herndon Case*, pp. 190, 211, 214-215. The first reported case in which Georgia courts applied Herndon precedent was Wolfe v. City of Albany, 104 Ga. App. 264, 121 S.E. 2d 333. The three-judge panel decision was reported in 8 Race Relations Law Reporter 1963; and the Carmichael case is in 267 F. Supp. 985 (N.D. Ga. 1967). The Georgia code in use in 1981 contains an anti-insurrection provision that is a 1968 revision of the 1866 law. The revision covers those who would teach, advise, or advocate the "duty, necessity, desirability, or propriety of

overthrowing or destroying the government of the State." See GA. CODE ANN. §§ 26-901—26-904.

37. CAL. GEN. LAWS ANN. Act 8428 (Deering); People v. Whitney, 57 Cal. App. 449 (1922), 207 P. 698 (1922); Harris v. Younger, 281 F. Supp. 507 (C.D. Cal. 1968); Younger v. Harris, 401 U.S. 37 (1971); and CAL. PENAL CODE §§ 11400 et seq. (West), which became operative July 1, 1977. See also Harris, *Black Power Advocacy: Criminal Anarchy or Free Speech* 56 CALIF. L. REV. 702 (1968).

38. 28 Cal. 2d 536 (1946), 171 P. 2d 885 (1946); Am. Civil Liberties Union v. Bd. of Educ., 55 Cal. 2d 167 (1961), 359 P. 2d 45 (1961); and Am. Civil Liberties Union of S. Cal. v. Bd. of Educ., 59 Cal. 2d 203 (1963), 379 P. 2d 4 (1963).

39. 236 La. 300 (1958), 107 So. 2d 648 (1958); Brief for Appellant at 24, Dombrowski v. Pfister, 380 U.S. 479 (1965). See also Briefs for *amicus curiae*, Pa. v. Nelson, 350 U.S. 497 (1956).

40. For a more detailed account see Appendix.

41. On the Oregon repeal see Eldridge Dowell, *A History of Criminal Syndicalism Legislation in the United States* (New York: Da Capo Press, 1969), p. 147. See also MINN. STAT. ANN. § 613.08 (West); N. Y. PENAL LAW § 240.15 (McKinney); OHIO REV. CODE § 2921.01 (Page); ALASKA STAT. §§ 11.50.010-11.50.930; and HAWAII REV. STAT. § 85. For information regarding states that have adjusted or repealed security statutes since 1970 see Appendix.

6. EXTENSION OF THE NETWORK

As the dual lines of U.S. Supreme Court precedent and the free speech application lag have persisted as central features in the opinions of a number of state supreme courts, state justices have applied the security statute precedents in a number of First Amendment cases involving statutes outside of the strictly defined security field. In the development of this pattern, state supreme courts have linked security statute precedents to rulings on political speech in decisions upholding the restriction of picketing, the licensing of public meetings, the enforcement of loyalty oaths and security investigations, and the control of civil rights and antiwar activities. Through this process courts have extended application of the precedents to cases involving the various issues of political speech and then have advanced the pattern further to include additional areas of First Amendment interpretation. This latter and wider network of control has included cases involving door-to-door solicitation, sound trucks, disturbance of the peace, censorship and obscenity, libel, group libel, and procedural considerations. These areas of interpretation in turn have had an effect upon the cases involving political speech directly.

Certain aspects of the application of Supreme Court security statute precedents to include situations involving various facets of meetings and assemblies have been discussed in relation to the dual lines of precedent and the free speech application lag. State court extension of the network of control in this area progressed until the Supreme Court, reflecting the Roosevelt appointments, provided precedents in 1939 in *Hague* v. *CIO* and in 1945 in *Thomas* v. *Collins*, which reinforced the position taken earlier in *De Jonge*.[1] Even after the High Court provided direction in this area, certain state courts continued to extend the network in assembly-related cases. In 1949 the New York Court of Appeals in *People* v. *Kunz* upheld a New York City ordinance that required a police commissioner's permit as a prior condition for public-worship meetings. Carl Jacob Kunz had held such a permit, but officials had revoked it on grounds that he had ridiculed other religious groups. The U.S. Supreme Court later overturned the New York ruling, but the state court decision reflected New York's reluctance to follow earlier Supreme Court direction on prior restraint and provided an example of network extension.[2] Circumstances similar to *Kunz* developed when a district court of appeals in Florida in 1961 denied a rehearing after a lower court had quashed a writ of *mandamus* request to compel Miami Beach to permit the use of a park to an organization seeking to honor the death of the park's namesake. The court denied the rehearing on grounds that the organization had held a riotous meeting on a previous occasion.[3] Ten years after the U.S. Supreme Court ruling in *Kunz*, the Florida network of control remained to enforce prior restraint of assembly.

State courts have also extended the network in other assembly-speech-press areas. In 1938 a California appeals court extended *Gitlow* speech-is-not-absolute precedent to uphold an ordinance prohibiting handbill distribution. The court ruled against a group of Spanish Civil War Loyalist sympathizers chaired by playwright Lillian Hellman. The judges distinguished the Los Angeles ordinance from the one recently discarded by the Supreme Court in *Lovell* v. *Griffin* on grounds that the Los Angeles regulation restricted distribution only in a limited number of locations. In this case judges applied a security statute precedent as well as the distinguishing technique to uphold extension of the network. The same year the Supreme Judicial Court of Massachusetts, Worcester, upheld a Worcester handbill-regulation ordinance on grounds of *Gitlow, Whitney, De Jonge,* and *Lovell* precedent that the free press was subject to reasonable rules to serve the public.[4] In contrast, in two cases during the early forties the Illinois Su-

preme Court reversed convictions involving licensing requirements for literature distribution. Both Illinois cases involved
members of the Jehovah's Witnesses, and the additional First
Amendment religious issue appears to have weighed the judgment in favor of the distributors. However, in neither case did the
justices declare the particular ordinance unconstitutional on its
face; so even though particular individuals achieved constitutional
protection, the Illinois network remained intact.[5] State court decisions restricting handbill distribution subsided after the early
forties; in 1943 the *Murdoch* v. *Pennsylvania* decision reinforced
Lovell v. *Griffin*. However, a variation of this network link sur-
faced again in the sixties in cases involving literature distribution
in shopping centers.[6]

In political speech cases that have involved charges of disturbance and riot, state courts have also extended security statute
precedents to expand the network. In the New Hampshire Supreme Court's *Chaplinsky* ruling of 1941, justices upheld the use
of the police power to restrict the defendant's "fighting words,"
which he had persisted in using in a circumstance that had become
increasingly inflammatory. The U.S. Supreme Court later upheld
Chaplinsky's conviction on the basis of the disruptive nature of the
words:

those which by their very utterance inflict injury or tend to incite an
immediate breach of the peace. . . . [S]uch utterances are no essential part
of any exposition of ideas, and are of such slight social value as a step to
truth that any benefit that may be derived from them is clearly outweighed
by the social interest in order and morality.[7]

The volatile nature of the circumstances proved to be a central
factor in the *Chaplinsky* rulings, and the New Hampshire court
relied on *Gitlow* and *Whitney* as well as the arguments for peace
and safety found in the *De Jonge* and *Herndon* opinions. However,
the New Hampshire statute that these precedents served to uphold was written in a vague and general manner: "No person shall
address any offensive, derisive or annoying word to any other
person who is lawfully in any street or public place, nor call him by
an offensive or derisive name, nor make any noise or exclamation

in his presence."[8] It was this type of state statute in combination with the application of state security statute rulings that worked to extend the network into areas of speech that did not involve threats of potential political overthrow.

The relationship between speech and violence continued to be a contributing factor in the maintenance of the network. In 1969 the Michigan Supreme Court held that a breach of peace statute was neither vague nor void on its face because it prohibited trouble and disturbance of the peace. In 1970 the Superior Court of Pennsylvania in a *per curiam* opinion affirmed a conviction for riot, inciting to riot, and conspiracy. A dissenting judge who favored a new trial relied in part upon *Herndon* precedent and pointed out some of the problems involved:

The jury should have been instructed that they could not find the conduct of this incident unlawful unless they found that it was conducted in a violent and turbulent manner, or for the purpose of arousing the crowd to violent and turbulent behavior, or with reckless disregard of the likelihood of such arousal.[9]

In addition to pointing to the close relationship between First Amendment issues and procedural protection, the judge's statement indicated how the issue of political speech could become involved with an area of the law that had not enjoyed First Amendment protection. The interaction between speakers and crowds and the creation of circumstances that states and courts have feared might become explosive have added to the extension of the network, often without careful consideration of the causal relationship between the words and the behavior of the crowd.[10]

In the censorship-obscenity area of First Amendment interpretation judges on state appellate benches have also added extensions to the network by applying or distinguishing from the security statute precedents. In a 1939 decision the Rhode Island Supreme Court denied *certiorari* in a case challenging an attempt by the Bureau of Police and Fire of the City of Providence to prevent the showing of a movie that allegedly contained communistic propaganda. The court opted for the exercise of the state police power and distinguished a circumstance involving movies from Supreme

Court decisions such as *Whitney*, *Stromberg*, and *Herndon*, which had involved direct speech. In 1945 the Supreme Judicial Court of Massachusetts, Middlesex, upheld an anti-obscenity statute citing *De Jonge* and *Gitlow* free-speech-is-not-absolute precedent. The justices also dealt with a vagueness challenge based on *Herndon* grounds and rejected that argument in favor of a test based on the effect of the materials on the public.[11]

During the fifties state appellate benches continued to apply security precedent in a manner that supported various types of state censorship boards. The Ohio Supreme Court in 1953 ruled that statutes creating the Board of Censors within the Department of Education was neither an unconstitutional delegation of legislative authority nor a violation of freedom of speech or press. Despite the 1952 Supreme Court anticensorship ruling regarding movies, provided in *Burstyn* v. *Wilson*, the Ohio justices relied on the *Gitlow* concept of nationalization, insisted there were exceptions to the rule of no prior restraint established in *Near*, and declared that freedom of speech and press did not cover all areas of expression. The next year the Court of Common Pleas of Ohio, Franklin County, used similar reasoning to hold that the statute creating the State Division of Film Censorship was clear and definite and that the board could prevent the showing of a film that it found to be obscene. Later in the decade the New York Court of Appeals continued to uphold the censorship authority of the Board of Regents. In an opinion later reversed by the U.S. Supreme Court the New York high bench upheld a statute applied as the basis for denial of a license for the showing of *Lady Chatterley's Lover* on grounds that the movie depicted adultery as proper behavior. The judges cited *Gilbert* police-power precedent claiming states to be in a better position than federal courts to understand local standards.[12]

A number of state courts continued to uphold anti-obscenity statutes during the sixties, but others moved to follow Supreme Court directives provided in decisions like *Butler* v. *Michigan* and *Roth* v. *U. S.*, both handed down in 1957.[13] In 1961 the Supreme Court of Florida upheld a conviction for obscenity, distinguishing *Herndon*, *Butler*, and *Winters* v. *New York* and declaring that "none of these cases are [*sic*] helpful to defendants." The Arizona

Supreme Court in 1962 also upheld an obscenity conviction on grounds that the element of scienter was implicit in the statute and the defendant had knowledge of the obscene nature of the materials.[14] In contrast, beginning in the late fifties a few state courts began to follow specific U.S. Supreme Court precedents in the area of censorship. In *Adams* v. *Hinkle* in 1958 the Washington Supreme Court declared the state's Comic Book Act void on its face on breadth and vagueness grounds indirectly related to *Herndon* precedent. The Washington justices relied primarily upon *Winters* v. *New York* and quoted directly from that Supreme Court ruling: "where a statute is so vague as to make criminal an innocent act, a conviction under it cannot be sustained." In addition the Washington court ruled against the statute on equal protection grounds since it had exempted comic sections of newspapers from the censorship.[15]

Other state courts began to follow a line of reasoning similar to that of Washington during the early and mid-sixties. In 1960 the Court of Appeals of Maryland applied *Herndon* precedent and held unconstitutional an anti-obscenity statute on grounds of vagueness and interference with an adult's right to read books on varying subjects. The next year the Pennsylvania Supreme Court held that the state Motion Picture Control Act violated procedural guarantees of jury trial and imposed a form of prior restraint. Again, the *Herndon-Winters* precedent applied. In *People* v. *Bookcase, Inc.*, in 1964 the New York Court of Appeals applied similar reasoning to discard a law attempting to restrict sale of materials to minors. The judges ruled that the statute was too vague to communicate a definite meaning. However, in 1966 the New York Appeals bench held that a statute restricting sale of materials to minors did not infringe constitutional rights even though the law did not contain a provision for proof of age. The judge held that the statute in question met the *Herndon* requirement of "ascertainable standards of guilt readily determined by men of reasonable intelligence."[16]

State appellate courts also discussed the Supreme Court ruling in *Dombrowski* v. *Pfister* in obscenity cases. In June 1970 the First District Court of Appeals of Florida refused to apply *Dombrowski* in a case requesting an interlocutory injunction to prohibit the continued sale of obscene materials. Judge Sam Specter pointed out the federalism overtones in a confused opinion in which he assumed that federal action had preceded state action in *Dombrowski*, just the reverse of the actual progression of events in the Louisiana case. In his confusion Specter distinguished the case at bar from *Dombrowski* for reasons indicating that the two sets of circumstances in Louisiana and Florida were very similar. In addition to his lack of understanding about the sequence of the Louisiana case, Judge Specter did not consider the Florida situation to constitute either bad faith or harassment.

In contrast to the Florida case the Chancery Division of the New Jersey Superior Court in August 1970 stopped an obscenity indictment on procedural grounds. The judge ruled that the movie *Man and Wife*, which had been declared not obscene, was to be shown and that the Monmouth County prosecutor was not to indict until a time when the movie might be declared obscene. The ruling considered the U.S. Supreme Court's emphasis on free speech and quoted *Dombrowski*:

Because of the sensitive nature of constitutionally protected expression, we have not required that all of those subject to overbroad regulations risk prosecution to test their rights. For free expression— of transcendent value to all society, and not merely to those exercising their rights— might be the loser.[17]

The cases discussed here that involve the censorship-obscenity issues demonstrate again state use of security statute precedent to extend the network until the time when specific Supreme Court guidance in the obscenity area provided repeated precedents to apply the Fourteenth Amendment in order to nationalize that area of First Amendment interpretation. These developments demonstrated not only state court expansion of another section of the network, but also the hesitancy of state courts to transfer speech and press protection from one substantive area to another, with or without specific Supreme Court direction.

Libel cases constituted another field of First Amendment interpretation that at times has involved political speech, a field in which state courts have utilized state security precedent to further the network. In 1945 the Florida Supreme Court affirmed a lower court ruling that held the Miami Herald Publishing Company in contempt for printing a cartoon and editorial critical of local judges. The justices, citing *Gitlow* and *Whitney* in regard to the nationalization process, ruled that freedom of the press did not protect what the court determined to be groundless charges of unfairness. Two dissenters pointed to what they considered to be the applicability of *Bridges* precedent and the failure of the state to show a clear and present danger. The next year the Court of Criminal Appeals of Texas ruled in a *habeas corpus* proceeding involving three newspaper people arrested for contempt for publishing material relating to a pending suit. The judges cited *Gitlow* as an antecedent to *Bridges* and held that a clear and present danger did exist in the circumstances of the case before them. The Louisiana Supreme Court in 1964 applied *Gilbert* and other strong police-power precedents to affirm the libel conviction of a defendant charged with slandering the district attorney of Iberia Parish. The Louisiana justices provided another example of extending the application of state security statute precedent to this area of First Amendment law. After the 1964 *New York Times* v. *Sullivan* ruling, however, certain state courts applied the public figure definition and the malice criteria to protect speech made in reference to local personalities. Supreme Court guidance on the specific subject of libel helped to short-circuit further application of security statute precedent and slowed further extension of this section of the network.[18]

In regard to the political speech-related issue of group libel restrictions, state courts have also applied security statute precedent. In a 1941 case the New Jersey Supreme Court considered a group libel statute in a case involving members of the German-American Bund accused of making anti-Semitic comments. The court applied the nationalization concept as well as the New Jersey Constitution to discard the law. The court based its reasoning in part on the argument, supported by the *Gitlow* opinion, that the state could regulate against abuses that menaced it. The justices then concluded that this doctrine did not apply to words that might endanger those other than the state, and they applied *Near* and *Cantwell* precedent to rule that the New Jersey statute was too broad. In *Beauharnais*, a better-known group libel case of the early fifties, Illinois Supreme Court justices upheld the restriction on grounds that attacks upon groups, in this case black persons, could not receive First Amendment protection. The U.S. Supreme Court, in a five-to-four vote, later agreed that the state police power provided a basis for the restriction and punishment of this type of speech.[19]

During the sixties, as more and more federal and state courts ruled for the protection of allegedly libelous statements regarding public figures, group libel laws also came under closer scrutiny. In 1966 an appeals court in Ohio discarded a Cincinnati ordinance that made it an offense to distribute materials ridiculing or showing contempt for a class, race, or religion. Even though the case involved the extremist, antiblack National States Rights party, the judge cited *De Jonge* and ruled that the ordinance presented an unconstitutional invasion of protected speech, press, and assembly rights. He commented, "The courts have been particularly zealous to permit the widest possible latitude of comment on religious and political affairs."[20]

As the network has expanded away from the core security statute area, the links have tended to weaken because the U.S. Supreme Court has provided more precise direction. For example, prior to the *Barnette* decision of 1943, certain state courts applied *Gitlow* precedent to uphold punishment of Jehovah's Witness children who did not participate in a flag salute. According to the New York Court of Appeals, the state could use the police power to "seek to prevent evil in its incipiency."[21] After *Barnette* dealt specifically with the flag salute issue, a number of state courts then followed the Supreme Court's guidance. The religious factor often divided Jehovah's Witness speech and press cases in state courts from cases involving political and economic speech and press. State justices appeared more willing to discard restrictions on speech and press if a religious group were involved than if the case concerned Socialists or other political critics.

In the area of labor relations state courts continued to extend the network even after the *Thornhill* and other decisions favorable to unions appeared in the early forties. The expansion continued especially if the cases involved organizations of public employees.

In 1941 the Court of Criminal Appeals of Texas upheld the conviction of a man arrested in a labor dispute, and the judges applied the
Whitney argument that "force and violence are not sheltered by
constitutional provision." Later in the decade a California appellate bench in 1947 ruled that the Los Angeles police commissioner's ban on police membership in outside unions did not infringe on
freedom of speech or equal protection. The judge ruled against the
application of *Herndon* and utilized *Gitlow* precedent in holding
that the state could take preventive measures against possible
disorder. Sixteen years later in 1963 the Michigan Supreme Court
applied similar reasoning and distinguished the pending case from
De Jonge, declaring that such regulation of police officers was
neither unreasonable nor arbitrary. However, by the mid-sixties
certain state supreme courts were declaring that public employment did not impose a restriction upon First Amendment freedoms. In 1965 the Oregon Supreme Court held that statutes
prohibiting state civil service employees from political candidacy
were unconstitutional and violated the First Amendment. The
justices based much of their reasoning on *NAACP* v. *Button*, but
they also cited the *Herndon* point on statutory vagueness. In 1969
the California Supreme Court ruled that the Los Angeles Board of
Education could not restrict teachers from circulating petitions
during their free lunch time unless the action constituted a threat
to the order and efficiency of the schools. Brandeis's concurring
opinion in *Whitney* provided part of the basis for the California
decision that "to avert violence and to preserve stable government there must be 'opportunity to discuss freely supposed grievances and proposed remedies'."[22]

School employees have also encountered other sections of state
enforcement of the network of control, and the results have often
been in contrast to the 1969 position of the California Supreme
Court. In 1961 the Florida Supreme Court ruled specifically in
regard to school teachers' contentions that a loyalty oath and
affidavit of non-communist activity required for employment violated both the state and federal constitutions. The justices held
such requirements did not violate basic rights of speech and press
and rejected *Nelson* reasoning in favor of the *Uphaus* line: "We
think the time is now passed when statutes of this type are subject

to question because of alleged pre-emption of the field of subversive control by the Federal Government." Later in the decade the Alaska Supreme Court held that teachers possessed free speech rights to criticize openly the school board, but the court also ruled that the exercise of such criticism could lead to nonretention. The justices distinguished the case from *Dombrowski* precedent because they reasoned that the dispute concerned false statements about the superintendent of schools.[23] At the end of the sixties, state courts continued a reluctance to apply First Amendment protection to public school teachers. Enforcement of the state networks was enhanced by the continued presence of dual lines of U.S. Supreme Court precedent and the facility of some state courts in distinguishing cases at bar from Supreme Court rulings that extended the area of First Amendment protection.

At times state appellate courts have applied state security precedents in areas that reach even further beyond the central area of the network; for example, the New York Court of Appeals cited *Gitlow* precedent as the basis for upholding a Rye ordinance prohibiting clotheslines. *Gitlow* also served as strong precedent for upholding conspiracy statutes and, along with other Supreme Court rulings, has been cited in procedural areas as well as in First Amendment cases. When defendants in a 1940 Georgia case contended that the *Herndon* void-for-vagueness concept should be applied in a case in which authorities searched an automobile without a warrant, the Georgia Supreme Court held that *Herndon* involved "no adjudication as to the rule of evidence." The California Supreme Court in 1942 applied *Whitney* and *De Jonge* reasoning regarding clear and present danger to endorse the Legislature's power to prescribe tests as conditions for Communist party participation in primary elections. According to Chief Justice Phil Gibson, "such groups constitute an immediate threat to the functioning of our institutions, including the continued exercise of the right of suffrage."[24]

Application of state security precedents or distinguishing the case at hand from them to extend the network into procedural areas continued into the fifties and sixties. In the late fifties the New York Court of Appeals chose to apply *Gilbert* precedent and rejected a challenge to state use of allegedly illegal wiretaps. Concentrating on the federalism issue of preemption rather than on Fourteenth Amendment nationalization precedent, Judge Charles W. Froessel reasoned that the Supreme Court in *Nelson* had not "prevent[ed] the State from prosecuting where the same act constituted both a federal offense and a state offense under the police power." In 1969 the New York Court of Appeals distinguished *Dombrowski* precedent to hold that university professors could be subpoenaed to appear before a grand jury without infringing upon Fifth Amendment protection against self-incrimination. The judges ruled as "specious" the argument "that teachers will be intimidated in their lectures merely because of the potential threat of being compelled to appear before a Grand Jury inquiry. If this allegation is true, the intimidation is attributable to something other than a violation of constitutional rights. *Keyishian* and *Pfister* are clearly inapplicable." The New Jersey Supreme Court also distinguished a procedural point from the *Dombrowski* precedent when in *Anderson* v. *Sills* it held that a lower court had granted improperly an injunction to stay action of local officials and police gathering materials relating to potential civil disorders. The justices concluded that there was no evidence that the procedure intended to inhibit First Amendment rights.[25]

Through the years numerous cases have demonstrated that state courts, in applying U.S. Supreme Court state security statute precedents, have extended the network beyond the security area. At times a U.S. Supreme Court decision in another substantive area of First Amendment interpretation has curtailed a particular line of network extension. However, the tendency of state appellate courts not to transfer First Amendment protection from one substantive area to another often has provided means for the extension of the network and for circumvention of High Court curtailment of state police power in one specific area. This durability of the network has provided a constant challenge to the development of the concept of protection of political speech and other related First Amendment topics.

NOTES

1. See Hague v. CIO, 307 U.S. 496 (1939), discussed in note 7, chapter 4; Thomas v. Collins, 323 U.S. 516 (1945), discussed in note 16, chapter 4; and De Jonge v. Or., 299 U.S. 353 (1937).

2. People v. Kunz, 300 N.Y. 273 (1949), 90 N.E. 2d 455 (1949) and Kunz v. New York, 340 U.S. 290 (1951). For a discussion of the Kunz case see C. Herman Pritchett, *Civil Liberties and the Vinson Court* (Chicago: University of Chicago Press, 1954), pp. 43-44.

3. State of Fla. v. City of Miami Beach, 132 So. 2d 349 (1961).

4. People v. Young, 33 Cal. App. 2d Supp. 747, 753 (1938), 85 P. 2d 232, 234 (1938) and Commonwealth v. Nichols, 301 Mass. 584 (1938), 18 N.E. 2d 166 (1938). See also Lovell v. Griffin, 303 U.S. 444 (1938), discussed in note 8, chapter 4.

5. Village of South Holland v. Stein, 373 Ill. 472 (1924), 26 N.E. 2d 268 (1940); and City of Blue Island v. Kozul, 379 Ill. 511 (1942), 41 N.E. 2d 515 (1942).

6. Murdoch v. Pa., 319 U.S. 105 (1943). See Food Employees Union v. Logan Valley Plaza, Inc., 391 U.S. 308 (1968), in which the Court majority held that private shopping centers could be picketed by a labor union. In Lloyd Corp. v. Tanner, 407 U.S. 551 (1972), the Court distinguished the instant case from Logan Valley because the former involved the distribution of antiwar materials rather than union information. Justice Lewis Powell explained that the materials in Logan Valley were directed at the owners of the shopping center, whereas the pamphlets in Tanner were aimed at the general public and could have been distributed in any of a number of public places. In Hudgens v. Nat'l. Labor Relations Bd., 424 U.S. 507 (1976), the Court held that pickets held no First Amendment right to enter an enclosed shopping mall for purposes of advertising their strike and remanded the case to be decided under the statutory criteria of the National Labor Relations Act. In the majority opinion, Justice Potter Stewart stated that the Court's position in Lloyd had "amounted to a total rejection of the holding in Logan Valley." 424 U.S. 507 at 518. The shopping center cases raised the issue of whether such facilities were to be considered private or public in nature and did not provide a direct parallel to the cases involving state laws and city ordinances imposing limitations on speech in public places.

7. State v. Chaplinsky, 91 N.H. 310 (1941), 18 A. 2d 754 (1941) and Chaplinsky v.N.H., 315 U.S. 568, 572 (1942).

8. 91 N.H. 310, 312, 18 A. 2d 754, 757-758.

9. People of Dearborn Heights v. Bellock, 17 Mich. App. 163 (1969), 169 N.W. 2d 347 (1969); and Commonwealth v. Belgrave, 217 Pa. Super. Ct. 297, 303-304 (1970), 269 A. 2d 317, 320 (1970).

10. Two U.S. Supreme Court cases that dealt with this issue were Terminello v. Chicago, 337 U.S. 1 (1949), and Feiner v. N.Y., 340 U.S. 315 (1951).

11. Thayer Amusement Corp. v. Moulton, 63 R.I. 182 (1939), 7 A. 2d 682 (1939); and Commonwealth v. Isenstadt, 318 Mass. 543 (1945), 62 N.E. 2d 840 (1945).

12. Superior Films v. Dep't. of Educ., 159 Ohio St. 315 (1953), 112 N.E. 2d 311 (1953); RKO Pictures v. Hissong, 123 N.E. 2d 441 (1954); Kingsley Int'l. Pictures Corp. v. Regents of the State Univ. of N.Y., 4 N.Y. 2d 349 (1958), 151 N.E. 2d 197 (1958). See also Burstyn v. Wilson, 343 U.S. 195 (1952) and Kingsley v. Regents, 360 U.S. 684 (1959). The latter U.S. Supreme Court decision reversed the New York Court of Appeals.

13. In Butler v. Mich., 352 U.S. 380 (1959), the Supreme Court unanimously discarded a state law that attempted to protect minors from unsavory books and magazines. Justice Felix Frankfurter declared that Michigan's attempt to "quarantine the general reading public against books not too rugged for grown men and women in order to shield juvenile innocence is to burn down the house to roast the pig." Later the same year, in Roth v. United States and Alberts v. Cal., 354 U.S. 476 (1957), the majority of the justices attempted to provide an obscenity test based on a California court definition, "Whether to the average person, applying contemporary community standards, the dominant theme of the material as a whole appeals to prurient interests."

14. Tracey v. Fla., 130 So. 2d 605 (1961) and State v. Locks, 91 Ariz. 394 (1948), 372 P. 2d 724 (1962). In Winters v. N.Y., 333 U.S. 507 (1948), the Vinson Court threw out on vagueness grounds a New York law that prohibited obscene materials focusing on "bloodshed, lust, or crime."

15. Adams v. Hinkle, 51 Wash. 2d 763, 783 (1958), 322 P. 2d 844, 857 (1958). The Winters opinion cited Herndon v. Lowry, 301 U.S. 242, 259 (1937).

16. Police Comm'rs. of Baltimore v. Siegel Enterprises, 223 Md. 110 (1960), 162 A. 2d 727 (1960); William Goldman Theatres, Inc. v. Dana, 405 Pa. 83 (1961), 173 A. 2d 59 (1961); People v. Bookcase, Inc., 14 N.Y. 2d 402 (1964), 201 N.E. 2d 14 (1964); and People v. Tannenbaum, 18 N.Y. 2d 268, 273 (1966), 220 N.E. 2d 783, 787 (1966).

17. Mitchum v. State, 237 So. 2d 72, 75 (1970); and Keuper v. Wilson, 111 N.J. Super. 502, 507 (1970), 268 A. 2d 760, 763 (1970), quoting from Dombrowski v. Pfister, 380 U.S. 479, 486 (1965).

18. Pennekamp v. State, 156 Fla. 227, 249 (1945), 22 So. 2d 875, 887 (1945), later overturned by the U.S. Supreme Court on Fourteenth Amendment grounds in 328 U.S. 331 (1946); Ex parte Craig, 150 Tex. Crim. 598 (1946), 193 S.W. 2d 178 (1946); and State v. Warren J. Moity, 245 La. 546 (1964), 15 So. 2d 149 (1964). Bridges v. Cal., 314 U.S. 252 (1941) is discussed in note 14, chapter 4. In New York Times v. Sullivan,

376 U.S. 254 (1964), the U.S. Supreme Court unanimously agreed that public officials must show malice in order to recover damages in libel suits. See also Tait v. King Broadcasting Co. and Irving Clark, 1 Wash. App. 250 (1969), 460 P. 2d 307 (1969); and Gibson v. Mahoney, 231 So. 2d 823 (1970). In the Tait case the Washington Court of Appeals ruled that a radio show host was not guilty of libel for calling the plaintiff a "local Fascist and Jew baiter." The court held that the statements had not been made with any knowledge of falsity or with any disregard of truth.

19. State v. Klapprott, 127 N.J.L. 395, 403 (1941), 22 A. 2d 877, 882 (1941); People v. Beauharnais, 408 Ill. 512 (1951), 97 N.E. 2d 343 (1951); and Beauharnais v. Ill., 343 U.S. 250 (1952). Near v. Minn., 283 U.S. 697 (1931), is discussed in note 8, chapter 4. In Cantwell v. Conn., 310 U.S. 296 (1940), the U.S. Supreme Court invalidated a statute on First Amendment free exercise grounds as well as Fourteenth Amendment grounds. The law granted the secretary of the Public Welfare Council the authority to decide whether prospective solicitors represented legitimate religious causes.

20. Cincinnati v. Black, 8 Ohio App. 2d 143, 148 (1966), 220 N.E. 2d 821, 824 (1966).

21. People ex rel. Fiske v. Sandstrom, 279 N.Y. 523 (1939), 18 N.E. 2d 840 (1939). See W.Va. State Bd. of Educ. v. Barnette, 319 U.S. 628 (1943).

22. Ex parte Frye, 143 Tex. Crim. 9 (1941), 156 S.W. 2d 531 (1941); Perez v. Bd. of Police Comm'rs. of Los Angeles, 78 Cal. App. 2d 638 (1947), 178 P. 2d 537 (1947); Am. Fed'n. of State, County, and Mun. Employees Local 201 v. Muskegon, 369 Mich. 384 (1963), 120 N. W. 2d 197 (1963); Minielly v. State, 242 Or. 490 (1966), 411 P. 2d 69 (1965); and Los Angeles Teachers' Union v. Los Angeles Bd. of Educ., 71 Cal. 2d 551, 559 (1969), 455 P. 2d 827, 832 (1969). NAACP v. Button, 371 U.S. 415 (1963), extended certain First Amendment protections to organizations as well as to individuals. In the Los Angeles Teachers' Union case the court found strong precedents in Pickering v. Bd. of Educ., 391 U.S. 563 (1968) and in Tinker v. Des Moines Independent School Dist., 393 U.S. 503 (1969), two cases that established that teachers and students do not relinquish freedom of speech rights.

23. Cramp v. Bd. of Pub. Instruction of Orange County, 125 So. 2d 554, 557 (1960), later overturned by the U.S. Supreme Court in 368 U.S. 278 (1961), and Watts v. Seward School Bd., 421 P. 2d 586 (1966).

24. People v. Stover, 12 N.Y. 2d 462 (1963), 191 N.E. 2d 272 (1963); Lash v. State, 244 Ala. 48 (1943), 14 So. 2d 229 (1943); McIntyre v. State,

100 Ga. 872, 876 (1940), 11 S.E. 2d 5, 8 (1940); and Communist Party of United States v. Peek, 20 Cal. 2d 536, 551 (1942), 127 P. 2d 889, 898 (1942).

25. People v. Broady, 5 N.Y. 2d 500, 509 (1959), 158 N.E. 2d 817, 822 (1959); Boikess v. Aspland, 24 N.Y. 2d 136, 142 (1969), 247 N.E. 2d 135, 138 (1969); Anderson v. Sills, 106 N.J. Super. 545 (1969), 256 A. 2d 298 (1969) and 56 N.J. 210 (1970), 265 A. 2d 678 (1970).

7. CONCLUSION

Preceding chapters have described state court application of major U.S. Supreme Court opinions involving state security statutes during the years 1920 to 1970. The persistent theme has been the continued existence of a series of networks of control made up of a variety of state statutes. At times these networks have remained dormant, and on other occasions law enforcement officials have activated them in attempts to control or even to prevent social protest and political criticism. Legislative and judicial support of these state networks of control not only has reinforced the state security statutes, but also has strengthened enforcement of statutes dealing with related areas, including trespass, loyalty oaths, vagrancy, flag salutes, picketing, door-to-door solicitation, noise and littering regulations, and conspiracy.

Existence of these individual state networks of control within a federal system in which the U.S. Supreme Court rules on specific cases appealed from a number of states creates a set of circumstances in which it is very easy for a state supreme court to sidestep application of a High Court precedent. State security statutes fall under several titles, but actually each state version of a particular security statute is only a slight variation of that of another state. This confusion of titles has combined with the basic factors of federalism to make it easy for a recalcitrant state supreme court to distinguish the case before it from a U.S. Supreme Court precedent that it wishes to ignore; and it allows a state to defy what is felt to be undue federal court interference in state matters.

TABLE 2   STATE SUPREME COURT NETWORK CASES APPLYING AT LEAST ONE OF THE PRECEDENTS UNDER CONSIDERATION

	1921-30	1931-40	1941-50	1951-60	1961-70	Total
State courts declared state laws unconstitutional	1[a]	1	5	6	4	17[a]
(Number of security statute cases)	(1)[a]			(3)		(4)
State courts upheld state law or action	6	15	15	19	22	77
(Number of security statute cases)	(4)	(7)	(3)		(1)	(15)
State courts ruled against application of statute to circumstances	2	3	15	4	15	39
(Number of security statute cases)			(1)	(1)	(1)	(3)
Total number of network cases[b]	9	19	35	29	41	133
(Total number of security statute cases)	(5)	(7)	(4)	(4)	(2)	(22)

[a]Includes *State* v. *Diamond*, in which application was thrown out because of conflict with New Mexico Constitution and not because of U.S. Supreme Court case precedent.
[b]Network total includes security statute cases. For reasons of consistency this table refers only to cases considered in the highest tribunal in each state. Intermediate appellate courts are not included.

State court resistance to the use of U.S. Supreme Court precedent is demonstrated in table 2, which provides an assessment of the number of network cases decided by the highest state courts. During the fifty-year period the 133 network of control cases that incorporate the Supreme Court precedents under consideration here fell into three categories: those which used Supreme Court precedent to declare a state law unconstitutional, those which ignored or distinguished from a precedent in order to uphold a state law or action, and those which applied High Court precedent only to the circumstances of a state case and left the statute intact. Between 1920 and 1970 there were seventeen cases in the first category, in which state courts applied at least one of the Supreme Court precedents in order to discard state statutes for unconstitutional intrusion upon First Amendment rights. Of those seventeen cases, only four involved the area of strictly defined security cases. In eighteen other cases involving security statutes, and in six others concerned with borderline security statutes related to antisubversive activities, state courts upheld state actions in all but three cases. In cases included in the latter category, state courts threw out application of a law in particular circumstances, but did not declare the law unconstitutional.

Another way of demonstrating state court reluctance to apply U.S. Supreme Court precedent in the network of control cases is to tally the total numbers in each of the three categories. As mentioned above, state courts used the ten precedents studied here to discard a total of sixteen network laws.[1] In seventy-seven cases courts upheld state law or action and in thirty-nine cases ruled that a particular statute did not apply to a specific set of circumstances, thereby reversing a conviction or otherwise discarding state action against a party without declaring a statute unconstitutional. In all but one of these thirty-nine cases the state courts applied at least one of the Supreme Court precedents under consideration in this study. These figures indicate that throughout the fifty-year period state courts have demonstrated a repeated resistance to discarding state network-of-control laws and an even greater resistance to declaring state security statutes unconstitutional. In 58 percent of the network cases and in 70 percent of the security cases state courts upheld state law or action.

Since there are so many statutory areas that touch upon the issue of free expression, the Supreme Court's development of protection of freedom of speech and expression has been piecemeal and has appeared gradually in a number of cases—*Gitlow*, *Stromberg*, *Near*, *Thornhill*, and a litany of others. Because of the gradual development of this core of First Amendment protection and the proliferation of free-expression issues, it has been possible for state courts to equivocate in their application of Supreme Court rulings within the broad First Amendment field.

A chronological summary of state court reaction to the Supreme Court precedents will demonstrate this reluctance on the part of many states. The *Gilbert* v. *Minnesota* decision of 1920 upheld that state's Sedition Law, and State courts applied that line of precedent consistently until the end of 1938. In twenty-eight network cases decided in state courts between 1921 and the end of 1940, justices upheld state action in twenty-one of the situations presented before them. State courts took advantage of the opportunity afforded by *Gitlow* and *Whitney* and the lack of majority opinion guidelines on clear and present danger to uphold state network laws on twenty-one occasions, eleven of which involved security statutes.

After 1940 the nationalization concept of *Gitlow* and the clear and present danger doctrine found in Brandeis's *Whitney* concurrence combined with the cognate rights thesis of *De Jonge* and the ascertainable standard of guilt requirement of *Herndon* to provide a basis for overturning state laws. Between 1941 and the end of 1950, state supreme courts did discard state statutes in five out of a total of thirty-five cases. Two of these discarded laws involved rights concerned with the activities of organized labor, and defense of this First Amendment position drew additional strength from the 1940 *Thornhill* decision. In the other three cases, the New Jersey Supreme Court voided that state's group libel law, using the curious First Amendment argument that the state could protect itself but other groups could not; the California Supreme Court discarded a loyalty oath required for use of school auditorium facilities; and the Supreme Judicial Court of Massachusetts ruled that portions of the ordinance restricting free speech on Boston Common were unconstitutional on their face.[2]

In another group of fifteen cases considered in the years between 1941 and the end of 1950, state high courts discarded the application of the state statute to particular circumstances without actually overturning any statutes. Three of these cases involved labor relations disputes;[3] and the remaining confrontations included a number of statutes involving licenses for Jehovah's Witness solicitation and restrictions placed upon freedom of the press. Mississippi was the only state in which the supreme court upheld a state security statute during this decade. In three cases the state court upheld the Mississippi Sedition Act; but after the U.S. Supreme Court declared the law unconstitutional in *Taylor* v. *Mississippi* in 1943, the Mississippi Supreme Court denied application of the law in *Counts* v. *State*, decided later the same year. In 1941 the Iowa Supreme Court considered a sedition case involving events at the Maytag strike at Newton and voted that the law did not apply in the case.[4]

Between 1951 and 1960, state courts operated within a security atmosphere heightened by the suspicions of the cold war era. States varied in their responses to Supreme Court precedent, especially in the wake of *Pennsylvania* v. *Nelson*, decided in 1956. However, only two state high courts in addition to Pennsylvania discarded state security statutes applying the lines of reasoning used in *Nelson*—the Michigan Supreme Court in *Albertson* v. *Millard* in 1956 and the Louisiana Supreme Court in *State* v. *Jenkins* in 1958. The Supreme Judicial Court of Massachusetts threw out application of its Sedition Act in the 1956 decision in *Commonwealth* v. *Gilbert*.[5] The neighboring New Hampshire Supreme Court, in a long series of cases involving the subversive investigation activities of the state attorney general, repeatedly upheld the state law and at times defied the Supreme Court's *Nelson* precedent.[6] In the twenty-nine network cases considered during the 1951-1960 period, nineteen state court decisions upheld state law or state action. However, in addition to state high courts' declaring security laws unconstitutional in Pennsylvania, Michigan, and Louisiana, state supreme courts threw out a loyalty oath requirement for residence in public housing in Wisconsin and a prior-restraint provision in the Washington Comic Book Law.[7] All in all, the fifties offered an era of state supreme court insistence that states should continue to protect themselves from critical speech despite the precedents of the U.S. Supreme Court which undergirded the concept of freedom of speech. Even though the decade of the fifties was one of the two decades in which state courts discarded state security statutes, courts declared these laws unconstitutional on the basis of technical preemption doctrine and not on First Amendment grounds. Consequently, the networks were not weakened to any great degree as state courts upheld state laws and actions in nineteen out of a total of twenty-nine cases.

During the decade that began in 1961, state high courts continued to uphold more network of control laws than they discarded. Between 1961 and the end of 1970, state high courts considered forty-one network of control cases. In twenty-two of these the courts upheld state law or state action in cases that reflected the issues of the sixties—civil rights marches, antiwar protests, black power speeches, teachers' strikes, police surveillance, and college student protest against the alleged sexism of *Playboy* magazine.[8] In four instances—two of them involving obscenity laws—courts discarded state network laws. In the other two cases the California Supreme Court again threw out a reconstituted version of the law requiring a loyalty oath from groups using school facilities and discarded another statute restricting the distribution of anonymous campaign literature.[9] In fifteen additional cases state supreme courts ruled against applying a statute to the circumstances involved in a case, but did not discard the statute. Perhaps the prime example of state recalcitrance was California's persistence in pursuing state supreme court approval of a provision in the Civic Center Act that required a loyalty oath of persons or groups using school facilities. After the supreme court had discarded two different versions of this law in 1946 and again in 1961, the California Legislature passed a provision requiring an oath of allegiance against criminal syndicalism rather than mere overthrow. In 1963 the California Supreme Court upheld the latter point on grounds that the U.S. Supreme Court had not declared the California Criminal Syndicalism Law unconstitutional in *Whitney*.[10]

Another area in which state courts have added to the uncertainty of the protection of First Amendment rights has been in the selective enforcement of state security statutes and the state courts' ability to distinguish their cases from U.S. Supreme Court precedents. Although it is very difficult to devise an all-inclusive general formula on this point, the most obvious observation is that courts have upheld security statutes more rigidly in times of social protest and political challenge than during calmer periods of political discussion. Authorities have enforced some security statutes only in controversial cases. The most notable example has been the New York Criminal Anarchy Law passed in the wake of President McKinley's assassination and applied in only two instances—in the post-World War I Red Scare and during the black power struggles of the late sixties. In the same respect the Ohio Supreme Court has considered and upheld that state's Criminal Syndicalism Law on only two occasions, in *State* v. *Kassay* in 1932 when the majority defied the 1925 *Gitlow* ruling and declared that the Bill of Rights did not apply to the states and again in the *Brandenburg* case during the sixties.[11] In the latter case the U.S. Supreme Court eventually declared the Ohio law unconstitutional.

Defenders of state security statutes who are countering arguments in the defense of the First Amendment might contend that selective enforcement would be preferable to the threat of continual enforcement, which with some broadly construed laws could mean subjecting large numbers of people to prosecution. However, selective enforcement and adjudication add to law enforcement a degree of arbitrariness that contradicts the very concept of law itself and detracts from the certainty that is a primary objective of a legal system. Selective application of state security laws has provided occasion for the use of political trials of particular individuals and groups that states have singled out as dangerous threats during periods of intense political confrontation.

A corollary to the selective application of state security laws has developed as states have applied statutes intended for particular types of protest to new variations of dissent, often involving circumstances that were not at issue when the laws originated. Examples of this development are numerous. States used the criminal syndicalism statutes to arrest Communists and Socialists in a number of cases, but only one U.S. Supreme Court case during the fifty-year period involved the Industrial Workers of the World, the group at which criminal syndicalism laws were aimed original-ly. After only one prosecution under its security law in more than fifty years, Georgia used the Reconstruction era's Anti-Insurrection Act to arrest Angelo Herndon and other Communists. Authorities have never used the New York law passed to curb anarchists for that specific purpose, but instead have applied it in an attempt to silence a member of the Left Wing Socialists and an adherent of the Progressive Labor Movement, associations that fell within the vague perimeters of the law. In still another instance of this type of application, during the sixties Ohio revived its 1919 Criminal Syndicalism Law to arrest participants in a Ku Klux Klan rally. The development of this corollary of selective enforcement and adjudication has added further elements of uncertainty to the First Amendment protection of dissenters and also has revealed the tendency of many states and many persons to lump together most forms of social protest, thus making the protesters and dissenters very vulnerable to the state action sanctioned by state security laws.

As the step-by-step process of extending Bill of Rights protection has proceeded through the years, it has become apparent that those concerned with the protection of political speech have encountered additional problems based upon the free speech application lag. As a particular area of dissent or protest has found Supreme Court-sanctioned First Amendment protection from state encroachment, newer forms of dissent or dissent focused upon a new variety of problems have not immediately received the benefit of previous Supreme Court free speech decisions. In fact, it appears that there has been very little transference of the application of Supreme Court decisions from one substantive category to another in state court cases involving security statutes. Consequently, each new protest movement or group of critics has had to begin at square one to fight its own battle for First Amendment protection.

The above observation can be illustrated best with two examples familiar to most observers of social protest. One well-known development that has demonstrated the reluctance of state courts to transfer application of rulings in security law cases arose in regard to picketing. The labor unrest of the depression years led to numerous contradictory state court rulings on the question of First Amendment protection of picketing, a series of developments that led ultimately to the U.S. Supreme Court decision in *Thornhill* v. *Alabama*. In that 1940 opinion Justice Frank Murphy declared, "In the circumstances of our times, the dissemination of information concerning the facts of a labor dispute must be regarded as within the area of free discussion that is guaranteed by the Constitution."[12] However, subsequent state judicial logic could not often see fit to extend that same principle regarding dissemination of information to picketing civil rights demonstrators or still later to students and others demonstrating in opposition to U.S. policy in Viet Nam. The civil rights workers and the antiwar leaders had to fight the picketing-as-free-speech battle anew and to seek U.S. Supreme Court sanction of picketing in these other areas of protest.

During the late fifties and throughout the decade of the sixties civil rights groups fought long and hard for Court recognition of their techniques of social protest. Well-known leaders like Martin Luther King, Jr., went to jail to secure Supreme Court sanction not only of picketing, but also of sit-ins, peaceful street demonstrations, and rallies—all of which received U.S. Supreme Court-applied First Amendment protection by the middle of the sixties. However, when the latter part of the decade produced the black power campaigns led by less well known and less polished leaders like H. Rap Brown and William Epton, state courts did not apply the earlier civil rights precedents to the new area of protest, even when the technique and the subject—racial equality and justice— were the same as in the earlier cases. Although some would argue that the black power movement was more violent and more controversial than the earlier civil rights struggles, history should remind these critics of the upheavals in Little Rock and Selma and the violence of Bull Connor's dogs and firehoses. True, King did preach nonviolence, a doctrine not always adhered to by his white opposition, and some later black power leaders did not; but courts had based the pro-civil rights opinions not upon doctrines of nonviolence but upon the constitutional principles of the First and Fourteenth Amendments, which were equally applicable to other forms and subjects of protest that did not in themselves constitute violence and might have been protected by a clear and present danger test.

Down through the years attorneys and others fighting for protection of free speech have encountered additional difficulties. One of these problems has involved the narrow nature of many state supreme court rulings. As indicated above, state courts often have discarded the application of a given security statute in a particular set of circumstances but have not declared the law unconstitutional. State supreme courts began exercising this practice to a great extent during the early forties and continued it into the sixties. In all fairness to state judges, it must be pointed out that in some instances the limited nature of a ruling can be tied to arguments made by attorneys involved in attempting to demonstrate how a statute did not affect a particular individual. Nevertheless, by 1970 the state high courts had ruled against applying a particular network of control statute in a total of thirty-nine cases but had actually discarded a state statute as unconstitutional in only seventeen cases.

Statutes voided through state supreme court application of the precedents from the ten U.S. Supreme Court cases studied here fall into several categories. As indicated earlier, three of the laws declared unconstitutional fall into the security statute classification. Pennsylvania in 1954 held its Sedition Law unconstitutional. The Pennsylvania court quoted at length from Chief Justice Hughes's discussion of free speech written for a unanimous Court in *De Jonge*:

The greater the importance of safeguarding the community from incitements to the overthrow of our institutions by force and violence, the more imperative is the need to preserve inviolate the constitutional right of free speech. . . . criminal sanctions for conduct hostile to our Federal Government must be promulgated, imposed and controlled uniformly for the Nation as a whole.[13]

When the *Nelson* case reached the U.S. Supreme Court in 1956, Chief Justice Warren's majority opinion relied upon the latter argument, bolstered by similar statements made by Justice Black in *Hines* v. *Davidowitz*, to uphold the Pennsylvania Supreme Court on grounds that the Pennsylvania Sedition Act had entered an area that the Smith Act had preempted.[14] The Supreme Court opinion in *Pennsylvania* v. *Nelson* in turn became the basis for voiding the other two state security statutes thrown out via application of the precedents discussed here. In 1956 the Michigan Supreme Court applied preemption and supersession arguments to overturn that state's Trucks Act since several of its sections attempted to regulate sedition against the U.S. Government as well as the State of Michigan. The Louisiana Supreme Court in 1958 invalidated that state's Subversive Activities Law on grounds that it was similar to the Pennsylvania Sedition Statute. The Louisiana Supreme Court went even further to declare that the Smith Act and other federal legislation had preempted the entire field of subversive activity, not merely laws prohibiting sedition against the United States. In another state security case frequently cited along with *Albertson* and *Jenkins—Commonwealth* v. *Gilbert*—the Supreme Judicial Court of Massachusetts did not declare the law unconstitutional.[15]

The largest number of network of control statutes declared unconstitutional related to the question of censorship and pornography. The *Adams* v. *Hinkle* opinion written by the Washington Supreme Court in 1958 voided that state's Comic Book Law on grounds that it was much too vague. The court applied the *Gitlow* nationalization precedent and the *Herndon* vagueness standard. The other three censorship cases involved state laws that imposed regulations upon allegedly obscene materials. Three state high courts applied *Herndon* vagueness standards to void three statutes in eastern seaboard states in the early sixties. The Maryland Court of Appeals in 1960 voided a Baltimore obscenity statute because it placed restrictions upon adults. In *William Goldman Theatres, Inc.* v. *Dana* the Pennsylvania Supreme Court in 1961 held that state's Motion Picture Control Act unconstitutional because it violated constitutional guarantees of fair trial and prohibitions against the use of prior restraint. On another occasion, the New York Court of Appeals voided obscenity statutes in that state. In 1964 in *People* v. *Bookcase, Inc.*, the court used *Herndon* precedent to discard a law that prohibited the sale of obscene materials to minors.[16]

Another group of network of control laws discarded by state supreme courts involved various versions of the loyalty oath. An often-cited 1946 California Supreme Court ruling in *Danskin* v. *San Diego Unified School District* threw out Section One of the California Civic Center Act, which had required that any group using school facilities sign a loyalty oath stating it did not advocate overthrow of the government. In Justice Roger Traynor's opinion for the California court he relied upon the precedent in Brandeis's *Whitney* concurrence and the majority opinions in *De Jonge*, *Herndon*, and *Taylor*. He also used Holmes's and Brandeis's *Gitlow* dissent, which a Supreme Court majority had adopted in *Bridges* v. *California* in 1941. Responding to the *Danskin* decision, the California Legislature attempted to rewrite the loyalty oath section of the Civic Center Act. In 1961 in *American Civil Liberties Union* v. *Board of Education* the California high court declared the new version unconstitutional as well. The opinion quoted *De Jonge*, declaring, "The holding of meetings for peaceful political actions cannot be proscribed."[17] In the other loyalty oath statute case the Wisconsin Supreme Court in 1955 in *Lawson* v. *Housing Authority of the City of Milwaukee* voided a requirement that occupants of public housing facilities sign an oath disclaiming any belief in overthrow of the government. The Wisconsin justices applied the nationalization principle of *Gitlow* as well as Brandeis's *Whitney* concurrence and Hughes's *De Jonge* opinion.[18]

Remaining network of control statutes declared unconstitutional in state courts fall into four categories: group libel law, political campaign regulations, labor union restrictions, and licensing requirements for public speaking. In the 1941 *State* v. *Klapprott* decision the New Jersey Supreme Court used the *Gitlow*, *Whitney*, and *De Jonge* majority opinions to invalidate a law prohibiting speech that promoted group hostility. In a rather unusual application of the precedents, the members of the New Jersey court found the statute to violate both the Fourteenth Amendment and the New Jersey Constitution because according to their interpretation the state might regulate abuses against itself but not against other organizations. In *Canon* v. *Justice Court for Lake Valley Judicial District* the California Supreme Court in 1964 relied upon Brandeis's *Whitney* concurrence and the *De Jonge* opinion to rule unconstitutional a law making distribution of anonymous campaign literature a misdemeanor.[19]

In the labor relations cases the California and Colorado Supreme Courts voided three state laws. In 1939 in *People* v. *Harris* the Colorado high court applied the two-year-old *Herndon* precedent regarding uncertainty in the standards of guilt to overturn a statute that penalized peaceful picketing. In 1944 in *American Federation of Labor* v. *Reilly* the Colorado court again faced questions of labor regulations and applied *Herndon* and *De Jonge* to declare restrictive sections of the state's Labor Peace Act unconstitutional as a violation of freedom of assembly and the National Labor Relations Act. In *Ex parte Blaney* in 1947 the California Supreme Court threw out a law restricting boycotts. The court used *De Jonge* and *Herndon* to declare that the statute was too vague to be enforced. In the final category the Supreme Judicial Court of Massachusetts in 1947 declared unconstitutional portions of a law requiring a mayor's permit to give public speeches in Boston Common. The court relied heavily upon the *De Jonge* concept of cognate rights and upon *Thornhill, Hague* v. *CIO, Lovell* v. *Griffin,* and *Thomas* v. *Collins.*[20]

In addition to the sixteen network of control laws, state courts voided seven statutes in other areas. Two of these cases dealt with regulations restricting an individual's personal life. In *Perez* v. *Lippold* in 1948 the California Supreme Court applied *Herndon* vagueness standards to declare an antimiscegenation ordinance to be a violation of Fourteenth Amendment equal protection. In a controversial case decided in 1969 the Supreme Judicial Court of Massachusetts in *Commonwealth* v. *Baird* used Brandeis's *Whitney* concurrence and *Herndon* vagueness arguments to invalidate a statute that prohibited the exhibiting of contraceptives. At the same time the Massachusetts court upheld a provision outlawing the free distribution of contraceptive devices.[21]

The other statutes that state supreme courts invalidated included an Oregon regulation that prohibited civil service employees from seeking public office and was declared unconstitutional on *Herndon* due-process grounds in 1966; a Nevada statute that allowed the district attorney to determine which auto thefts were to be considered felonies and was thrown out in 1968; two Montana reckless driving regulations discarded in 1956 and 1959 on narrow technical standards; and a Florida statute that singled out bottle clubs for a \$25-a-day licensing fee and was invalidated in 1960 through application of *Whitney's* equal-protection categorization ruling.[22]

At least partial explanation for state supreme court development along these lines can be found in the example that the U.S. Supreme Court set in not always considering First Amendment issues in a direct line of development and in setting down two lines of interpretation regarding freedom of speech. In the 1927 *Fiske* decision the Court declined to apply the Kansas Criminal Syndicalism Act to Fiske's circumstances and provided a statement so confusing that it led one prestigious law journal to note incorrectly that the Court had declared the law unconstitutional.[23] In the *Whitney* case, handed down the same day as *Fiske*, the attorneys for Miss Whitney had challenged the constitutionality of the California Criminal Syndicalism Statute and lost the appeal partly because the Court was not willing to support such a direct confrontation between the First Amendment and the state police power. In still another example, the Supreme Court had two opportunities in which it might have reversed or modified the *Gilbert* v. *Minnesota* ruling on grounds of congressional preemption of the sedition field. Yet in *Taylor* the Supreme Court ignored the *Gilbert* precedent altogether and based much of its opinion on arguments relating to free exercise of religion, and in *Nelson* the Court distinguished the case at bar from *Gilbert* on the basis of the argument that the state exercise of the police power justified the Minnesota law but not the Pennsylvania statute,[24] which was more closely connected to the concept of national defense and therefore subject to congressional preemption. In a sense state supreme courts followed the High Court's example and did not always consider all First Amendment interpretations made by the High Bench. Furthermore, some states, most notably Georgia after the 1937 *Herndon* decision, continued to apply a state security statute even when it had been ruled to be in violation of the Fourteenth Amendment. It was not until 1968 that the Georgia Legislature modified the Anti-Insurrection Law following the federal district court ruling in *Carmichael* v. *Allen*. In another example, the Mississippi Supreme Court in *Counts* v. *State* in 1943 ruled only that the state's Sedition Law could not be applied to Jehovah's Witness statements critical of the war even though the U.S. Supreme Court had declared the law unconstitutional on clear and present danger grounds in *Taylor*.[25]

Civil liberties history of First Amendment protection of free speech has also revealed the difficulties that defense attorneys have encountered in establishing trial records that might provide a substantial basis for appeal. These problems were particularly acute during the twenties and thirties. In the *Gilbert* trial, defense attorneys' procedural objections to the "parrot chorus"and the testimony of other state witnesses went unheeded and resulted in a conviction based upon shaky evidence. Anita Whitney's attorney died during the early stages of her trial, and subsequent counsel tried unsuccessfully to break new ground in challenging the entire statute on First Amendment grounds. Had Whitney's counsel argued for a clear and present danger application, as Brandeis later suggested in his concurring opinion, the appeal might have yielded different results. An inexperienced, young, local attorney represented Angelo Herndon and made errors that a more experienced advocate might have avoided in the racially prejudiced atmosphere of the Atlanta of the 1930s. Even though Herndon was ultimately victorious, it took five years and two U.S. Supreme Court decisions to gain him his freedom and to secure a ruling against the Georgia Anti-Insurrection Law.

However, it must be pointed out that the trial records at times worked to the advantage of defendants whose cases reached the High Court. In the *Fiske* and *De Jonge* cases the respective state prosecutors had decided prematurely that they had open-and-shut cases against the defendants and, as a result, produced vague indictments. Challenges to the application of the criminal syndicalism statutes in these particular instances produced unanimous Supreme Court decisions against the state action. If there is a general observation to be made here, it is to reinforce a point made earlier: challenges to the constitutionality of state security laws were not as successful as challenges to their application. The Supreme Court moved step by step, not by leaps and bounds; and narrow and more technical legal challenges won more civil liberties points than substantive arguments regarding free speech.

It was this very step-by-step process used by the U.S. Supreme Court that left room for much contradictory and confusing state application of precedents. Additional room for confusion and hence avoidance of Supreme Court precedent occurred because the Court, during several decades of attempting to provide guidance in the area of state security laws, presented conflicting lines of precedent. The Court demonstrated this development most dramatically in the duality of the *Gilbert* and *Nelson* rulings and also in the contrast of the *Gitlow* and *Whitney* opinions with the *De Jonge* and *Herndon* decisions. Those contradictions persisted until 1969, when the *Brandenburg* ruling removed the *Whitney* precedent and—along with it—part, but not all, of the conflicting line of precedent. Despite the development of a considerable body of law protecting First Amendment free speech from state encroachment, the Court has removed only the *Whitney* precedent and left other rulings that have supported state action. Just a few years prior to *Brandenburg* the Court refused *certiorari* in a case involving the same statute as had convicted Gitlow, and the High Bench never did clarify successfully the inconsistency of the *Gilbert* and *Nelson* rulings. The duality persists.

Another significant observation that can be made by viewing the historical development of the network of control is the extent of the complications within the federal system itself. What might be termed a gradually developing tangle of federalism in the interpretation of security laws grew to a high level in *Dombrowski* and then flourished into a jungle of complicated interpretation. Much of the development of this confusing body of legal pronouncement appears to have been related to the procedural points made by various courts in interpreting precedents in state security cases. As shown in table 3, the U.S. Supreme Court opinions in state security cases produced procedural points of law as well as substantive First Amendment rulings. In subsequent use of these two types of precedents, state supreme courts appear to have been more creative and flexible in finding ways to transfer procedural points to situations that differed from the precedent cases.

In *Gilbert* v. *Minnesota* the majority ruled that the state police power could be used to preserve domestic peace and that free speech did not enjoy the absolute protection of the First Amend-

TABLE 3   PROCEDURAL APPLICATIONS DEVELOPED IN STATE SECURITY STATUTE CASES BEFORE THE U.S. SUPREME COURT

CASE	*PROCEDURAL APPLICATION*
Gilbert v. *Minnesota* 7-2, 1920	Double jeopardy protection not immune from concurrent jurisdiction
Gitlow v. *New York* 7-2, 1925	Presumption to be made in favor of validity of statute State to be primary judge of validity
Whitney v. *California* unanimous, 1927	State may classify and categorize despite equal protection of 14th Amendment
Fiske v. *Kansas* unanimous, 1927	Trial court must adhere to facts in case
De Jonge v. *Oregon* unanimous, 1937	No conviction on a charge not included in indictment
Herndon v. *Lowry* 5-4, 1937	No reasonable standard of guilt Void for vagueness "judgment of legislature is not unfettered"
Taylor v. *Mississippi* unanimous, 1943	No procedural ruling
Pennsylvania v. *Nelson* 6-3, 1956	Smith Act preempted field of sedition legislation involving United States
Dombrowski v. *Pfister* 5-2, 1965	Void for vagueness Federal courts could intervene when rights deprived; to wait constituted chilling effect
Brandenburg v. *Ohio* unanimous, 1969	No procedural ruling

Substantive rulings are summarized in Table 1.

ment. Both of these points fell within the substantive side of the analysis. However, McKenna's *Gilbert* opinion also led to a considerable number of state court decisions that applied the police power ruling in a far more procedural sense, resulting in opinions upholding concurrent jurisdiction of state and federal authorities and even sustaining procedures that raised serious questions of double jeopardy. Both of these applications of *Gilbert* precedent produced questions about federalism that subsequent judicial bodies would have to solve.

The well-known 1925 *Gitlow* decision produced the first majority ruling applying the Fourteenth Amendment to the states, a pronouncement that had both substantive and procedural ramifications. In dealing with the substantive issues, the Court held that Gitlow's words did not require free speech protection, and the majority did not apply Holmes's test of clear and present danger. In later state court use of *Gitlow* precedent, state justices repeatedly relied upon a procedural point stating that when an individual challenged a law, presumption was to be made in favor of the validity of the statute in question. This High Court ruling provided considerable support for the power and judgment of the state legislature and made it very difficult for an individual to challenge successfully a state law on First Amendment or any other civil liberties grounds. It took the development of a considerable number of clear and present danger rulings as well as the appearance of a large body of equal-protection doctrine to balance the credence that *Gitlow* gave to the wisdom of the state. Heavy state court reliance upon this particular point in *Gitlow* also helps to explain the great difficulty that persons or groups have had in successfully challenging the constitutionality, rather than the mere application, of a state security statute.

The *Fiske* case of 1927, which involved the Kansas Criminal Syndicalism Law, provided only a brief opinion that Kansas had applied the statute to Fiske unconstitutionally. However, the unanimous opinion also stated that a court must adhere to the factual evidence in a case and that the trial record must show that the evidence produced supported the conviction. Much of the subsequent application of *Fiske* precedent relied upon this statement of procedure. In the *Whitney* opinion, delivered the same day as *Fiske*, the justices declined to apply a clear and present danger test to the California Criminal Syndicalism Law, thus repeating the ruling that the Court did not consider free speech to be an absolute right. However, the *Whitney* opinion also gave much credence to the procedural device of state categorization and classification; and until 1960, state courts used this precedent to uphold classification of numerous categories of regulation. In so doing, state legislatures and courts relied heavily upon Justice Sanford's statement in *Whitney*:

It is settled by repeated decisions of this Court that the equal protection clause does not take from a State the power to classify in the adoption of police laws, but admits of the exercise of a wide scope of discretion, and avoids what is done only when it is without any reasonable basis and therefore is purely arbitrary; and that one who assails the classification must carry the burden of showing that it does not rest upon any reasonable basis, but is essentially arbitrary.[26]

Supreme Court support of state legislative action in *Whitney* reinforced the credence that the *Gitlow* decision gave to the validity of state statutes. Although after 1925 the Supreme Court ruled repeatedly that the Fourteenth Amendment protected the Bill of Rights from the encroachment of state law, these statements in defense of the First Amendment seemed to conflict with the *Gitlow* and *Whitney* procedural points regarding state legislative action. These circumstances demonstrated a crucial problem in federalism. If the state legislation is to be presumed to be valid and the state can classify persons and actions into categories that it considers reasonable, then how can the United States Constitution protect individuals and groups from the excesses of state power?

Perhaps part of the answer to the above question lies in subsequent historical development. In the two 1937 rulings, *De Jonge* v. *Oregon* and *Herndon* v. *Lowry*, the Court granted protection to the substantive areas of free assembly and free speech; but those decisions also provided state courts with less well known procedural precedent. After 1946, state supreme courts began to rely upon a technical *De Jonge* point that a court could not produce a conviction on a charge not included in the indictment, a procedural contention involving civil liberties questions. One statement made in the five-man majority opinion in *Herndon*—"judgment of the legislature is not unfettered"[27]—provided state supreme courts with an alternative to the *Gitlow* reliance upon the presumption of legislative wisdom. Also, the reasonable-standard-of-guilt and void-for-vagueness portions of the *Herndon* opinion became important precedents for subsequent state courts. Although basically procedural rulings, these concepts are closely intertwined with the protection of the substance of free speech.

The 1943 Supreme Court ruling in *Taylor* v. *Mississippi*, a Sedition Law case, resulted in a clear and present danger application in the area of freedom of religion. However, this case did not overrule *Gilbert* and did not become a crucial precedent in subsequent state court litigation in either the substantive or procedural area—except as a basis for protection of the activities of the Jehovah's Witnesses. By contrast, the decision in the well-known 1956 Sedition Law case, *Pennsylvania* v. *Nelson*, provided the basis for considerable controversy in both national and state legislatures and offered considerable fuel for the fires of the lingering federalism controversy. In a sense there was no substantive First Amendment ruling in *Nelson*, even though Chief Justice Earl Warren gave the usually procedural point of preemption a substantive flavor in his Opinion of the Court. By contending that "a state sedition statute is superseded regardless of whether it purports to supplement the federal law,"[28] Warren and the majority informed the states that they could not concern themselves with the question of sedition against the United States and provided a precedent that seemed in some ways to contradict the *Gilbert* ruling. The *Nelson* opinion left unclear the answer to the question of whether states could prohibit sedition against themselves, thereby providing to some a precedent for a continuation of laws against certain groups considered to be subversive. But a few other state courts read the *Nelson* message as a signal that in the federal system sedition legislation was an area for congressional—not state—concern.

State courts reacting quickly and positively to the *Nelson* decision included the Supreme Judicial Court of Massachusetts, which argued against the application of that state's sedition law in *Commonwealth* v. *Gilbert*, and the Michigan Supreme Court, which overturned several sections of the Trucks Act, a law regulating communist-front activity. However, other state courts insisted that the upholding of their laws did not violate *Nelson* precedent. In 1957 the Florida Supreme Court insisted on exempting a case from the High Court's *Nelson* ruling on the grounds that the state statutes under consideration concerned only the security of the state and not that of the United States. The New Hampshire Supreme Court was most determined to distinguish its cases from the *Pennsylvania* v. *Nelson* precedent. In 1956 the New Hampshire justices stated in *Kahn* v. *Wyman* that the U.S. Supreme Court opinion did not preclude the New Hampshire attorney general's investigation of subversive activities. In 1957 in *Wyman* v. *De Gregory* the New Hampshire court used the previous year's opinion to justify contempt proceedings against De Gregory for refusing to cooperate with loyalty investigations. Again in 1957, the New Hampshire high court upheld its subversive investigation law in *Wyman* v. *Uphaus* by insisting that a number of cases fell outside the sweep of the *Nelson* ruling. Two years later the U.S. Supreme Court confused the area of jurisprudence bordering on state security statutes still further by upholding the New Hampshire law in *Uphaus* v. *Wyman*.[29]

In the three High Court cases of the sixties under consideration in this study only the Supreme Court ruling in *Dombrowski* v. *Pfister* has been used to any great extent as a precedent. In that 1965 ruling the Court held five-to-two that the Louisiana Anti-Subversive Activities Act was unconstitutional on its face because it was overly broad and could not meet a void-for-vagueness test. On the procedural side the Court held that federal courts could intervene in cases involving state laws having civil liberties overtones because to force citizens to wait until all state legal channels had been exhausted could have a "chilling effect" on free expression. The procedural portion of the *Dombrowski* opinion became by far the most influential and controversial area of that ruling. It helped to create a tremendous backlash of opinion shared by state judicial authorities and by some members of the federal bench, including the man who was to become chief justice of the United

States—Warren Burger. The complicated nature of the *Dombrowski* opinion written by Justice William Brennan heightened the conflict over the state-federal court clash within the federal system and led to considerable confusion in interpretation, which has created a maze of procedural points for federal as well as state courts.

Since the U.S. Supreme Court did not grant *certiorari* in *Epton* v. *New York*, that case cannot be considered in this analysis of substantive versus procedural rulings. However, the refusal of *certiorari* served to allow the old *Gitlow* ruling to stand as a precedent for state attempts to curtail social protest and political criticism. The 1969 *per curiam* ruling in *Brandenburg* v. *Ohio* provided further protection for free speech by declaring the Ohio Criminal Syndicalism Law unconstitutional and overturning *Whitney* v. *California*. In *Brandenburg* the Court finally applied the clear and present danger test to criminal syndicalism laws, nearly fifty years after those laws and that test originated.

It would appear that the very nature of the system of federalism has created a great part of the difficulty in providing Fourteenth Amendment Bill of Rights guarantees. Research in this study has reinforced the premise that state appellate courts have been less responsive to First Amendment considerations than have the federal courts and the Supreme Court in particular. In each of the ten precedent-setting cases studied here, all but *Dombrowski* went the state-appellate-court route; and in only one of those, *Pennsylvania* v. *Nelson*, did the state high court declare a state law unconstitutional. In other instances the state courts did not rule in favor of state protection of forms of free speech until the U.S. Supreme Court provided leadership in applying a cause-and-effect relationship to the question of free-speech protection against state law. No state has relinquished its authority easily, and many states have guarded jealously their authority to determine what speech could be protected by the First and Fourteenth Amendments, long after the Supreme Court had ruled that the Bill of Rights applied to the states on the issue of freedom of expression. In all of the Supreme Court cases that are included in this study and came before the Court after *Whitney* in 1927, the High Court ruled favorably toward a state security statute in only one, *Epton*

v. *New York.* However, as has been pointed out, many state courts continued to uphold security laws.

State reluctance to relinquish authority in this area is demonstrated further by the annotations in a number of state codes that indicate the applicability of a U.S. Supreme Court decision to sections that the legislatures have chosen not to repeal or modify in compliance with High Court ruling. Further evidence of this development is demonstrated by the fact that in this study Oregon was the only state directly involved in a Supreme Court security statute decision that repealed its statute immediately after the Supreme Court declared the law unconstitutional. New York modified its Criminal Anarchy Law by removing its application to action against the United States, but did so eleven years after the *Pennsylvania* v. *Nelson* ruling. In 1963 the Minnesota Legislature repealed the 1917 Sedition Act but retained its Criminal Syndicalism Law. California revised its Criminal Syndicalism Law only slightly after *Brandenburg* v. *Ohio* overturned the *Whitney* opinion based upon that California law. As a result of *Brandenburg,* Ohio repealed its Criminal Syndicalism Statute, effective January 1, 1974. In *Dombrowski* v. *Pfister* authorities took action under portions of a law that the Louisiana Supreme Court declared unconstitutional in 1958 and that had been revised by the legislature and that remains on the books.[30]

Difficulty in securing state court compliance with U.S. Supreme Court opinions in the free speech area led Dombrowski and the other officials of the Southern Conference Educational Fund who were harassed by the Louisiana officials to seek redress in the federal courts. In their case the ultimate result was successful, but the intricacies of Justice Brennan's *Dombrowski* opinion created even more questions and greater confusion, so subsequent developments in no way insured the federal-court route as a haven from state courts unwilling to provide First Amendment protection.[31]

Over the years since 1930 the Supreme Court has discarded a number of state speech-related statutes in the area of security legislation as well as other points in the network of control. Despite this large body of case law designed to protect the First Amendment from state encroachment, many states persist in maintaining a network of control that can be activated at numerous points, should the state officials decide the circumstances warrant restrictions. A survey of state statutes and codes made in 1981 indicates that thirty-six—or 72 percent—of the states continue to maintain provisions that fit this study's definition of a security statute affecting civilians.[32] This survey does not take into account the numerous other statutes that the state might also activate to interfere with politically oriented First Amendment freedoms.

During the period under discussion here there existed a considerable tension between the individual liberties of expression based upon the First Amendment and the state legislative attempts to protect the security and authority of the government; in addition, tension at times grew between the operations of the national and state governments. This study has dealt with the history of those tensions in light of the issue of freedom of political speech versus the security of state government. The ebb and flow of historical circumstances have produced alternating periods of crisis and stability for the protection of free speech and other civil liberties. Like any civil liberty, freedom of speech does not become an issue of law until it is restricted or denied. It should come as no surprise to historians or to anyone else that liberty of expression is far more likely to go unchallenged, either by an existing statute or the passage of a new one, during periods of political calm and social and economic stability than during times of war or intense difference of opinion on domestic issues. Ironically, it is during those treacherous periods of intense conflict of opinion that freedom of expression is all the more necessary to ensure continuation of a constitutional system that attempts to protect individual rights.

However, as pointed out in these chapters, far too often the network of control can be activated to counter the system of freedom of expression created by courts and legislatures during earlier periods of relative calm. The history of U.S. Supreme Court decisions in the area of free speech and state security statutes, considered apart from state court developments, does not reveal the more limited extent to which states have protected First Amendment civil liberties. Results of this research point to a definite need for historians and other students of legal and constitutional developments to investigate at the state as well as the national level of judicial pronouncement. Even though the U.S. Supreme Court declared a number of state security statutes unconstitutional in the years after 1930, it did so repeatedly without removing the precedents that had upheld earlier security laws. The history of the U.S. Supreme Court and state supreme courts during this period has provided two lines of precedent in freedom of expression cases. If one considers the Supreme Court decisions that upheld state security statutes, the Court has overturned only *Whitney*, leaving the *Gilbert* and *Gitlow* line of precedent to detract from the certainty of interpretation that is among the primary goals of the law. The hit-and-miss nature of the state application of U.S. Supreme Court precedent may have aided the causes of individual litigants, but it has done little to strengthen the certainty expected from the body of the law. As the founder and long-time chairman of the American Civil Liberties Union, Roger Baldwin, stated repeatedly, "No civil liberties victory ever stays won."[33] The persistence of the network of control guarantees the validity of his statement.

NOTES

1. The New Mexico Supreme Court applied the state constitution in the seventeenth case included in table 2.

2. The Colorado Supreme Court discarded a picketing regulation in AFL v. Reilly, 113 Colo. 90 (1944), 155 P. 2d 145 (1944); and the California Supreme Court did so in Ex parte Blaney, 30 Cal. 2d 643 (1947), 184 P. 2d 892 (1947). State v. Klapprott, 127 N.J.L. 395 (1941), 22 A. 2d 877 (1941), involved the New Jersey Group Libel Law; Danskin v. San Diego Unified School Dist., 28 Cal. 2d 536 (1946), 171 P. 2d 885 (1946), discarded the loyalty oath portion of the Civic Center Act; and Commonwealth v. Gilfedder, 321 Mass. 335 (1947), 73 N.E. 2d 241 (1947) dealt with free speech on Boston Common.

3. Hotel and Restaurant Employees Int'l. Alliance v. Greenwood, 249 Ala. 265 (1947), 30 So. 2d 696 (1947); Montgomery Ward and Co. v. United Retail, Wholesale, and Dept. Store Employees, 400 Ill. 38 (1938), 79 N.E. 2d 46 (1948); and State ex rel. Culinary Workers Union v. Eighth Judicial Dist. Court, 66 Nev. 166 (1949), 207 P. 2d 990 (1949).

4. In Taylor v. State, 194 Miss. 1 (1943), 11 So. 2d 663 (1943), the Mississippi Supreme Court upheld the sedition provision in a tie vote. See

also Taylor v. Miss., 319 U.S. 583 (1943); Counts v. State, 15 So. 2d 287 (1943); and State v. Sentner, 230 Iowa 590 (1941), 298 N.W. 813 (1941).

5. Commonwealth v. Nelson, 377 Pa. 58 (1954), 104 A. 2d 133 (1954); Pa. v. Nelson, 350 U.S. 497 (1956); Albertson v. Millard, 345 Mich. 519 (1956), 77 N.W. 2d 104 (1956); State v. Jenkins, 236 La. 300 (1958), 107 So. 2d 648 (1958); and Commonwealth v. Gilbert, 334 Mass. 71 (1956), 134 N.E. 2d 13 (1956).

6. Nelson v. Wyman, 99 N.H. 33 (1954), 105 A. 2d 756 (1954); Kahn v. Wyman, 100 N.H. 245 (1956), 123 A. 2d 166 (1956); Wyman v. Uphaus, 100 N.H. 436 (1957), 130 A. 2d 278 (1957); and Wyman v. De Gregory, 100 N.H. 163 (1957), 137 A. 2d 512 (1957).

7. Lawson v. Housing Authority for Milwaukee, 270 Wis. 269 (1955), 70 N.W. 2d 605 (1955); and Adams v. Hinkle, 51 Wash. 2d 763 (1958), 322 P. 2d 844 (1958).

8. For the controversial *Playboy* case see State v. Nelson, 178 N.W. 2d 434 (1970).

9. William Goldman Theatres, Inc. v. Dana, 405 Pa. 83 (1961), 173 A. 2d 57 (1961); People v. Bookcase, Inc., 14 N.Y. 2d 402 (1964), 201 N.E. 2d 14 (1964); Am. Civil Liberties Union v. Bd. of Educ., 55 Cal. 2d 167 (1961), 359 P. 2d 45 (1961); and Canon v. Justice Court for Lake Valley Judicial Dist., 61 Cal. 2d 446 (1964), 393 P. 2d 428 (1964).

10. Danskin v. San Diego Unified School Dist., 28 Cal. 2d 536 (1946), 171 P. 2d 885 (1946); 55 Cal. 2d 167, 359 P. 2d 45; and Am. Civil Liberties Union of S. Cal. v. Bd. of Educ., 59 Cal. 2d 203 (1963), 379 P. 2d 4 (1963).

11. Harris, *Black Power Advocacy: Criminal Anarchy or Free Speech*, 56 CALIF. L. REV. 702 (1968); People v. Gitlow, 234 N.Y. 132 (1922), 136 N.E. 317 (1922); Gitlow v. N.Y., 268 U.S. 652 (1925); People v. Epton, 19 N.Y. 2d 496 (1967), 227 N.E. 2d 829 (1967); State v. Kassay, 126 Ohio St. 177 (1932), 184 N.E. 521 (1932); and Brandenburg v. Ohio, 395 U.S. 444 (1969).

12. Thornhill v. Ala., 310 U.S. 88, 102 (1940).

13. 377 Pa. 58, 75-76 (1954), 104 A. 2d 133, 141-142 (1954), quoted Chief Justice Hughes in De Jonge v. Or., 299 U.S. 353 (1937).

14. 350 U.S. 497 and Hines v. Davidowitz, 312 U.S. 52 (1941).

15. 345 Mich. 519, 77 N.W. 2d 104; 236 La. 300, 107 So. 2d 648; and 334 Mass. 71, 134 N.E. 2d 13. In 1962, after the 1959 U.S. Supreme Court opinion in Uphaus v. Wyman, 360 U.S. 72 (1959), the Louisiana Legislature reinstated the Subversive Activities Control Law in a form slightly different from the original. See Brief for Appellants and Appellants-Intervenors at 23-24 and Jurisdictional Statement at 7, 26, Dombrowski v. Pfister, 380, U.S. 479 (1965) and LA. REV. STAT. ANN. §§ 14.115, 14.359 (West).

16. 51 Wash. 2d 763, 322 P. 2d 844; Herndon v. Lowry, 301 U.S. 242 (1937); Police Comm'rs. of Baltimore v. Seigel Enterprises, 223 Md. 110 1960), 162 A. 2d 727 (1960); 405 Pa. 83, 173 A. 2d 59; 14 N.Y. 2d 402, 201 N.E. 2d 14.

17. 28 Cal. 2d 536, 171 P. 2d 885; and 55 Cal. 2d 167, 172, 359 P. 2d 45, 47.

18. 270 Wis. 269, 70 N.W. 2d 605; 268 U.S. 652; and Whitney v. Cal., 274 U.S. 357 (1927).

19. 127 N.J.L. 395, 22 A. 2d 877; and 61 Cal. 2d 446, 393 P. 2d 428.

20. People v. Harris, 104 Colo. 386 (1939), 91 P. 2d 989 (1939); 113 Colo. 90, 155 P. 2d 145; 30 Cal. 2d 643 (1947), 184 P. 2d 892 (1947); Commonwealth v. Gilfedder, 321 Mass. 335 (1947), 73 N.E. 2d 241 (1947); Hague v. CIO, 307 U.S. 496 (1939); Lovell v. Griffin, 303 U.S. 444 (1938); and Thomas v. Collins, 323 U.S. 516 (1945).

21. Perez v. Lippold, 32 Cal. 2d 711 (1948), 198 P. 2d 17 (1948); and Commonwealth v. Baird, 355 Mass. 746 (1969), 247 N.E. 2d 574 (1969).

22. Minielly v. State, 242 Or. 490 (1966), 411 P. 2d 69 (1966); Lapinski v. State, 84 Nev. 611 (1968), 446 P. 2d 645 (1968); City of Billings v. Herold, 130 Mont. 138 (1956), 296 P. 2d 263 (1956); Town of White Sulphur Springs v. Voise, 136 Mont. 1 (1959), 343 P. 2d 855 (1959); and Segal v. Simpson, 121 So. 2d 790 (1960).

23. Fiske v. Kan., 274 U.S. 380 (1927) and 76 U. PA. L. REV. 201 (1927).

24. Gilbert v. Minn., 254 U.S. 325 (1920); Taylor v. Miss., 319 U.S. 583 (1943); and 350 U.S. 497.

25. GA. CODE ANN. §§ 26-901—26-904; Carmichael v. Allen, 276 F. Supp. 985 (N.D. Ga. 1967); and Counts v. State, 15 So. 2d 287 (1943).

26. 274 U.S. 357, 369.

27. 301 U.S. 242, 258.

28. 350 U.S. 497, 504.

29. 334 Mass. 71, 134 N.E. 2d 13; 345 Mich. 519, 77 N.W. 2d 104; Gibson v. Fla. Legislative Investigating Comm., 108 So. 2d 729 (1958); 100 N.H. 245, 123 A. 2d 166; 100 N.H. 163, 137 A. 2d 512; 100 N.H. 436, 130 A. 2d 278; and 360 U.S. 72.

30. Notations in reference to the Illinois affidavit and loyalty oath required of state employees indicate that provisions were declared unconstitutional in Snyder v. Bd. of Trustees of U. of Ill., 286 F. Supp. 927 (N.D. Ill. E.D. 1968) and in Thalberg v. Bd. of Trustees of U. of Ill., 309 F. Supp. 630 (N.D. Ill. E.D. 1969). See ILL. ANN. STAT. ch. 127 § 166a (Smith-Hurd). LA. REV. STAT. ANN. §§ 14.115, 14.359 (West) still includes sections of the Internal Security Act discarded in *Dombrowski*.

Mississippi retains its Criminal Syndicalism Statute despite the decision in Ware v. Nichols, 266 F. Supp. 546 (N.D. Miss. 1967), which discarded the law. See also Eldridge Dowell, *A History of Criminal Syndicalism Legislation in the United States* (New York: Da Capo Press, 1969), p. 147 and Appendix I; N.Y. PENAL LAW § 240.15 (McKinney), which indicates a 1967 change in the statute to apply only to New York state government rather than to "all organized governments;" CAL. PENAL CODE § 11400 et seq. (West); and MINN. STAT. ANN. § 609.405 (West). Since 1970 the following states have repealed security statutes: Arizona, 1978; Indiana, 1977; Maine, 1971; Michigan, 1978; New Jersey, 1978; Ohio, 1974; and South Dakota, 1976. See Appendix for additional details. See also Epton v. N.Y., 390 U.S. 29 (1968) and Brandenburg v. Ohio, 395 U.S. 444 (1969).

31. Although Dombrowski may have provided a brief period of optimism regarding the use of the federal courts as a means to avoid state court litigation in First Amendment cases, events subsequent to 1970 quickly ended those hopes. In 1971, with only Justice William O. Douglas dissenting, the U.S. Supreme Court ruled on a three-judge panel decision appealed from the U.S. District Court for the Central District of California. The case involved the same Criminal Syndicalism Law as Whitney; and the High Bench declared in Younger v. Harris, that in the interest of comity and federalism federal courts should abstain from interfering in pending state court proceedings. In the Opinion of the Court, Justice Hugo Black asserted that "the existence of a 'chilling effect', even in the area of First Amendment rights, has never been considered a sufficient basis, in and of itself, for prohibiting state action" and that the Dombrowski decision should not be regarded as having upset the settled doctrines that have always defined very narrowly the availability of injunctive relief against state criminal prosecutions (401 U.S. 37, 51-53 [1971]).

As one law review commentator stated, Younger presented a legal Catch-22, "if you have not been prosecuted, you have not shown any injury," and therefore do not merit federal declaratory or injunctive relief; "but as soon as you are prosecuted, Younger comes into play" to trigger state court action. See Sedler, *Dombrowski in the Wake of Younger: The View From Without and Within*, 1972 WISC. L. REV. 1, 56. The wake of the Younger decision brought a body of state and federal court action denying requests for Dombrowski type of relief in the federal courts. These developments are discussed in detail in Kennedy, *I Used to Love You But It's All Over Now: Abstention and the Federal Courts' Retreat from Their Role as Primary Guardians of First Amendment Freedoms*, 45 SO. CALIF. L. REV. 847 (1972) and Fiss, *Dombrowski*, 86

YALE L. J. 1103 (1977). As Fiss commented at 1104, "By the spring of 1976, Dombrowski seemed only a formal vestige of another era."

The Younger ruling was only one in a series of Burger Court developments that have served to restrict access to the federal courts and to leave many First Amendment questions within state jurisdiction. In 1976, Congress followed the Supreme Court's lead and passed a statute limiting the creation of three-judge panels to circumstances involving reapportionment or specific congressional requirements, such as those stipulated in the Civil Rights Acts of 1964 and 1965. This legislation ended the use of three-judge federal panels in First Amendment cases. See H8145, S13424, 94th Cong., 2d Sess. (1976) and "3-Judge Court Use for U.S. Cases Out," *New York Times*, August 13, 1976, p. A9.

Combined action of the federal courts and Congress has done much to place First Amendment civil liberties focus on the state courts. Although some commentators, including Justice William Brennan, have expressed some optimism regarding the role that state courts might play in this area, the preceding chapters have demonstrated that without U.S. Supreme Court leadership state benches are not inclined to provide strong First Amendment protection. For further discussion of the future role of state courts in this area see Brennan, *State Constitutions and the Protection of Individual Rights*, 90 HARV. L. REV. 489 (1977) and Jaglom, *Protecting Fundamental Rights in State Courts: Fitting a State Peg to a Federal Hole*," 12 HARV. CIV. RTS. AND CIV. LIB. L. REV. 63 (1977).

32. See Appendix.

33. Baldwin is quoted in Charles L. Markmann, *The Noblest Cry* (New York: St. Martin's Press, 1965), p. 432.

APPENDIX: STATE SECURITY STATUTES, 1981

State	Type of Law					Jurisdiction			Citation
	Sedition	Criminal Anarchy	Criminal Syndicalism	Other	None Indexed	State	U.S.	Organized Government In General	
Alabama		x						x	ALA. CODE § 13-6-45-13-6-46.
Alaska					x				ALASKA STAT. §11.50.010-11.50.030 repealed 1978.
Arizona					x				ARIZ. REV. STAT. ANN. Sedition law removed in 1978 criminal code revision.
Arkansas		x		x		x	x		ARK. STAT. ANN. §41-3953 includes treason.
California			x					x	CAL. PENAL CODE §11400 et seq. (West).
Colorado		x		x		x	x	x	COL. REV. STAT. §18-11-101—18-11-103 includes treason and insurrection.
Connecticut	x			x					CONN. GEN. STAT. ANN. §27.8 (West) pertains only to military.

State	Type of Law					Jurisdiction			Citation
	Sedition	Criminal Anarchy	Criminal Syndicalism	Other	None Indexed	State	U.S.	Organized Government In General	
Delaware				x				x	DEL. CODE ANN. tit. 20, §3501-3502 requires Communist registration.
Florida	x	x				x	x		FLA. STAT. ANN. §876.01-876.04 (West).
Georgia	x					x			GA. CODE ANN. §26-901—26-904.
Hawaii				x					HAWAII REV. STAT. §85 includes "loyalty" regulations.
Idaho					x				IDAHO CODE.
Illinois				x		x			ILL. ANN. STAT. ch. 127, §166a (Smith-Hurd) includes loyalty oath for state employees, thrown out in federal court.
Indiana									IND. CODE ANN. (Burns) indicates security laws repealed 1977.

State	Type of Law				Jurisdiction				Citation
	Sedition	Criminal Anarchy	Criminal Syndicalism	Other	None Indexed	State	U.S.	Organized Government In General	
Iowa				x		x			IOWA CODE ANN. §718.1 (West) refers to "Insurrection" which is a 1976 revision of the sedition law.
Kansas			x						KAN. STAT. ANN. §21-3802—21-3804.
Kentucky				x		x			Treason provision in state constitution.
Louisiana		x		x		x	x		LA. REV. STAT. ANN. §14.115, 14.359-14.390 (West) includes the Subversive Activities Control Law.
Maine									ME. REV. STAT. ANN. indicates repeal of insurrection section in 1971.
Maryland				x					MD. ANN. CODE indicates sedition and subversion placed under a special assistant attorney general.

State	Type of Law					Jurisdiction			Citation
	Sedition	Criminal Anarchy	Criminal Syndicalism	Other	None Indexed	State	U.S.	Organized Government In General	
Massachusetts	x					x	x		MASS. ANN. LAWS ch. 264, §11 (Michie/Law. Co-op).
Michigan									MICH. COMP. LAWS ANN. §750.46 repealed in 1978.
Minnesota			x					x	MINN. STAT. ANN. §609.405 (West).
Mississippi			x					x	MISS. CODE ANN. §97-7-21—97-7-27 includes the provision despite federal court ruling.
Missouri				x					MO. ANN. STAT. §41.140 pertains only to military.
Montana			x					x	MONT. CODES ANN. §45-8-105.
Nebraska									NEB. REV. STAT. contains no laws in 1979 edition.

State	Type of Law					Jurisdiction			Citation
	Sedition	Criminal Anarchy	Criminal Syndicalism	Other	None Indexed	State	U.S.	Organized Government In General	
Nevada		x	x					x	NEV. REV. STAT. §203.115-203.117.
New Hampshire				x		x	x	x	N.H. REV. STAT. ANN. §648 is 1973 version of 1951 statute.
New Jersey									N.J. STAT. ANN. §148-12—148-19 (West) repealed in 1978.
New Mexico	x					x	x	x	N.M. STAT. ANN. §10-1-12, 20-11-90.
New York		x				x			N.Y. PENAL LAW §240.15 (McKinney).
North Carolina					x				N.C. GEN. STAT.
North Dakota					x				N.D. CENT. CODE.
Ohio									OHIO REV. CODE ANN. §2921.04-2921.10 (Page) repealed, effective January 1, 1974.

State	Type of Law					Jurisdiction			Citation
	Sedition	Criminal Anarchy	Criminal Syndicalism	Other	None Indexed	State	U.S.	Organized Government In General	
Oklahoma			x			x	x	x	OKLA. STAT. ANN. tit. 21, §1261-1263, 1267.1 (West).
Oregon				x					OR. REV. STAT. §390.338 applies to sedition and mutiny in military.
Pennsylvania	x					x	x		18 PA. CONS. STAT. ANN. §4207 (Purdon).
Rhode Island		x				x	x	x	R.I. GEN. LAWS §11-43-12—11-43-14.
South Carolina				x					S.C. CODE §25-7-20—25-7-60 includes treason and sabotage.
South Dakota				x		x			S.D. CODIFIED LAWS §22-8-1 includes treason against the state; criminal syndicalism law repealed 1976.
Tennessee	x					x	x		TENN. CODE ANN. §39-4405.

State	Type of Law					Jurisdiction			Citation
	Sedition	Criminal Anarchy	Criminal Syndicalism	Other	None Indexed	State	U.S.	Organized Government In General	
Texas				x		x	x		TEX. CIVIL STAT. ANN. §6889-3A (Vernon) regulates Communist party activity.
Utah			x					x	UTAH CODE ANN. §76-8-901—76-8-904.
Vermont		x				x			VT. STAT. ANN. tit. 13, §3405.
Virginia				x		x	x	x	VA. CODE §18.2-485 refers to insurrection involving race; §18.2-481 deals with treason.
Washington		x				x			WASH. REV. CODE §9.05.
West Virginia				x		x			W. VA. CODE. §61-1-4 deals with insurrection and armed invasion; §61-1-1 deals with treason.

State	Type of Law					Jurisdiction			Citation
	Sedition	Criminal Anarchy	Criminal Syndicalism	Other	None Indexed	State	U.S.	Organized Government In General	
Wisconsin	x					x	x		WIS. STAT. ANN. §946.03 (West).
Wyoming					x				WYO. STAT. ANN.

175

LIST OF CASES

UNITED STATES SUPREME COURT

Tinker v. Des Moines Independent School District, 393 U.S. 503 (1969)
Townley v. Minnesota, 257 U.S. 643 (1921)
United States v. Robel, 371 U.S. 415 (1963)
Uphaus v. Wyman, 360 U.S. 72 (1959)
Watkins v. United States, 354 U.S. 178 (1957)
West Virginia State Board of Education v. Barnette, 319 U.S. 628 (1943)
Whitney v. California, 274 U.S. 357 (1927)
Winters v. New York, 333 U.S. 507 (1948)
Yates v. United States, 355 U.S. 66 (1957)
Younger v. Harris, 401 U.S. 37 (1971)

LOWER FEDERAL COURTS

Carmichael v. Allen, 276 F. Supp. 985 (N.D. Ga. 1967)
Dombrowski v. Pfister, 227 F. Supp. (E.D. La. 1964)
Hague v. CIO, 25 F. Supp. 127 (D. N.J. 1938)
Hague v. CIO, 101 F. 2d 774 (1939)
Harris v. Fred Chappell, Sheriff, Harris v. Pace, Aelony v. Pace, 8 Race
    Rel. L. Rep. 1355 (1963)
Harris v. Younger, 281 F. Supp. (C.D. Cal. 1968)
Mc Surely v. Ratliff, 282 F. Supp. 848 (E.D. Ky. 1967)
Snyder v. Board of Trustees of University of Illinois, 268 F. Supp. 927
    (N.D. Ill. E.D. 1968)
Thalberg v. Board of Trustees of University of Illinois, 309 F. Supp. 630
    (N.D. Ill. E.D. 1969)
Ware v. Nichols, 266 F. Supp. 546 (N.D. Miss. 1967)

STATE COURTS

Alabama
Hotel and Restaurant Employees International Alliance v. Greenwood,
    249 Ala. 265 (1947)
Lash v. State, 244 Ala. 48 (1943)
Patterson v. State, 234 Ala. 342 (1937)
Shuttlesworth v. City of Birmingham, 43 Ala. App. 68 (1965)
Shuttlesworth v. City of Birmingham, 281 Ala. 542 (1967)

Alaska
Watts v. Seward School Board, 421 P. 2d 586 (1966)

Arizona
State v. Locks, 91 Ariz. 394 (1948)

Kentucky
Braden v. Commonwealth, 291 S.W. 2d 843 (1956)

Louisiana
State v. Cade, 244 La 534 (1963)
State v. Cox, 244 La. 1087 (1963)
State v. Jenkins, 236 La. 300 (1958)
State v. Warren J. Moity, 245 La. 546 (1964)

Maryland
Hammond v. Lancaster, 194 Md. 462 (1950)
Melville v. State, 10 Md. App. 118 (1970)
Police Commissioners of Baltimore v. Siegel Enterprises, 223 Md. 110
    (1960)

Massachusetts
Commonwealth v. Baird, 355 Mass. 746 (1969)
Commonwealth v. Davis, 162 Mass. 510 (1895)
Commonwealth v. Gilbert, 334 Mass. 71 (1956)
Commonwealth v. Gilfedder, 321 Mass. 335 (1947)
Commonwealth v. Isenstadt, 318 Mass. 543 (1945)
Commonwealth v. Nichols, 301 Mass. 584 (1938)

Michigan
Albertson v. Millard, 354 Mich. 519 (1956)
American Federation of State, County, and Municipal Employees Local
    201 v. Muskegon, 369 Mich. 384 (1963)
People of Dearborn Heights v. Bellock, 17 Mich. App. 163 (1969)

Minnesota
State v. Gilbert, 141 Minn. 263 (1918)

Mississippi
Benoit v. State, 194 Miss. 74 (1943)
Counts v. State, 15 So. 2d 287 (1943)
Cummings, v. State, 194 Miss. 59 (1943)
Taylor v. State, 194 Miss. 1 (1943)
Thomas v. State, 160 So. 2d 657 (1964)

Montana
City of Billings v. Herold, 130 Mont. 138 (1956)
Town of White Sulphur Springs v. Voise, 130 Mont. 1 (1959)

North Carolina
Pentuff v. Park, 194 N.C. 146 (1927)

Ohio
Cincinnati v. Black, 8 Ohio App. 2d 143 (1966)
RKO Pictures v. Hissong, 123 N.E. 2d 441 (1954)
State v. Fletcher, 22 Ohio App. 2d 83 (1970)
State v. Kassay, 126 Ohio St. 177 (1932)
Superior Films v. Department of Education, 159 Ohio St. 315 (1953)

Oklahoma
Emch v. City of Guymon, 75 Okla. Crim. 1 (1942)
Shaw v. State, 76 Okla. Crim. 271 (1943)
Walrod, Ex parte, 78 Okla. Crim. 299 (1941)
Wood v. State, 76 Okla. Crim. 89 (1943)

Oregon
Minielly v. State, 242 Or. 490 (1966)
State v. Boloff, 138 Or. 568 (1931)
State v. De Jonge, 152 Or. 315 (1935)
State v. Denny, 152 Or. 541 (1936)

Pennsylvania
Commonwealth v. Belgrave, 217 Pa. Super. Ct. 297 (1970)
Commonwealth v. Lazar, 103 Pa. Super. Ct. 417 (1931)
Commonwealth v. Nelson, 377 Pa. 58 (1954)
Commonwealth v. Reid, 144 Pa. Super. Ct. 569 (1941)
Commonwealth v. Watson and Russell, 215 Pa. Super. Ct. 499 (1969)
Commonwealth v. Widovich, 295 Pa. 311 (1929)
William Goldman Theatres, Inc. v. Dana, 405 Pa. 83 (1961)

Rhode Island
Thayer Amusement Corporation v. Moulton, 63 R.I. 182 (1939)

Texas
Craig, Ex parte, 150 Tex. Crim. 598 (1946)
Frye, Ex parte, 143 Tex. Crim. 9 (1941)

Washington
Adams v. Hinkle, 51 Wash. 2d 763 (1958)
Fornili v. Auto Mechanics' Union Local No. 297 of International Associa-
    tion of Machinists, 200 Wash. 283 (1939)

BIBLIOGRAPHY

CASES

As the footnotes indicate, the main core of research is based upon court cases. These citations are arranged in federal and state categories in the list of cases.

STATUTES AND CODES

Citations for state statutes and codes are included in the Appendix. Federal statutory materials include the following:

Alien Registration Act. U.S. Code, vol. IV (1976).
Civil Rights Act of 1866. U.S. Code, vol. X (1976).
Communist Control Act. U.S. Code, vol. XI (1976).
Internal Security Act. U.S. Code, vol. XI (1976).
Repeal of Sedition Act of 1918. Statutes at Large, vol. XLI (1921).
Rules for Judiciary and Judicial Procedure. U.S. Code, vol. VII (1964).

BRIEFS AND COURT MATERIALS

Brandenburg v. *Ohio*, 395 *U.S.* 444 (1969). *Transcript of Proceedings. Brief for Appellant. Brief for Appellees in Opposition to Jurisdiction. Jurisdictional Statement.*
De Jonge v. *Oregon*, 299 *U.S.* 353 (1937). *Transcript of Record. Brief for Appellant. Appellee's Brief.*
Dombrowski v. *Pfister*, 380 *U.S.* 479 (1965). *Transcript of Record. Original Brief for Appellees. Brief for Appellants and Appellants-Intervenors. Jurisdictional Statement. Briefs for* Amicus Curiae.

Epton v. *New York*, 390 *U.S.* 29 (1968). *Respondent's Brief in Opposition to Writ of* Certiorari. *Motion to Dismiss.*

Fiske v. *Kansas* 274 *U.S.* 380 (1927). *Transcript of Record. Brief for Plaintiff in Error. Brief for Defendant in Error.*

Gilbert v. *Minnesota*, 254 *U.S.* 325 (1920). *Transcript of Record. Brief for Plaintiff in Error. Brief of Defendant in Error.*

Gitlow v. *New York*, 268 *U.S.* 652 (1925). *Brief for Plaintiff in Error.*

Herndon v. *Lowry*, 301 *U.S.* 242 (1937). *Transcript of Record. Brief for Appellant. Brief for Appellee.*

Pennsylvania v. *Nelson*, 350 *U.S.* 497 (1956). *Transcript of Record. Reply Brief for Petitioner. Brief for Respondent. Brief for the United States as* Amicus Curiae. *Brief of the Commonwealth of Massachusetts as* Amicus Curiae. *Brief of* Amicus Curiae, *Latham Castle, Attorney General of the State of Illinois. Brief of the State of New Hampshire as* Amicus Curiae *in Support of the Petition for Writ of* Certiorari *to the Supreme Court of Pennsylvania. Brief for the American Civil Liberties Union as* Amicus Curiae. *Brief for the Civil Liberties Committee of the Philadelphia Yearly Meeting of the Religious Society of Friends,* Amicus Curiae. *Brief of Individual* Amici Curiae.

State v. *Gilbert*, 141 *Minn.* 263 (1918); 169 *N.W.* 790 (1918). *Indictment. Record. Brief for Appellant.*

Taylor v. *Mississippi*, 319 *U.S.* 583 (1943). *Transcript and Record. Brief of Plaintiff in Error. Appellants' Brief. Brief for State of Mississippi. Brief for the American Civil Liberties Union,* Amicus Curiae.

Whitney v. *California*, 274 *U.S.* 357 (1927). *Brief for Plaintiff in Error. Brief of Defendant in Error.*

BOOKS

Belknap, Michal R. *Cold War Political Justice.* Westport, Conn.: Greenwood Press, 1977.

Biddle, Francis. *In Brief Authority.* Westport, Conn.: Greenwood Press, 1976.

Brissenden, Paul F. *The IWW: A Study of American Syndicalism.* New York: Russell and Russell, 1957.

Caute, David. *The Great Fear.* New York: Simon and Schuster, 1978.

Chafee, Zechariah, Jr. *Free Speech in the United States.* Cambridge, Mass.: Harvard University Press, 1967.

Danielski, David J., and Tulchin, Joseph S. *The Autobiographical Notes of Charles Evans Hughes.* Cambridge, Mass.: Harvard University Press, 1973.

Davis, Benjamin J. *Communist Councilman from Harlem*. New York: International Publishers, 1969.

Dowell, Eldridge. *A History of Criminal Syndicalism Legislation in the United States*. New York: Da Capo Press, 1969.

Dubofsky, Melvyn. *We Shall Be All*. Chicago: Quadrangle, 1969.

Emerson, Thomas I. *The System of Freedom of Expression*. New York: Random House, 1970.

Emerson, Thomas I.; Haber, David; and Dorsen, Norman. *Political and Civil Rights in the United States*, vol. 1. Boston: Little, Brown, 1967.

Folsom, Gwendolyn. *Legislative History: Research for the Interpretation of Laws*. Charlottesville: University of Virginia Press, 1972.

The Founding Convention of the IWW: Proceedings. New York: Merit Publishers, 1969.

Fraenkel, Osmond K. *The Supreme Court and Civil Liberties*. New York: Oceana, 1960.

Freeland, Richard M. *The Truman Doctrine and the Origins of McCarthyism*. New York: Knopf, 1972.

Friedman, Lawrence. *A History of American Law*. New York: Simon and Schuster, 1973.

Gellhorn, Walter. *American Rights: The Constitution in Action*. New York: Macmillan, 1960.

————, ed. *The States and Subversion*. Ithaca, N.Y.: Cornell University Press, 1952.

Goldman, Eric F. *The Crucial Decade*. New York: Knopf, 1956.

Harper, Alan D. *The Politics of Loyalty*. Westport, Conn.: Greenwood Press, 1969.

Harris, Richard. *Freedom Spent*. Boston: Little, Brown, 1976.

Hurst, James W. *The Growth of American Law*. Boston: Little, Brown, 1950.

Jaffe, Julian F. *Crusade Against Radicalism*. Port Washington, N.Y.: Kennikat Press, 1972.

Josephson, Matthew, and Josephson, Hannah. *Al Smith: Hero of the Cities*. Boston: Houghton Mifflin, 1969.

Kalven, Harry, Jr. *The Negro and the First Amendment*. Columbus: Ohio State University Press, 1965.

Kelly, Alfred H., and Harbison, Winfred A. *The American Constitution*. 5th ed. New York: Norton, 1976.

Konefsky, Samuel J. *The Legacy of Holmes and Brandeis*. New York: Macmillan, 1956.

Konvitz, Milton. *Fundamental Liberties of a Free People*. Ithaca, N.Y.: Cornell University Press, 1957.

McAuliffe, Mary S. *Crisis on the Left: Cold War Politics and American Liberals*. Amherst: University of Massachusetts Press, 1978.

Markmann, Charles L. *The Noblest Cry*. New York: St. Martin's Press, 1965.

Martin, Charles H. *The Angelo Herndon Case and Southern Justice*. Baton Rouge: Louisiana State University Press, 1976.

Murphy, Paul L. *The Constitution in Crisis Times, 1918-1969*. New York: Harper & Row, 1972.

———. *The Meaning of Freedom of Speech*. Westport, Conn.: Greenwood Press, 1972.

———. *World War I and the Origin of Civil Liberties in the United States*. New York: Norton, 1979.

Murray, Robert K. *Red Scare*. Minneapolis: University of Minnesota Press, 1955.

Nelson, Steve. *The 13th Juror*. New York: Masses and Mainstream, 1955.

Patterson, William. *The Man Who Cried Genocide*. New York: International Publishers, 1971.

Preston, William, Jr. *Aliens and Dissenters*. Cambridge, Mass.: Harvard University Press, 1963.

Pritchett, C. Herman. *Civil Liberties and the Vinson Court*. Chicago: University of Chicago Press, 1954.

Reitman, Alan, ed. *The Pulse of Freedom*. New York: Norton, 1975.

Schmidhauser, John. *The Supreme Court as Final Arbiter in Federal-State Relations, 1789-1957*. Chapel Hill: University of North Carolina Press, 1958.

Shapiro, Martin. *Freedom of Speech: The Supreme Court and Judicial Review*. Englewood Cliffs, N.J.: Prentice-Hall, 1966.

Tarr, G. Alan. *Judicial Impact and State Supreme Courts*. Lexington, Mass.: Lexington Books, 1977.

Theoharis, Athan. *Seeds of Repression*. Chicago: Quadrangle, 1971.

Wasby, Stephen L. *The Impact of the United States Supreme Court: Some Perspectives*. Homewood, Ill.: Dorsey Press, 1970.

———. *The Supreme Court in the Federal Judicial System*. New York: Holt, Rinehart and Winston, 1978.

JOURNAL ARTICLES

Bloom, Herman J. "Validity of Criminal Syndicalism Statute." *Michigan Law Review*, 7 (May 1937), 1171-1173.

Boudin, Louis B. " 'Seditious Doctrines' and the 'Clear and Present Danger' Rule." *Virginia Law Review*, 38 (January 1952), 143-186.

Bratton, William W., Jr. "The Preemption Doctrine: Shifting Perspectives on Federalism and the Burger Court." *Columbia Law Review*, 75 (April 1975), 623-654.

Brennan, William J., Jr. "State Constitutions and the Protection of Individual Rights." *Harvard Law Review*, 90 (January 1977), 489-504.

Brewer, Bradley R. "*Dombrowski* v. *Pfister*: Federal Injunctions Against State Prosecutions in Civil Rights Cases—A New Trend in Federal-State Judicial Relations." *Fordham Law Review*, 34 (1965), 71-106.

Campbell, Robert V. "Supremacy Clause and Preemption— Pennsylvania Sedition Act Declared Invalid." *Southern California Law Review*, 30 (December 1956), 101-107.

Chafee, Zechariah, Jr. "Walter Heilprin Pollak." *Nation* 151 (October 12, 1940), 319.

Cramton, Roger C. "*Pennsylvania* v. *Nelson*: A Case Study in Federal Pre-Emption." *University of Chicago Law Review*, 26 (1958-1959), 85-108.

———. "The Supreme Court and State Power to Deal with Subversion and Loyalty." *Minnesota Law Review*, 43 (May 1959), 1025-1082.

Emerson, Thomas I. "Freedom of Expression in Wartime." *University of Pennsylvania Law Review*, 116 (April 1968), 975-1011.

Fiss, Owen M. "*Dombrowski*." *Yale Law Journal*, 86 (May 1977), 1103-1164.

Foster, George, Jr. "The 1931 Personal Liberties Cases." *New York University Law Review* 9 (September 1931), 64-81.

Harris, Paul. "Black Power Advocacy: Criminal Anarchy or Free Speech." *California Law Review*, 56 (May 1968), 702-755.

Hunt, Alan R. "Federal Supremacy and State Anti-Subversive Legislation." *Michigan Law Review*, 53 (January 1955), 407-438.

Jaglom, André R. "Protecting Fundamental Rights in State Courts: Fitting a State Peg to a Federal Hole." *Harvard Civil Rights and Civil Liberties Law Review*, 12 (Winter 1977), 63-111.

Jenson, Carol E. "Loyalty as a Political Weapon: The 1918 Campaign in Minnesota." *Minnesota History*, 43 (Summer 1972), 42-57.

Josephson, Harold. "The Dynamics of Repression: New York During the Red Scare." *Mid-America*, 59 (October 1977), 131-146.

Kalven, Harry, Jr. "The Concept of the Public Forum: *Cox* v. *Louisiana*." *Supreme Court Review* (1965), 1-32.

Kennedy, James H. "I Used to Love You But It's All Over Now: Abstention and the Federal Courts' Retreat from Their Role as Primary Guardians of First Amendment Freedoms." *Southern California Law Review*, 45 (Summer 1972), 847-887.

Linde, Hans H. " 'Clear and Present Danger' Reexamined: Dissonance in the *Brandenburg* Concerto." *Stanford Law Review*, 22 (June 1970), 1163-1186.

McAuliffe, Mary S. "Liberals and the Communist Control Act of 1954." *Journal of American History*, 63 (September 1976), 351-367.

Mendelson, Wallace. "Mr. Justice Black's Fourteenth Amendment." *Minnesota Law Review*, 53 (March 1969), 711-727.

Miller, Peter P. "Freedom of Expression Under State Constitutions." *Stanford Law Review*, 20 (January 1968), 318-335.

Murphy, Walter F. "Lower Court Checks on Supreme Court Power." *American Political Science Review*, 53 (December 1959), 1017-1031.

Prendergast, William. "State Legislatures and Communism: The Current Scene." *American Political Science Review*, 49 (September 1950), 556-574.

Purcell, Edward A. "American Jurisprudence Between the Wars: Legal Realism and the Crisis of Democratic Theory." *American Historical Review*, 75 (December 1969), 424-446.

Rogge, John O. "State Power Over Sedition, Obscenity and Picketing." *New York University Law Review*, 34 (May 1959), 817-860.

Sedler, Robert A. "Dombrowski in the Wake of Younger: The View from Without and Within." *Wisconsin Law Review* (1972), 1-61.

———. "Standing to Assert Constitutional *Jus Tertii* in the Supreme Court." *Yale Law Journal*, 71 (March 1962), 599-660.

Shenas, Peter. "Doctrine of Pre-emption: State Sedition Act Superseded by Federal Smith Act." *UCLA Law Review*, 4 (December 1956), 118-121.

Stickgold, Marc. "Variations on the Theme of *Dombrowski* v. *Pfister*: Federal Intervention in State Criminal Proceedings Affecting First Amendment Rights." *Wisconsin Law Review* (1968), 369-412.

Strong, Frank R. "Fifty Years of 'Clear and Present Danger': From Schenck to Brandenburg—and Beyond." *Supreme Court Review* (1969), 41-80.

Tighe, Ambrose. "The Legal Theory of the Minnesota 'Safety Commission' Act." *Minnesota Law Review*, 3 (1918), 10-19.

Warren, Charles. "The New 'Liberty' Under the Fourteenth Amendment." *Harvard Law Review*, 39 (February 1926), 431-465.

White, Jack L. "Protection of Freedom of Speech Under the Fourteenth Amendment." *Michigan Law Review*, 35 (June 1937), 1373-1375.

Zifkin, Walter. "Federal Pre-emption of State Sedition Laws." *Southern California Law Review*, 33 (Fall 1959), 92-97.

JOURNAL NOTES

"Clear and Present Danger Re-examined." *Columbia Law Review*, 51 (January 1951), 98-108.

"Conduct Proscribed as Promoting Violent Overthrow of the Government." *Harvard Law Review*, 61 (July 1948), 1215-1224.

"Constitutional Law—Civil Liberties—Validity of State Statutes Restricting Right of Assembly of Radical Organizations." *Columbia Law Review*, 37 (May 1937), 857-860.

"Constitutional Law—Criminal Syndicalism Statutes—Right of Peaceable Assembly." *University of Chicago Law Review*, 4 (April 1937), 489-490.

"Constitutional Law—Due Process: Freedom of Speech and Assembly—Conviction Under Insurrection Statute for Soliciting Members for Communist Party." *Harvard Law Review*, 50 (June 1937), 1313.

"Constitutional Law—Due Process—Power of State to Prohibit Peaceable Assembly Under Auspices of Communist Party." *University of Pennsylvania Law Review*, 85 (March 1937), 523-533.

"Constitutional Law—Fourteenth Amendment—'Liberty' as Including Freedom of Speech." *Virginia Law Review*, 14 (November 1927), 49-55.

"Constitutional Law—Freedom of Speech—The Justifying of Acts of Violence as Criminal Syndicalism." *University of Pennsylvania Law Review*, 81 (June 1933), 977-999.

"Constitutional Law: Liberty of Assembly Under the Fourteenth Amendment." *California Law Review*, 25 (May 1937), 496-499.

"Constitutional Law—State Investigatory Power in the Field of Sedition." *New York University Law Review*, 32 (November 1957), 1302-1308.

"Criminal Law—Insurrection and Sedition—Criminal Syndicalism." *New York University Law Review*, 14 (March 1937), 369-375.

"Criminal Syndicalism Statutes Before the Supreme Court." *University of Pennsylvania Law Review*, 76 (December 1927), 198-203.

"Effectiveness of State Anti-Subversive Legislation." *Indiana Law Journal*, 28 (1953), 492-520.

"Legislation: Federal Sedition Bills: Speech Restriction in Theory and Practice." *Columbia Law Review*, 35 (June 1935), 917-927.

"Legislation: State Control of Political Thought." *University of Pennsylvania Law Review*, 84 (January 1936), 390-399.

"Limiting State Action by the Fourteenth Amendment: Consequences of Abandoning the Theory of First Amendment Incorporation." *Harvard Law Review*, 67 (April 1954), 1016-1030.

"State Control of Subversion: A Problem in Federalism." *Harvard Law Review*, 66 (December 1952), 327-334.

"The Supreme Court as Protector of Political Minorities." *Yale Law Journal*, 46 (March 1937), 862-866.

MISCELLANEOUS

"Florence Ellinwood Allen." *Who Was Who in America*. Chicago: Marquis Who's Who, Inc., 1968. Vol. 4, p. 22.

Jenson, Carol. "Agrarian Pioneer in Civil Liberties: The Nonpartisan League in Minnesota During World War I." Ph. D. Dissertation, University of Minnesota, 1968.

Le Sueur, Arthur. Papers, 1910-1954. Minnesota Historical Society, St. Paul.

New York Times. "3-Judge Court Use for U.S. Cases Out," August 13, 1976.

Nonpartisan Leader. Vols. 1-2, 1915-1916.

Nonpartisan League. Papers, 1913-1927. Minnesota Historical Society, St. Paul.

Report of the Minnesota Commission of Public Safety. St. Paul: State of Minnesota, 1919.

"Southern Conference Education Fund." In *Encyclopedia of Associations*, 11th edition, edited by Margaret Fish, p. 701. Detroit: Gale Research, 1978.

U.S. Congress. Senate. *Civil Liberty in Wartime*. S. Doc. 434, 65th Cong., 2d Sess., 1918.

INDEX

About the Author

CAROL E. JENSON is Professor of History at the University of Wisconsin-LaCrosse. Her articles have appeared in the *International Journal of Women's Studies*, *Minnesota History*, and the collection, *Women of Minnesota*.